Sussex.   H
The rise and fall of British
documentary.

THE RISE
AND FALL
OF BRITISH
DOCUMENTARY

THE RISE
AND FALL
OF BRITISH
DOCUMENTARY

The Story of

the Film Movement

Founded by John Grierson

by
ELIZABETH SUSSEX

UNIVERSITY OF CALIFORNIA PRESS
Berkeley • Los Angeles • London

University of California Press
Berkeley and Los Angeles, California

University of California Press, Ltd.
London, England

ISBN 0-520- 02869-4
Library of Congress Catalog Card Number: 74-16719
Printed in the United States of America

For my parents, John L. Hardie and Mary Hardie — Scottish educationalists — who taught me what perseverence is and generously incurred the consequences during my frequent retreats to Dumfriesshire over the three years that this book was being prepared.

Contents

Preface

When John Grierson founded the British Documentary Movement in the 1930s it was a revolutionary thing, the first real opportunity in Britain to explore in practical terms the possibilities of film as an art. The idea seems to have attracted quite a following from its earliest years. Writing in 1932, the critic C. A. Lejeune mentions the existence all over the country of "professionals and amateurs shooting, cutting and editing in what they believe to be the Grierson manner, inverting sequences here, fashioning hortatory captions there; working with immense enthusiasm and a considerable capacity for a cinema whose first principles they don't in the least understand. . . ." Lejeune's sceptical tone gives in itself a good indication of the difficulties that confronted Grierson in keeping his venture financed. The main problem was always money. Grierson got it from Government Departments, and in order to win their confidence he created for documentary a prestige image which has clung to it almost unaltered over the years and gradually become a myth.

It was because I felt that this myth was obscuring many of the most interesting aspects of the subject in the context of the 1970s, preventing rational reassessment of the actual achievement, concealing perhaps the real story, that I set out with a tape recorder to interview as many members of the original movement as possible. I got the maximum cooperation, hospitality, help of all kinds, interviews that sometimes lasted several days — and that is the basis of this book.

My method was to ask each interviewee to tell his story from beginning to end, and then to fit all the stories together. The editing proved a formidable task starting as it did from miles of tape all of which had to be transcribed in order to decide what not to use, but it was the only way in which I could be certain of acquiring a composite picture of everything that was going on at any given moment. The composite picture was rarely quite the same as that of any single individual, except perhaps at the beginning where there were surprises of a different kind — for the famous movement began with a bunch of amateurs, using second-hand equipment which may have been a false economy despite the shoestring budget on which they operated, going off to make films (which were strongly influenced by Russian theory) with virtually no knowledge of the job. By their own admission most of their work before 1934 was amateur, and this is confirmed by the surviving films of that period which I was able to see. Grierson was shrewd enough to bring in Robert Flaherty, whose name itself conferred some honour on the movement, but the film that resulted, *Industrial Britain,* like Grierson's own famous *Drifters,* is disappointing today for what might seem the unlikeliest of reasons, i.e., a lack of social content.

This is the reality. The myth comes over very clearly in Forsyth Hardy's selection from Grierson's writings for the book *Grierson on Documentary.* In an article about the Empire Marketing Board Film Unit's achievement from 1930 to 1933, Grierson writes: "Wright was the best lyrical documentary director in the country, Elton the best industrial, and Legg the best all-rounder. One or two others, it seemed, would presently be heard from." In 1933, the year when Grierson wrote this for *Cinema Quarterly,* there were of course hardly any recognised documentary directors in the country apart from Wright, Elton, Legg and one or two others working under Grierson at the EMB, and the article was part of Grierson's campaign to ensure the survival of his film unit after the dissolution of the Empire Marketing Board. It puts a different complexion on things to be clear about this, makes the unit's continued existence perhaps a braver more impressive thing, and yet in the first edition of *Grierson on Documentary,* published in 1946, Forsyth Hardy did not even include the dates when the various articles first appeared. In general Forsyth Hardy's selection favoured the propaganda rather than the factual line, so that there are curious omissions, for instance Grierson's glowing account of the acquisition of sound equipment at the GPO (quoted on pages 44-46 of this book) which comes over with undiminished enthusiasm after forty years and which explains so much about the new documentary and the excitement it aroused.

The attraction of British documentary in its early years was not that it achieved success but that it achieved the freedom to stumble in a number of interesting directions almost by accident. Stuart Legg, for example describes how he failed to get anywhere with a film about the plum harvest in the Vale of Evesham; in the end somebody else finished it. "It was obviously a black mark against me," says Legg, "but Grierson was very good about that sort of thing, and he gave me a lot of material to cut which had been shot in coal mines. He asked me to make a two-reeler. And this was the beginning of *Coal Face....*"

Coal Face still stands as one of the movement's most significant experiments. It was taken over by Cavalcanti who gave it a soundtrack of a kind unprecedented in British documentary. It preceded *Song of Ceylon* and *Night Mail,* and was the first film on which W. H. Auden and Benjamin Britten

worked together. Ironically, however, it is practically impossible to hear the
sound on most of the prints available for viewing today, and this is another extraordinary aspect of the story. They made all their major experiments in
sound in the mid-thirties with recording equipment which was inferior to the
best that existed at the time and which added to the track a noise of its own
that went "acchh." With *Coal Face* you have to use imagination to hear what
is actually there. In less obvious ways you have to be imaginative about viewing the entire output of the documentary movement, because there is a feeling
that it was always reaching out towards something that it never quite achieved
except in the work of Humphrey Jennings (from which Grierson dissociated
himself, but which would probably never have existed without him).

Perhaps the most deadening aspect of the myth is that it prevented any
sensible admission of the gap between expectations and achievement. In the
interviews for this book, however, the gap is finally acknowledged. How good
were the films? I can say that the majority of them were not particularly
good by present-day standards, knowing that I have the full support of at least
some of my interviewees. I have given indications throughout the book of the
way certain films struck me, but where my opinion exactly coincided with
other opinions quoted I saw no need for repetition. People were in the main
modest about their work, more ready to criticise than to praise, and their
cumulative judgements seem to me fair.

Many film critics believe that British documentary is due for a complete
reassessment. They are right, but any reassessment based merely on an analysis of individual films would seem to me a futile exercise in this case, proving
only that the excitement of pioneering work diminishes when the work ceases
to be new. What I think really needs analysis is the decline of a movement that
had such obviously promising beginnings, and this is what these interviews,
to an almost incredible extent, provided. For the first time the people directly
concerned have not only admitted that the movement failed, but listed reasons
for the failure, what Grierson called "the dereliction."

This is where the composite picture was particularly revealing. No single
interviewee could ever have explained it all, because everybody's view of it
was coloured by which side he happened to be on. We discover that there was
a division of opinion in the documentary movement at a very early stage in its
development, and that alongside all the idealistic pioneering efforts another,
very different, story was relentlessly unfolding. The seeds of the trouble were
planted soon after the brilliant Cavalcanti's arrival at the GPO in 1934. They
made a comedy called *Pett and Pott* which seems naive and self-conscious
today but which did contain some interesting experiments with sound. You
could say that it represented one of the many aesthetic lines that was never
developed by the movement. Nobody cared for it very much, but the reasons
for this were poles apart. Cavalcanti disliked it because it was too amateurish,
"a sound picture" rather than a film. Basil Wright adopted a characteristically

middle position, paying a characteristic compliment to Grierson: "We got away with *Pett and Pott* because Grierson was a great salesman, and he told everybody what a wonderful film it was, and made sure that nobody ever saw it." John Taylor defined it quite frankly as "the beginning of the division. . . . Documentary was supposed to be for the service of people. It wasn't supposed to be in the entertainment industry as far as I'm concerned anyway."

By 1937, when Grierson left the GPO Film Unit and British documentary had still to reach its wartime peak, there were two factions in the movement — those who shared Grierson's view that documentary was for the service of people, and those who like Cavalcanti wanted it to be in the entertainment industry. It was this division, I think, that finally proved fatal, but what I find even more interesting is that everybody saw what was happening, and yet it still happened. Was it inevitable? We can only examine the facts and wonder. Was there a way out?

Although this book is obviously influenced by my opinion, in the editing of the interviews as well as in the linking comments, my aim was primarily to provide enough documentary evidence to enable readers to reach their own conclusions. If these conclusions differ from mine, if they reflect as many varying attitudes as did the members of the movement themselves, I shall think my job well done.

E.S.

London,
Hallowe'en 1974

Acknowledgments

The author wishes to thank everyone who gave an interview for this book, also all those who helped in various ways at the British Film Institute and National Film Archive – in particular Paddy Whannel, former head of the BFI Education Department, who provided essential viewing facilities. Thanks are also extended to Ian Cameron whose idea the book originally was, to Lindsay Anderson for insisting that facts alone are not enough, to Robert Vas for constant encouragement, and to Tom Milne for reading the manuscript and giving the only reaction every author wants.

Photographs and film stills by courtesy of Ian Dalrymple, Edinburgh Film Guild, Sir Arthur Elton, Pat Jackson, Stuart Legg and Film Centre, Paul Rotha, *Sight and Sound,* Basil Wright.

Interviewees in Order of Appearance

John Grierson (1898-1972). Founded the British Documentary Movement after making his pioneering film *Drifters* (1929). Also set up the National Film Board of Canada.

Basil Wright (b. 1907). Grierson's first recruit in 1929. Director of *Song of Ceylon* (1934) and key collaborator on *Night Mail* (1936). Continued in documentary mainly as producer. Also writer.

John Taylor (b. 1914). Grierson's brother-in-law. Began in documentary when he left school in 1930 and has continued in it ever since.

Paul Rotha (b. 1907). Worked briefly with Grierson's film unit in 1931. Thereafter independent documentary producer and director, e. g., *World of Plenty* (1943), *Land of Promise* (1946), *The Life of Adolf Hitler* (1962). Also film historian.

Edgar Anstey (b. 1907). Joined Grierson in 1931 and has since remained in documentary. 1949-1974: head of the British Transport Film Unit.

Sir Arthur Elton (1906-1973). Joined Grierson at the same time as Edgar Anstey. Remained in documentary all his life. Associated with the Shell Film Unit from 1936 until his death.

Stuart Legg (b. 1910). Joined Grierson in 1932, and also worked with him in Canada. Has since given up film-making for writing.

Harry Watt (b. 1906). Joined Grierson in 1932. Directed notably *Night Mail* (1936), *North Sea* (1938), *Target for Tonight* (1941), and then left documentary for features.

Alberto Cavalcanti (b. 1897). Joined Grierson in 1934 as director already well-known for his avant-garde film work in France. At the GPO his experiments in sound included *Coal Face* (1935) and *Night Mail* (1936). In 1940 he left documentary and went to Ealing Studios.

Pat Jackson (b. 1917). Joined Grierson's film unit straight from school in 1934.

Director of *Western Approaches* (1944). After the war went into feature films.

W. H. Auden (1907-1973). The poet. A member of the GPO Film Unit for a short time in 1935-1936.

Ian Dalrymple (b. 1903). Producer at the Crown Film Unit, 1940-1943.

1

The Movement Moves In

JOHN GRIERSON was born in 1898 in a village near Stirling in Scotland. He grew up as one of a large family (two sisters, Marion and Ruby Grierson, were later to follow him into documentary film making). His father was a village dominie, his grandfather a lighthouse keeper. During the First World War he served on minesweepers, and in 1923 he took an M.A. degree at Glasgow University, with distinctions in English and moral philosophy. The following year he went to the United States on a Rockefeller research fellowship in social science.

The story of British documentary begins with his decision at this period to cut out a career not in politics nor in journalism, but in films.

Grierson: I grew up in the Clydeside movement. I've been in politics all my life. Nobody who ever grew up in the Clydeside movement forgets. Under no circumstances do we forget. But whether I went into politics in the ordinary sense was another matter. I was offered a couple of constituencies before I left the university, and the thing that interested me — not that I'd have got in, but I was offered the chance to stand for them — they were by two different parties. That tickles me — two different parties!*

No, I thought I'd do a better political job the way I did, and I was very interested in this question of putting the working class on the screen, of bring-

*There is a long and bitter history of workers' protest on Clydeside, going back to the great lock-out in the shipyards in 1867 when employers successfully demanded renunciation of Trade Union membership. In 1915 a huge unofficial strike of engineering workers on the Clyde seriously threatened the production of armaments for the war, and the committee responsible for organizing this became the spearhead of a national "Workers' Committee" movement which often ran counter to official Trade Union policies. In 1919 a general strike for a forty-hour week in the Clyde area was defeated by a large display of military force by the Government. This is the background to which Grierson refers, but it should be emphasised that his personal involvement in it was obviously slight. As he himself indicates, his political astuteness was always of the sort that eluded identification with any specific party line.

ing the working class thing alive in another form than we were getting on the soapboxes of Glasgow Green. That wasn't good enough for me, the soapbox. You see, I worked in a factory down the Clyde, and I didn't think that we could live off platforms, platform relationships. And I think I saw early the possibility of other forms. Of course I was interested in the journalistic form first of all, that is the yellow newspaper form. I've always been interested in the yellow newspaper. But then of course Flaherty was a turning point. *Nanook* hit Glasgow round about 1922, I think. I was on to it by 1924, that film could be turned into an instrument of the working class.

From then on, there was no question of where one's duty lay. But it was an idea that didn't develop in Glasgow or in England. It was an idea that developed in America. I spent three years, 1924 to 1927, based in Chicago, and I was very concerned then with what was happening to the immigrants. There was no question that it started out in a political conception, a political social conception.

Now, if you think of the cinema, the motion picture, round about the twenties, you have a tradition of it's being used for theatrical purposes and developing quite a big tradition in comedy and also in theatrical shapes, through people like DeMille and D. W. Griffith and so on. You get the use of the film extending into musical comedy when sound comes along. But apart from entertainment, dramatic entertainment, you have very little use of the cinema's native and natural powers – for example, in the matter of getting around. There's nothing like the camera for getting around. That's what makes it unique, the fact that it can travel from place to place. It can see round corners, more or less. It can see upways, downways, all the way round. It can put a telescope at the end of a lens. It can, of course, look through a microscope. In other words, it's capable of an infinite variety of observations. But in taking the picture of the twenties, it had not greatly invaded the field of its possibilities.

There were newsreels. These were very superficial accounts of pageants, fires, disasters, parades, national celebrations, army celebrations, things of that kind. There was something in the way of an occasional travelogue – many travelogues, if you like – but rather superficial visits to one place or another. There was an occasional film made of an expedition, for example, Scott's visit to the South Pole (there was a splendid film made of that, and as early as 1912).* And there was Flaherty's beginning in the making of films in far places with *Nanook of the North.* There were various minor scientific uses of the camera. But, by and large, very, very little had been done to use the cinema in its powers of observation of the real.†

*Herbert Ponting's *The Great White Silence,* later re-edited with sound track as *Ninety Degrees South.*

†Grierson's omission of Dziga Vertov, who was making his Kino-Pravda newsreels in 1922 and his Kino-Eye films in 1924, was probably deliberate because he always argued that Vertov made no real contribution to working-class documentary traditions.

There was a whole world undiscovered, a whole area of cinematic possibility undiscovered. All we did in documentary was we occupied Oklahoma. I saw this thing. I saw here was a territory completely unoccupied. I thought I was going in for newspapers, but obviously newspapers were very expensive and I couldn't see myself buying up a few newspapers. But here were newspapers — as it were, the whole power of newspapers — going for nothing. The only thing was to find a way of financing it. And, of course, the great event in the history of documentary was that we didn't go to Hollywood for money. We went to governments for money and thereby tied documentary, the use of the realistic cinema, to purposes.

Grierson first used the word "documentary" in a review of Flaherty's Moana *in 1926.*

Grierson: I suppose I coined the word in the sense that I wasn't aware of it's being used by anybody else. I mean, to talk about a documentary film was new, and I know I was surprised when I went over to Paris in 1927 and found them talking about *"films documentaires."* Now, I must have seen that before, but I wasn't aware of it. When I used the word "documentary" of Bob Flaherty's *Moana,* I was merely using it as an adjective. Then I got to using it as a noun: "the documentary;" "this is documentary." The word "documentary" became associated with my talking about this kind of film, and with me and a lot of people round me. There was a period (I think you'll find some very curiously mixed evidence on this subject) when some of them tried to get rid of the word "documentary," because it was felt to be very ugly. And Caroline Lejeune in *The Observer* kept saying, "Why the devil do we hang on to this gruesome word 'documentary'?" I said at the time, "Well, I think we'd better hang on to this word because if it's so ugly nobody will steal it." And that, of course, is what happened. It was so ugly that nobody would steal it.

There was a time when they suddenly realised I was on to something of a very, very great proprietory order, and somebody came and offered me something like £350,000 to do a certain operation which would involve liquidating the government relationship with the thing and selling out.* But we didn't liquidate the government relationship. We liquidated every possibility of its stopping. That was a good warning to me. But we kept to documentary

*In an obituary tribute to Grierson in the London *Times,* Paul Rotha wrote that when the Empire Marketing Board (EMB) film unit was dissolved, "Grierson could easily have sold the whole of its skilled talents and possibly its valuable library of films to the Gaumont-British organisation, which had its eyes fixed on the educational film market. He refused, preferring instead the government service under the aegis of the Post Office. Spurred by vested trade interests, and with the aid of the British Film Institute of that time, Conservative politicians frequently attacked both the EMB and GPO film units without success. . . ."

because it was, as I say, an ugly word that nobody would steal, and it always was one of our defences against commercialisation.

There was of course an earlier use of the word, which I used at one time. I was invited — oh, many, many years ago — to open some new wing or section of the Maritime Museum, and I couldn't quite understand how I could be so privileged because I had been in the British navy, all right, but I hadn't been in the British navy in any grandiose way. I'd been an able seaman and such. Anyway, I found that they were interested in the documentary movement because the documentary movement would, of course, be the photographic side of the records of the British navy and of the maritime world, which were very rich. But in the course of thinking how I should open this thing I came across an extraordinary fact, that the first sponsorship for the development of photography was for one Fox Talbot, who came from Lacock Abbey and who, I think, was associated with a development on coloured paper round about 1834. He was a captain in the navy, and I think his father was a captain in the navy, and I somehow think that there was a Fox Talbot at Trafalgar somewhere. Anyway, Fox Talbot developed this photographic process under the auspices of the British navy. And at the time I was making up the spiel and speech for the Maritime Museum, I came across a quotation (they were explaining to the Treasury why they were spending money on developing and training people in this new thing called photography) — "so that our captains and mariners may bring back documentary evidence of the wonderful things they will have seen in their voyages across the Southern Seas," or something to that effect. "So that they will bring back documentary evidence." So I could really claim for the navy this relationship with the documentary word and the documentary movement!

In fact, the first use of the documentary approach was a total disaster, because it was associated with the Franklin expedition into Hudson Bay, and I think there were as many as fourteen people aboard that ship, officers and petty officers, trained in photography, because I've actually seen a photograph of them all gathered together. And there they all were, the first documentary people in the world, and they all perished on the Franklin expedition.*

So there's a little piece of semihistory. I'm sure you'll find it's right, somewhere along the line. But Fox Talbot — 1834 when he first began — 1838, 1840, these are the dates in which he's recognised as having made particular steps forward in the photographic history.

However, the word *documentary* belongs to everybody now . . . .

The Empire Marketing Board was set up in May 1926 as a government department to promote trade with the Commonwealth. As its secretary, Stephen Tallents (1884-1958, knighted in 1932) pioneered the field of public

*Sir John Franklin died on 11 June 1847 on an expedition in search of the northwest passage.

relations. Under him the EMB evolved new techniques in marketing, adver-tising, and research, of which the formation of a film unit was only a minor part. In describing his approach to what he called "the art of national projec-tion" in a pamphlet The Projection of England *(first published in 1932 and reprinted by Film Centre in 1955), Tallents wrote: "I am convinced, and not without experience, that, when new work has to be undertaken in a novel field, the only sensible prescription is to pick out the best team that can be found, to put them to grips with their problem, and to leave them, free of undue pressure or interference, to follow, like Socrates, whithersoever it leads, the argument in which their own intimate handling of the material will quickly engage them."*

In February 1927 John Grierson returned to England from America and went to see Tallents, who had him appointed as a films officer at the EMB. Walter Creighton had already been commissioned to make a film, which even-tually emerged as One Family, *a seven-reel fantasy about the gathering of the ingredients for the king's Christmas pudding, described by Sir Arthur Elton as "very old-fashioned in our opinion, society ladies playing Britannia, and the Empire cake, Buckingham Palace and so forth" and by Harry Watt as "abysmally vomit-making." According to Elton, it "has disappeared and never been seen since, though I believe there might be a copy hidden still in Canada."*

Grierson, with Creighton, spent two years converting Whitehall to the idea of film making. Then he got what remained of the EMB production bud-get to direct the documentary Drifters.

From the outset, John Grierson had a marked flair for publicity, and Drifters *was accorded the then considerable honour of a screening at the Film Society, which in those days attracted London's intellectual élite. In the pro-gramme on Sunday, 10 November 1929, at the Tivoli Palace, Strand, it was preceded by Jean Epstein's* The Fall of the House of Usher *and followed by Walt Disney's* The Barn Dance *and the first-ever British showing of Eisenstein's* Battleship Potemkin, *which had previously been banned, even for private screenings, by the Conservative government. Eisenstein was in the audience and Aldous Huxley and a strong representation from the British documentary move-ment of the future, including Basil Wright, Paul Rotha, Stuart Legg, Arthur Elton.*

Elton: *Drifters* was an immense revelation to everybody who saw it at the time. Films had been going through a particularly irritating, a particularly artificial, phase. There were some magnificent American silent films, at the end of the good gangster silents. But the British film industry was fatuous, I think one can say. And *Drifters* was a revelation to us all, a revelation of Grierson's own theories that life at home is just as interesting as life in fiction, if only you can be made to see it so.

Does it stand up as one of the great films? It probably doesn't now. But can you look at *Potemkin* with as much interest now? A dimension has been

John Grierson, circa 1929.

lost. Of course, you do have to see the early films with an orchestra playing and all that kind of stuff. They did demand a kind of showmanship. Some of our later films can be seen anywhere without any showmanship; that is certainly true. I cut a version once for the BBC (which they ought to have still) with music. And Forsyth Hardy, I think, made one. It's fair to say that you should see it done with music, with Fingal's Cave, which I think was the music Grierson selected.

But *Drifters* did prove something which many people have contended and showed it to us on the screen, and that was of fundamental importance. I don't believe that Grierson — and I don't think he would mind my saying this — is himself a dedicated or a very creative film maker, as such. Diaghilev couldn't dance, after all, and he was a very strong influence in the ballet, and Grierson must be regarded as a Diaghilev in this. (I don't think he'd be very pleased with the analogy. Nevertheless, I think there's an element of truth in it.)

Wright: It's very unfortunate for Grierson that *Drifters* was made just at the change-over from the presynchronous sound days to the synchronous sound days, or, as they say (and I don't like saying), from the silent film to the sound film (because there never was such a thing as the silent film). This film, to begin with, had a great success in the theatres; it was very widely shown, with a very good score. In the big cinemas they had a musical score which had been well designed by an orchestral director, and in the other theatres they had a turntable score which was also very well calculated. But now, you see, it's a sort of archival picture, and most people see it without any sound, which is an awful thing to do to any silent film, except the ones which the makers specify there shouldn't be any sound on, like Stan Brakhage and Maya Deren and one or two experimentalists. Of course there are some films which retain tremendously vivid effect and some which don't. Flaherty's *Moana,* I think even silent, still has a tremendous impact, whereas *Drifters* doesn't. But at the time it was very much up to the mark. Grierson had got the whole idea of Eisenstein's montage, not in the sense of just imitating a cutting technique but knowing what Eisenstein was about. . . . I was terribly thrilled with *Drifters.* I said, "This is the sort of film I want to make."

As a result of Drifters, *the EMB film unit was formed in London for continuous production. BASIL WRIGHT who had come down from Cambridge in June 1929 wanting to get into films, was Grierson's first recruit.*

Drifters (1929).

Wright: I saw *Drifters* at the Film Society on the Sunday. On Monday I started ringing up my friends, saying, "Do you know anybody who knows Grierson?" so I could get at him. On the Tuesday I received a letter from Grierson out of the blue, saying that he'd seen an amateur film I'd made at some amateur film festival and would I go and see him? That was that. By the end of November I was installed in a dank basement somewhere near Victoria, cutting some material for him.

While I was at Cambridge, I got this sudden discovery of the art of the film through seeing Dupont's *Variety,* Hitchcock's *The Lodger,* and Pudovkin's *Mother* (which we saw in a secret projection, unknown to the authorities, arranged by Bertrand Russell). I was so thrilled I really abandoned all ideas of being an artist in any other field except this. My twenty-first birthday was coming up, and I told my family that if every single one of them kicked in something, surely they could manage to get me a camera and a projector, which were very expensive in those days. This was a Kodak 16 millimetre camera with a projector to go with it. And so I started making experimental films like mad all the rest of the time I was at Cambridge. I was absolutely sold on the whole thing, and in fact it was lucky I did make these films because that was how I got the job from Grierson. He liked the cutting of one of them. (All my amateur films were destroyed by Field Marshal Goering during the war. It's the only decent thing he ever did. He dropped a bomb on Druce's Repository in Baker Street.)

Grierson: I got £2,500* to make *Drifters,* and I think I got £7,500 for a picture called *Port of London,* and *Port of London* was merely used as an excuse to create the unit. So we kept that running. I think I had £7,500 for the first year. Maybe I had it for the second year. I don't know how long, but there was always this mythical film that I kept on pretending was going to be made. We did a few shots. I may say we never wasted any of the shots, because it turned out later that our shooting in the Port of London had become extremely valuable as background, when it came to background projection [i.e., *for feature films*]. We were the people who provided the back shots of the docks and the stuff that went into the porthole. So that all came out of the famous *Port of London* illusion, the idea that I was making my second great epic. I was in fact creating the documentary film movement. It was done on that.

Wright: The first thing I had to do was to make what was called a poster film. Sir Stephen Tallents had the idea of putting up triptych poster frames all over England, beautifully made from Empire wood with room for three different posters in them. He was getting all the best artists of the day — McKnight Kauffer and all those people — to design things about the Empire. (Some of

---

* Paul Rotha remembers that *Drifters* was made for less than £2,000.

these frames are still in existence, I think, and they were used afterwards by the GPO and other people, and a lot during the war.) Arising from this, Grierson said to Tallents, "All right, while you're doing your poster campaign, why shouldn't we have poster films?" Everyone was very much influenced by the way the Russian directors were integrating their subtitles into the montage of their films, by intercutting them in short pieces, splitting up sentences, varying the type size from very small to very big, and so on. So I was given some very rusting cans full of mostly very, very old instructional films about cocoa in the Gold Coast (Ghana, as it is today), and Grierson said, "OK. Sell the British public the idea that cocoa comes from one of our great colonies, the Gold Coast, and do it in (I can't remember) either five or seven minutes.

So there I was wrestling with this unknown material. It was the first time I'd ever touched 35 millimetre film. Nobody told me what to do or how to do it. I had to find it all out for myself. And he said, "I will give you five pounds for the whole job, and it's your responsibility to get the titles made." He told me about somebody who could do titles, who turned out to be Philip Harben, who subsequently became famous as a television chef. I went up to his place and we did a sort of mini-animation, making trick titles. We took them to a very small, cheap laboratory, and the laboratory destroyed the negative, so there were no titles. At my own expense I had to go somewhere else and have them made on cards, so that when I'd finished I was two pounds out of pocket.

But this little film, I can't remember much about it except that it was rather a lot of frenzied cutting. It took you very quickly from the growing to the harvesting and then, fortunately, they used to have at Accra a tremendous thing — the small boats used to have to go out to the big cargo boats to load, and the weather was always rough and there were all these natives rowing away. . . . So I managed to get quite a nice sequence which I intercut with titles. Grierson was quite pleased with it.

From then on we continued using this silent montage technique because it was about this time that Grierson prepared the English version of Victor Turin's *Turksib*. We did the titles for that, and Turin used titles very much in this way, particularly at the end, because he had to solve the problem that he'd made the film but the railway wasn't finished. You know, "Next year the Trans-Siberian railway will be complete," all intercut with engines and things dashing about. It was very exciting at the time.

Well, there were all sorts of fiddly things like that, and there were other young men around who'd been doing a few jobs like that for him. The next thing was the brilliant idea of Grierson's that, as Canada was one of the largest countries in North America, something could be built up out of that about the development of the North American continent, a sort of vivid little history for schools. By some ingenious skullduggery of his own, he managed to get Hollywood firms — chiefly Paramount, I think — to let us have the use for a limited period of material from all the big epics of the twenties — *The Covered Wagon,*

The Iron Horse, Pony Express, and so on. So there we were in the cutting
room bashing away at a film which was called *Conquest.* I forget how long it
ran, but over half an hour anyhow, and I was the sort of editor-in-chief on this,
but there were only two people. I mean, I would get to work and Grierson
used to come in and curse me every two days. Actually during this time John
Taylor joined us, and he used to do some of the dirty work for me. The film
came up quite interestingly. It was made of this material plus a lot of material
we got from the Canadian Motion Picture Bureau (or whatever it was called
at the time) — mostly tourist material, but useful stuff. And there were bits
of *Turksib* lying about the cutting room, so I cut in some of that. Then there
was a row because the Russians said we couldn't use their film. I had to go to
Kings Cross or Euston or somewhere and shoot sort of double-in shots for
the *Turksib* ones I'd used and cut those in instead.

The film of course no longer exists because under the contract we had
to return the American films — the bits we'd used — to the owners eighteen
months later or something of that sort. But it was widely shown, and the
great thing was that it got extremely favourably reviewed. It rather put us on
the map.

*JOHN TAYLOR (brother of Margaret Taylor, whom Grierson married
in 1930) joined the EMB film unit when he left school in 1930 at the age of
fifteen and a half.*

Taylor: When I went there, there was Basil Wright and a man called J.
D. Davidson. We were the three original ones. They started increasing the staff
very quickly, and they nearly always argue about who got where first. I can't
see that it matters one way or another. But all these people like Elton, Anstey,
Rotha, Grierson's sister Marion Grierson, Evelyn Spice, J. N. G. Davidson (an
Irishman), Jeakins (another cameraman), Miss Long, Miss Plant, came over
the next year and a half or two years, I suppose. There were a number of small
boys — Jonah Jones, Chick Fowle and Fred Gamage — and they were taught
in a slightly haphazard way, but they were taught to do everything.

The original offices were in a place called Dansey Yard, off the bottom
end of Wardour Street. They had two small cutting rooms and a lavatory, with
a projector in the lavatory. The next offices were two rooms on the top floor
of 175 Wardour Street — very small rooms, you know, with a lot of people
working in them. There were cutting benches and desks, all more or less mixed
up together, and the cutting room was also the projection room. There was
very little money.

They put all the boys through the same kind of thing. You started off
as a messenger boy, and you did the projection and the joining — and the joining in those days was a very laborious business. Technically I think the whole
thing was rather far behind even the cinema trade at that time. I don't know
for certain, but I suspect the studios used Bell & Howell joiners, which are

these big mechanical things with levers and pedals, and they make a very good overlap join. But all the smaller companies had little hand joiners. The film was quite thick nitrate film, and you had to make this overlap which could vary between two-sixteenths of an inch — maybe not as much as that — on a good join, and about five-sixteenths on a bad join. It's only a detail, but it was a very laborious kind of thing, and we used to make the joins on bits of blotting paper on the bench. The thing was, the people weren't really technically very much up in the world. They were a bit backward. I mean, it was very early days, anyway.

EMB and GPO films were shot on 35 millimetre film.

Taylor: Kodak had brought out 16 millimetre and the amateurs were using 16 millimetre, but it was considered poor quality, and you couldn't use it except for 16 millimetre projection. Most of the stuff they did [*i.e., at the EMB*] was for 35 millimetre projection.

The camera equipment they had was mostly old stuff. They had a Bell & Howell camera and a Debrie Super Le Parvo, which were hand-turned cameras. They also relied a lot on a small clockwork camera called a De Vry: the small one took hundred-foot spools; the other took four-hundred-foot rolls. But they were hand-turned cameras, and the tripods also were hand-turned, geared tripods, which were very cumbersome. I mean, they were all right for kind of set studio things, but to try and operate them on this kind of documentary work really wasn't very satisfactory. Grierson, I think, most likely all his life had a kink about using second-hand equipment, you know. And it wasn't really very sensible.

Anyway, the boys in the place were trained in a kind of haphazard way to clean and operate cameras and do the projection and do the joining and make the tea and all this kind of thing. Basil and that age group went more or less straight into film making with no real training at all. Grierson also, you see, didn't know a lot about the film industry. He'd made one film, but his technical knowledge wasn't really very strong. He edited *Drifters,* and he was a very good editor — well, you can see how well *Drifters* is edited. A lot of the emphasis in those days was on editing.

Sound didn't come into it for quite a while. Don't forget, it was early days of sound. The equipment was terribly crude, compared with modern equipment, and they always were working on very low budgets. The total budget was very small. I shouldn't think they used sound for the first year I was there, or two maybe. At the time, you see, a great controversy went on, that sound was just a flash in the pan and was interfering with the real art of film making, which was cutting and silence and so on. There was tremendous opposition to sound from all the kinds of intellectual film makers. I mean they resisted it.

Wright would most likely be more accurate on this, but certainly the early films he worked on (*Conquest,* and he re-edited *Matterhorn* and, I think, a film called *Down Channel*) were silent films, conceived as silent films. I think they were all committed to the silent film as the only way films could be made and didn't want sound. They'd most likely all argue with this now. But there was definitely opposition to sound. It was dragging this high art form down into a kind of commercialism, a kind of showmanship.

Wright: There are two factors involved. When sound came in, people concerned with the art of the film were horrified because they felt people hadn't yet learned how to use the construction of film, the Eisenstein theories of montage and so on, and now they were suddenly faced with the sound system, which was going to lock the camera, stop the whole idea of editing. So there was, from the point of view of the film aesthete, the cineaste (which included people like myself, to begin with — this was in the late twenties), a great feeling of horror and disaster that this thing was happening. Then there was the famous manifesto issued from the Soviet Union by Eisenstein, Pudovkin, and Alexandrov (which you can find in detail in Jay Leyda's *Kino* and in Marie Seton's *Eisenstein*) in which they said in effect (although probably in the long run they got it wrong) that sound was OK. So, with these great artists saying that, we had to begin to think, "OK, sound is a good thing," particularly because they used the magic word "asynchronism." That is, you didn't have to have people's lips moving all the time. But the actual addition of a sound track to the picture was a good thing, and there they were right. (I think it was 1929. You've got to remember that sound was already coming up in 1926, and of course the Russians were very late in coming to it, simply because of the physical difficulty of getting sound apparatus.)

The next thing is that we hadn't any money, and therefore we had no access to sound-recording equipment from the time when Grierson started to set up his unit at the end of November 1929 until we moved into Blackheath Studios in January 1934. It's a long time!

Now in the meantime, right at the beginning, I did a compilation film about Canadian timber, a film called *Lumber*, for which my friend Dennis Arundel wrote a special score which was minutely synchronised with the picture. It was recorded at the Stoll Film Studios, and this was the first English documentary sound film with music specially written for it. But this was unique, and I think it was a bit too expensive for us to do, really, at that time. It was a good score, but it was lost. *Lumber* was one of six films which had to be enlarged when we got a contract with Gaumont-British for what was known as the Imperial Six. We made a number of one-reelers, and when we got this distribution contract, they wanted them as two reels, and then of course the recording and the commentary was put on by Gaumont-British.

The first film I ever directed, *Country Comes to Town,* was made as a one-reeler and had to be blown up into a two-reeler. This happened to nearly all the films at that time, including Flaherty's *Industrial Britain,* which was one of the Imperial Six. All of them had the sound put on by the distributors. Grierson, I know, went to the studios and did what he could to control them, but in fact he had no basic control. I think a good deal of the wording of the commentaries of some of the films, we had some control over, but Grierson in the end was left with studio people who were slapping Beethoven's *Coriolanus* Overture on here or bits of somebody else's music on there, standard stuff. Now this may have given John Taylor, when he was very young, the impression that we didn't like the sound film, and in that case he was right, because we hated the way they put the sound onto these films.

And this brought us to the point at which we realized that theatrical distribution was not the whole thing, as far as we were concerned. It was during a long period of this trial and error in an attempt to get theatrical distribution that Grierson gradually developed the idea of nontheatrical, and you can never put a date on that. You'd never put a date on it because this was simply a development from not being able to get theatrical distribution. At a certain point he made the famous pronouncement [*that there was more seating capacity outside the theatres than there was inside the theatres*] , but what we were going through was a whole process of development in which firstly it was difficult to get sensible theatrical distribution and secondly the importance of the specialized audience (the audience which was waiting for you in a hospital or a teacher-training college or a factory or something of that sort) became realised. Then you thought, if these people are in a hospital or a teacher-training college, why do you expect them to go and see your film in a cinema? They go to the cinema to see Greta Garbo. Therefore, let them see the film when they want to see it, when they're learning. This is how it gradually evolved. It's not like Saul on the way to Tarsus.

PAUL ROTHA, prior to joining the EMB film unit, had trained at the Slade School of Art and worked as a painter, designer, and art critic for The Connoisseur. *During 1928 he was an assistant in the art department of British International Pictures at Elstree until he was fired for writing an article (published in* Film Weekly *in November 1928) in which he said, "in England there is little creative set designing." He then wrote the first history of the cinema in the English language,* The Film Till Now, *which was published in 1930, when he was twenty-three and which, he says, threw him "completely out of favour with the film industry."*

Rotha: Like a lot of other people, I was deeply impressed with John Grierson's film *Drifters* when it was shown at the Film Society in 1929. I was very impressed. Well, it so happened that I used a small coffee shop in Gerrard Street just off Wardour Street, which by the way I regret to say like everything else has been pulled down. But anyway, Grierson was there one morning at the same time as I was sipping my coffee. He was with Basil Wright, who later was to become a close colleague of mine, coworker. And I took my courage in my hands and went across to Grierson and said, "I wrote *The Film Till Now*." He said "Oh, did you?" just like that. He never says much more than that. I said "Well, I'd like to come and work with you." He said "What have you done?" I said "Well, I've had a year at Elstree . . . ."

Paul Rotha in 1929. Photo by Francis Bruyiere.

I joined Grierson for a short time in April 1931, and I was with the Empire Marketing Board film unit for about five months, and I enjoyed every minute of it. We were experimenting. I was working mainly on what we called at that time the poster films, which were, I suppose you can say, the predecessors of the TV commercial. Basil Wright and I were making these.

We had to make a film a week. We had fifteen pounds to make a film with — not fifteen hundred or fifteen thousand, but fifteen quid — and we were given a subject. I can remember one on Empire timber, how much better it was than the other timber, and we just had to think up some kind of abstract design, abstract image, to explain or dramatize Empire timber. We used to shoot these films mainly at night, because in those days film was combustible, and we used the cutting room as our studio. We couldn't do it in the daytime because of the fire-licensing people. When we knew the fire officers were off duty late at night, we turned the place into a studio. We shot all night and went to breakfast in Lyons Corner House in the morning.

I think our interest at that time, the small group of us, was in the main an aesthetic interest. We were interested in montage and so on. We couldn't care less about Empire butter or Empire timber or whatever it was. It wasn't until later that we developed the sociological and political inspiration.

In his second book, Celluloid: The Film Today, *published in September 1931, Rotha wrote of the EMB film unit: "An outstanding feature of the output of this unit is the variety of short poster films produced to advertise the natural wealth of the Empire. These are directed and edited with an almost complete freedom in technique so long as their advertising message is clearly and powerfully expressed. . . . Some of the material for these pictures is specially photographed, others are composed from old material selected for the purpose, but in either case editing and cutting − the basic factors of film making − are their strength. For the expression of some particular contents, abstract effects and trick photography are employed so as to give an added power to the appeal of the film. It is interesting to note that the abstract film, usually considered as a highbrow article to be left well alone, is in this case harnessed to a purpose and is the better for it. . . .*

"Such short abstract films are not shown in the ordinary commercial cinemas, but on continuous automatic projectors at exhibitions and scattered in prominent places, such as big stores and railway stations, throughout the country."

Rotha: But, came September of that year − I don't know why or how, but you get two people in a room sometimes and they agree to disagree, and although Grierson and I have remained the greatest and closest of friends, and I admire and respect the work he has done over all these years − it was perfectly clear there wasn't room in the Empire Marketing Board film unit for both Grierson and myself. So, Grierson being the boss, I went.

Wright: Rotha, who is one of my oldest friends, and indeed we are almost twins, as it were (our birthdays are a few days apart), is I think very much a lone wolf, or an individualist. I don't think Paul really likes working for other people, although other people like working for him. You see, when he finally during the war set up his two organisations, Paul Rotha Productions and Films of Fact, he got a group of the most enthusiastic youngsters, boys and girls, around him. And the results were absolutely terrific. I don't think that his personality and Grierson's could have comfortably coexisted at that time, and, as you know, he went off and very quickly made one of the big pioneer documentary films, the one for Imperial Airways, *Contact,* which was the beginning of the Shell idea, because it was through Jack Beddington of Shell that the *Con-*

tact film ever got made. It was a really big sponsored film of its time and a very interesting one. So Paul really remained independent all through the first half of the thirties. Then of course he joined up with Donald Taylor, and they ran Strand Films very successfully until, again, you got this clash of personalities, because both of them had their own ideas and something had to give. I'm sure Paul would agree with this if I was saying it when he was in the room.

Grierson: The point is that he [Rotha] came to us not as a documentary man at all. He didn't believe in documentary films in these days. He'd just left BIP as assistant art director, and in fact his entire affection at that time was with abstract films. And I wanted to operate — I think he began the thing — an abstract unit. I've always wanted to have an abstract and cartoon unit around because in government sponsorship you are always involved in messages which you don't want to put in documentary form but you can make amusing with abstract films or cartoon films. So Rotha was the beginning of a process that finished up with Norman McLaren and people like that. He was with us for a while, and I think he left us because we ran out of money for abstract films. He made a film for the Tomato Marketing Board; he made another for the Egg Marketing Board. I think we bought up the rights of Moholy-Nagy's famous abstract machine, and we used that for making abstract films that drew attention to egg marketing or tomato marketing or something of that kind. Now he left us because we were out of resources for abstract film making, but he was the beginning of the whole process that was taken up again when I brought in Len Lye. And then Norman McLaren of course carried on with the same idea in Canada, with the result that you have today at the National Film Board, without any question, the greatest animation centre in the world. That is with all respect to the Bugs Bunny group and one or two others that are very important. The Pink Panther group are very good; there are three or four good groups in America. But the great one is of course the animation group in Canada. So it all came out of the Paul Rotha thing.*

But the next thing that happened was that Paul Rotha, having left us, got excited about the documentary idea, which seemed very curious. The next thing we knew, he was making a documentary film. And he made *Shipyard*, which was a very good picture indeed. Now he came into documentary as a convert from outside, after having been with us not in the documentary process but on the arty-tarty side of things.

*In his book *Documentary Diary* (London: Secker & Warburg, 1973) Rotha writes of the poster films: "Grierson liked to think in hindsight that they were the forerunners of the trick colour films made later by Len Lye and Norman McLaren. He recalled that he bought the rights of a short film of a remarkable abstract light machine constructed by Moholy-Nagy, the Hungarian photographer, of Bauhaus fame. Bits of this film were interpolated in some of the EMB Poster films. Grierson believed that this experimental work began when I joined his Unit in 1931 but I disclaim the responsibility."

*ARTHUR ELTON and EDGAR ANSTEY joined the EMB film unit at
the same time in 1931 as a result of answering an advertisement that had appeared in the* Times *agony column.*

*Anstey, who trained in science, had been working as a junior scientific
assistant in the Building Research Station under the Department of Scientific
and Industrial Research and "eagerly looking out for something more' creative
to do." He was a member of the Film Society, already very interested in the
Russian cinema and the work of people like Ruttmann, Pabst, Cavalcanti,
aware of Grierson through the writings of Caroline Lejeune in* The Observer.

Anstey: The first thing – there was no sort of training really that was
followed by everybody – was to learn to join pieces of film together and to
run the projectors (not 16 millimetre, but 35 millimetre projectors) in order
to get a kind of basic idea of what the medium was about. I was trained in this
by Marion Grierson, John Grierson's sister. Everybody spent a certain amount
of time doing these very simple things. Then, from that one started to take old
material – there were a lot of old Canadian films which Grierson had somehow
acquired (they'd come, I think, to the Empire Marketing Board, and they'd
been made for the promotion of Canada, things Canadian, travel to Canada) –
and we used to re-edit them into new shapes and forms, sometimes rather
highbrow and extraordinary. But this was done as kind of practice. It wasn't
hoped that very much would come in the way of finished films. There was one
very good film, I think made by Basil Wright that did in fact come out of that
process [i.e., *Conquest*].

Then I went off – and some would have said prematurely – entirely on
my own to make a film on the Labrador coast. What had happened was that
the Admiralty was embarking on a survey of the Labrador coast. It seems a
little odd, but at the time it had never been fully surveyed, and they told Sir
Stephen Tallents (Stephen Tallents, as he was then) there was an opportunity
for somebody to go and film this survey. Grierson asked me if I would like to
go, and naturally I was surprised, delighted. Tallents was a bit sceptical, but I
think was finally converted, because I'd done a little still camerawork, but I
hadn't had a movie camera in my hand at this time. Grierson sent me down to
St. James's Park, I remember, and I spent half a day photographing statues
from very low angles – the kind of shooting we believed in, in those days, the
sort of looming figure above the lens, – very significant stuff. I would have
had a second half-day doing this, but something or other happened to prevent
it. So this was virtually all the film training that I had, and I went off with a
lot of film and some lights, because there were going to be some interiors in
the ship, and some paper on which I was going to write my script. Grierson and
his wife, Margaret Grierson, took the stock down to the boat, the *Challenger*,
and we started at Portsmouth. And I took this very kindly, that he was seeing
me off personally, and away I went to learn by trial and error.

All kinds of things happened. We ran on a rock, and I went off and tried to make a film on a Grand Banks trawler, but the weather was too cold and the camera jammed up because I think there must have been rather unsuitable oil being used. (I had two De Vry cameras, and they both gummed up from the low temperature and, I suppose, the oil being too thick). This also prevented my getting a lot of material I wanted on the *Challenger* itself and shots of the *Challenger* running on the rock. But I left the ship and spent some time in the village of Nain in Labrador, and I was rather pleased with this material of Eskimo life.

I was able to develop some tests which I could look at, but it took some time to get the rest of the material back to England and processed and then I used to get cabled reports. Some were encouraging, some not nearly so encouraging. But out of it came two silent films, *Unchartered Waters* and *Eskimo Village*. The prints were shown in the Imperial Institute, I remember, but the negative and all the prints, as far as I know, were lost at the beginning of the war, when there was a great turn-out of material, out of London, to get it distributed round the country because of the fire risk.

There wasn't [in these films] any serious attempt at characterisation of the kind you find in Flaherty because we regarded this as a bit romantic. We were all pretty serious-minded chaps then, you know, and we believed, like the Russians, that you should use individuals in your film in a not exactly dehumanized way but a sort of symbolic way. This is the horny-handed fisherman and this is the housewife waiting and here are the innocent children exposed to the forces of nature and so on. So the characters in *Eskimo Village*, and indeed the characters on the *Challenger*, were always sort of symbolizing man in the abstract, as compared with Flaherty, who did develop much more characterisation and was ready to show human quirks and a certain number of weaknesses as well as strengths.

The ordinary working people in our early documentaries never showed any weaknesses at all, except perhaps when we got on to *Housing Problems* later, when they were allowed to show some humour and peccadilloes, perhaps. But this is one of the big contrasts between the treatment of people in the early documentaries and later — not only in England; the same is true I think of Cavalcanti in France and Ruttmann in Berlin and the Russians. Man was always the heroic symbol, really, unless he was a sort of wicked kulak or exploiter of land. We didn't in our films deal with such people, but the ordinary workingman was seen as a heroic symbol. And Flaherty began to move a little bit — not very much — away from that. And then if you come right up to date and contrast the Free Cinema* approach with ours, I think we were often horrified to find ordinary people as anti-heroes, in many of the Free Cine-

*See Epilogue.

ma films. I was horrified by *Together,* perhaps still would be, I don't know. It seemed to me to be absolutely wrong in terms of what East End life is really like. Perhaps it was my idea which was a romantic one, but I found a certain viciousness and cruelty amongst the people in the East End shown in that film, which still deeply shocks me. Perhaps these are my sort of romantic beginnings, this belief that the workingman can only be an heroic figure. If he's not heroic, he can't be a workingman, almost.

ARTHUR ELTON read English literature and psychology at Cambridge (where he wrote film criticism for Granta *and belonged to a group that included Ian Dalrymple, Angus McPhail, Ivor Montagu) and joined the script department at Gainsborough under Michael Balcon in 1927 through a scheme to bring university graduates into the film industry, which, in his words, "regarded them like wild beasts and flattered itself that it parted itself as far as possible from any university education." At Gainsborough he worked as an assistant of various kinds and then as "representative is perhaps too grand a word, to the company in Germany on a series of Anglo-German films which I think were of very little interest." Also, at the instigation of Ian Dalrymple, he started to make a documentary about London which was never finished. On being made redundant when the studio burned down, he applied successfully for a job at the EMB.*

Elton: I began with a film called *Shadow on the Mountain.* I'm not sure if it still exists; I think it does. It was a film which tried to explain the essential elements behind Professor Stapledon's research into grasses, in order to rehabilitate the grasslands on the Welsh mountains.

I knew nothing whatever about films, nothing whatever, and Grierson fired me off with a hand-cranked Debrie camera, me and an assistant — I think, J. N. G. Davidson. Jack Miller was certainly the cameraman. And off we went. I'd no idea how long the shots ought to be or whether they ought to fit — anything at all — so, guided by Jack Miller, we began. And we made a film which was not completed, which was based obviously — heaven knows what it looks like now — but when I made it, it was clearly derived from *Turksib.* The sheep and the oncoming of winter were crosscut in those kinds of ways to make one understand the importance of it.

My second film was *Upstream.* This was about the salmon industry in Scotland, on the East coast of Scotland, about a particular technique of fishing for salmon. It ended up with a quite celebrated sequence of salmon going upstream, and that sequence still appears to be the only sequence of salmon leaping available in Great Britain, so it constantly appears in library form at the BBC. I'm sure there must be much better salmon stuff in Canada, but so far as Britain goes, they appear still to use it, and it's now at least forty years old.

After The Country Comes to Town, *Basil Wright photographed and directed* O'er Hill and Dale, *about the life of a shepherd in the border country. It went out as one of the Imperial Six, but its commentary is quieter and more personal than those of the others.*

Wright: I had finished editing the film, and it had gone off into the awful morgue of Gaumont-British, or wherever it was, and Grierson rang me up (I was doing something else, in Liverpool, I think) and said, "Just write the commentary for that film and stick it in the mail tonight, will you?" So I did, and they used it. They didn't alter it very much, and I'm very glad of that because that's a very personal film. Only one person was concerned in that film. I must have been quite a strong young man, because I walked about on the top of those hills with old Martin, the shepherd, and I had a large tripod, a huge lens case, a big 35 millimetre camera, and the spare magazines. And I carried all this bloody stuff around without an assistant or anything for two and a half weeks through hail and storm and sunshine, up and down dale, across the mountains with this old boy. And I used occasionally to say "Mr. Martin (he had to be treated with great respect) would you mind stopping?" or, even worse, "would you mind doing that again?"

Nowadays it would be much easier, actually, because you'd have a tiny little camera which you could just hold in one hand. You'd have a tape recorder which you'd put in your pocket. Nothing else. Oh, and a zoom lens, for Gawd's sake, a zoom lens! Everybody has the things we'd have sold our souls for in those days!

There were no unions then, and we were, all of us, highly exploited labour. It's interesting, we — in fact, the documentary people — were very much in on getting the film trades union *[ACTT]* established, but not because we felt ourselves exploited, because we felt the people in the studios were being exploited. In a sense, it was always a disadvantage of documentary to have to face up to the union regulations, although there's been a lot of nonsense talked about that. In my experience, I've always been able to go to ACTT and say, "Look, Paul Rotha and I have got this contract with UNESCO. He's going to Mexico. I'm going to Thailand. We're going to make this big feature film about the work of the United Nations.* Now if you're going to make both of us take crews with us, the film will never be made." And they say, "Well, never mind about that. Just specify exactly what you're going to do." What I'm trying to say is that people talk a lot of nonsense about documentary being crippled by having to pay enormous units and so on. It has never really been true if you approach the union in the right way.

In the first two years at the EMB film unit the top salary seems to have been about £4 a week. Grierson's senior recruits started at around that figure.

**World Without End* (1953).

Anstey: I think when I went to Labrador I was still earning £4 a week. I'm sure I did some direction at £4 and then when I got up to £5 a week, which I did after two or three years, I thought I was doing extremely well. And there was no overtime; you worked all the hours there were.

Wright: I was living at home and I had a slight private income, and I could get by. But the pay in documentary was never good. You accepted the pay for the privilege of working in documentary and getting creative freedom. And it was a double freedom because we were most of us politically conscious, and we felt that there was a social contribution to be made. The whole secret of the thing for Grierson was that the people who wanted to be very aesthetic had to toe the line in terms of the budget. Their money was coming from the Government or from some big organisation, so therefore they had a sense of responsibility in expenditure. But this also added up to the fact that one was making films in which some measure of social comment was possible, much more so than in the feature films of the day. If today, looking back, the social comment seems to be fairly small, it looked much bigger at the time because there was nowhere else where you could say things like that through cinema.

Grierson: I would be paid at least first-division wages because I would never work for anything other than first-divison wages. That would, at that time, be a thousand plus. Whatever pay employed first-class travelling I would have; otherwise I wouldn't have worked for any government. So I must have been paid a thousand pounds a year: that was the breaking line between the first division and the second division. And anyway, my vanity — academic vanity — wouldn't have allowed me to take a second-division thing. That was very important for documentary, the vanity. The intellectual vanity, the academic vanity, was total from the beginning. So much so that, you see, these first people in documentary were first-class. Stuart Legg and Basil Wright and Arthur Elton were first-class minds. And there was a time when we used to say that you couldn't get into documentary unless you had a double first, and from Cambridge too, which was supposed to be great snobbery. That was because I couldn't get Anthony Asquith. I tried to get Anthony Asquith at one time, but he didn't come. So from then on they decided to hell with the Oxford people, and we started this line: you need double firsts, and from Cambridge!

Compared with most professional salaries, £4 a week in 1930 was near the bottom end of the scale. It cost more to send a boy to Eton, where annual fees were £230. An engine driver could bring in as much as £4.10s. and an able seaman £9 weekly. On the other hand, most skilled workers had to get by on less than £4. Cabinetmakers, carpenters, upholsterers, stonemasons, plumbers earned around £3.10s. Building labourers got less than £3. Agricul-

tural labourers and many unskilled and semiskilled workers got less than £2. Moreover, between 1930 and 1933 the wages for all these jobs dropped by a shilling in the pound or more.

Grierson's earning were roughly on a par with those of an inspector for schools. By contrast, Sir John Reith, Director General of the BBC, commanded in 1930 a salary of £6,000 per annum, which was £1,000 more than that of Prime Minister Ramsay MacDonald.

2

The Spell of Flaherty

The American director and photographer Robert Flaherty, whose influence on early British documentary with Nanook of the North *(1921) and* Moana *(1925) has already been indicated, worked with the EMB film unit for a short period in 1931. This was another of Grierson's highly successful bids for prestige. The name* Flaherty *has cast a halo round the British documentary movement ever since.*

Grierson: Flaherty first of all came over because he had failed to get entry to Russia. He wanted to make a film about the Russian woman, and he couldn't get the necessary finance and he was pretty short of opportunity − money probably − in Berlin. He called me up.

I couldn't at that time technically get him, as an American, appointed a member of the film unit, but I fixed up a sort of job for him to instruct us in special photographic approaches to the difficult English climate, which at that time was supposed to be a very great drawback to film making. Well, I knew Flaherty's theories and of course you didn't need sunlight really. You only needed a key in black and a key in white, and with all the grades between, you could get your range. He came over as a kind of instructor in photography, but it was understood also that he would make a film on the English craftsman.

Well, Flaherty was a very peculiar fellow to work with. He had a very peculiar approach to film making. He kept on making tests, tests, tests, tests. The point was Flaherty's real film making finished with shooting, making photographs. He just loved discovering things with the camera, but I always had a feeling that he didn't even like looking at what he had shot. He just liked going on shooting. So he went on shooting and shooting − test, test, test, test. And there came a point where I had really to call it a day because he'd spent the money. And there we were with Flaherty's tests, and really glimpses of Britain. He wasn't shooting to any line. He simply wouldn't get down to any line, whether it was British craftsmanship or anything else, but he had such a wonderful eye that we had a lot of material. So several of us −

Arthur Elton, Basil Wright, and I — went out with separate cameras and shot things, and we made a continuity. We made a picture of British craftsmanship, first of all of the old-fashioned sort in glassblowing and pottery making, and then related it to the craftsmanship behind the making of the Rolls Royce engine. So we tried to get across the idea that British craftsmanship and all its qualities were resident in the modern British industrial product.

At that time sound was coming in, and unfortunately — it was one of those steps that one takes simply because it was a time when it suited me to do well for the Treasury — I sold the idea of the series of six pictures with sound to be distributed by Gaumont-British, and the key one was *Industrial Britain.* And the sound was put on at Gaumont-British, and it was, I'm afraid, a commentary by an actor, Calthrop, which sounded very very West End actory and altogether out of the spirit of Flaherty's shooting and out of the spirit of our film making. But there it was. It was the beginning of sound. It had a commentary and it had some lush music and there it was. It was a great success, and it carried with it another five pictures to a great commercial success. And this was very important at that time because nontheatrical was certainly growing all this while, but the theatrical thing was still very much a matter that excited the Treasury and excited our people in Whitehall. I never had the same feeling for the theatrical success that anybody else had, but there it was. And that picture's gone on being circulated ever since. It's still running around in America, still running around in New Zealand and elsewhere, and it has some very, very lovely pictures by Flaherty of the faces of British craftsmen, and probably that's the most notable thing about it today. But it is a film that has many things not by Flaherty at all. It's got some of my own shooting of steel works, some of Basil's shooting is there, and it represents the kind of thing that we could do at that time because we all sort of fitted into each other. We could all cut together or shoot together or whatever.

The amount of money put aside for Flaherty was £2,500, so I probably fired him by the time he spent £2,400. So we'd finish it off with another hundred or two, you may take it from me. We'd finish it within the £2,500, all right. That would be higher than any other picture because it was rather a budget for Flaherty, not a budget for us. I mean the highest film was *Night Mail,* I think, with £1,800. No, we didn't deal with £2,500 as a rule. (The first picture with £2,500 was *Drifters,* and there never was another in my knowledge that cost as much as that. That meant hiring a boat for a long time, a much more complex thing. But I came out inside the money.)

Apart from that, we made another five pictures out of Flaherty's bits and pieces, so that we had in the long run at least six pictures from Flaherty for the £2,500. And in a way it was the only case of Flaherty's being a total commercial success, because with the other five pictures we had, of course, a very big circulation, apart from the theatres. I remember one picture was just of one man making one pot. It was one of the most beautiful films I ever saw in my life. It was a silent picture called *The English Potter,* and every now and then the COI tries to bring it up to date and makes more of a mess of it, not realising the original thing which was simply Flaherty during one day's test-shooting doing one man making one pot. It was the quintessence of Flaherty, because there's nothing to beat Flaherty behind a camera.

But, right from the beginning, we weren't concerned about single pictures. We were concerned about covering territories and opening up new territories in film making. We weren't concerned about making one film about housing but making dozens of films about housing, not one film about nutrition but dozens of films about nutrition.

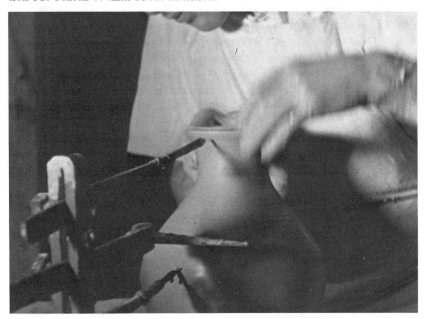

Industrial Britain (1933).

Taylor: I was the production assistant on *Industrial Britain.* I mean, I looked after the camera and the lights. You didn't have electricians. There were three of us. There was a man named Golightly who was the production manager and drove the car, and there was Flaherty and me. We had two one-thousand-watt lamps, and we just used to trundle around Wedgewood's and Rolls Royce and so on shooting stuff.

Elton: J.P.R. Golightly was a strange little man — I think a forestry expert or something like that — wandering about Dartington Hall in a state of great depression, when Grierson met him somehow or other and was struck by him and engaged him as a kind of production manager. He looked after all Grierson's affairs, his money and the unit's money, and really kept the whole place on a very level position, and Grierson was an erratic administrator. (I think he would certainly agree. He would think the only possible sensible way of administering is to administer erratically.) Golightly produced a kind of keel on the whole operation, made it balance itself, which it wouldn't, I think, without him. So he was a very important functional character but not a creative one. He was a sportsman, a fisherman, countryman. He went with Grierson to Canada, came back with Grierson, died some years ago. He had tuberculosis very badly — operated on, very weak; Grierson looked after him.

Grierson: When I fired Flaherty, there was a wonderful moment. We'd had a marvellous dinner — it was Saturday night — up in the Grand Hotel in Birmingham, and oh, a very respectable evening was being had by one and all. Finally I said to Bob, I said, "By the way, Bob, by the time we pay for this darned dinner we'll have spent two thousand four hundred and so and so pounds. Your number's up," said I. And he said, "Oh but John, you've got to get me more money." He said, "I'm not going on with this picture unless I get the promise of another £7,500." I said, "Well, I accept your resignation Bob. Regretfully I accept your resignation because there's no £7,500. This is Treasury money, and by the time we have this last drink, Bob, it's just about through." Then he gave me a long song and dance about how we must get the boys together, and there came a moment when he said, "Go down Whitehall and tell them who I am, John." I said, "Bob, do you know what they think you are down in Whitehall?" He said, "No." I said, "They think you're a photographer." At which dear, great, wonderful Bob Flaherty — he was a great, majestic fellow — he gets up. He puts his fist right up to the sky and he shouts, "Oh fuck them, fuck them."*

Anstey: I did the editing of *Industrial Britain* under Grierson's supervision, a lot of it in Merrick Square, where he had a house. He was ill in bed, and I remember rigging up a rewind over the bed. He had a cutting room in the basement, and I would do some editing, and then we would look at it on a hand-wound 35 mm. projector. Or I would put the rewind across his bed, and he would sit and pull it to and fro in order to announce that there was some vital shot which I hadn't included. And I would diffidently say that I hadn't noticed this shot, and he would roar with rage and accuse me of having lost the shot. This was constantly happening because Grierson had a great facility for remembering shots which hadn't been made. And he would never admit that the shot didn't exist, because, you see, he was the greatest of all editors, in a way, because he knew what the shot was that he needed. I

*This story is apocryphal. Stuart Legg remembers that the dinner took place at the Midland Hotel, Manchester. J.P.R. Golightly told Paul Rotha of a similar dialogue between Flaherty and Grierson on an earlier occasion. Maybe something like it happened more than once.

mean, he would think, "Well, Flaherty must have shot that, the old bastard. Couldn't possibly have been there without shooting that." Flaherty often could. He didn't always make obvious shots, you see. Or Grierson would remember a shot that was in the cut already, which I'd put in, but remember it as being much more magnificent and wonderful because he'd seen perhaps how it might be used and, as I'd used it, it didn't have the right effect. But he had a real instinct for building something out of nothing with film. The only person who had it comparably in my experience was Louis de Roche-mont, a very much underestimated chap, whom I worked with on *March of Time,* when I went to New York. He had the same ability to take a lot of material and sit down himself and make something from it, something quite different from what anybody ever intended.

Wright: I still think it's a marvellous film [i.e., *Industrial Britain*] . I still do. I think the shooting is marvellous: the magic with which that old boy Flaherty could anticipate a movement, start to move his camera just before the potter was going to move his hands; the feeling of the people in that; the beauty of the photography, too — marvellous greys in that film, not many blacks but marvellous greys. All this seems to me to completely overpass the inept sound track put on by the distributors. Well, maybe the *Coriolanus* Overture is as good as any for some of those shots. It's not for me to argue.

After Industrial Britain *Flaherty was commissioned by Gaumont-British to make* Man of Aran. *John Taylor went to Aran with him.*

Robert Flaherty on the Aran Islands.

Taylor: We left London, I think, on the 28th of December, 1931, and went to Aran, where we were shooting for twenty months. I did everything for the first year: I mean, I did the laboratory and developing and printing. But you see, Flaherty had done his developing and printing on *Moana* and New York out on location as well, and he taught me what to do. We had terrible troubles with the laboratory. I did second camera. I mean, there's a percentage of the stuff like the storm sequence and the shark sequence shot on two cameras, and I was working the other one. And every day we used to have about five Leica rolls of stills (which would be about 150 stills) which every night had to be developed and printed. I did the accounts, which I did very inefficiently, and we had a generator which I ran. Because the EMB taught you to do everything, you knew how to do all these things. There was nothing very complicated, but you did get a training there that covered everything you could possibly need, except accounting. They didn't train you in accounting, which was a great pity.

We used to get £500 a month from Gaumont-British in notes – I can't remember whether they were white five-pound notes or white ten-pounds – in a registered envelope. Flaherty used to take three or four of them and give me the rest. I was seventeen. I used to just put it in my pocket and spend it. At the end of the-month we used to have to send in accounts, and I would gather up all these torn and bedraggled bills and write it down. I could hardly write. And then I'd have maybe £200 I couldn't account for. And I'd say to Flaherty, "What do I do with this?" And he'd say, "Put miscellaneous expenditure." And I'd write "Miscellaneous," which was the first word I learnt to spell – "Miscellaneous expenditure, £250." We used to send these accounts in, and Gaumont used to accept them, you know.

He was a wonderful man, Flaherty, in all sorts of ways. He really is the nearest thing to a genius, I think, who's been in the thing. Grierson, of course, was quite exceptional but in a different way. Flaherty was such an incredible character on top of everything else. I've never met anything like him before or since.

STUART LEGG *joined the EMB film unit in 1932. He had rejected the idea of a comfortable slot in his father's firm of solicitors and decided to become an engineer before going to Cambridge, where he read engineering. At Cambridge, in partnership with British Instructional Films headed by Bruce Woolfe, he made a film* Cambridge, *which got theatrical distribution. Woolfe paid for the sound, and Legg, who describes it as "the sort of nonsense one does in one's youth with one's own money," paid for the picture. Spike Hughes wrote the music, and the poet James Reeves played the part of a dishevelled don on his way to a lecture after a heavy night.*

After coming down from Cambridge, Legg had been working for about six months at Publicity Films, as an assistant to Walter Creighton (who earlier made One Family*), when he sought out an interview with Grierson.*

Legg: We sat in the theatre at 37 Oxford Street, which was the EMB premises then, and he said, "Well, I can't give you a real job, but I have one film which has been asked for from outside, and you can have that to make."

It was a film for the Chesterfield Education Authority. At least, it wasn't for the authority, but it was being made by a schoolmaster personally about the Chesterfield education system. It had a budget of £250. So I made this film with a cameraman with whom I subsequently worked on many occasions – an awfully nice chap called Gerald Gibbs. The two of us really made it together, and I think we were within the budget. It was called *The New Generation.* I scripted it and I directed it. He shot it and I cut it. It was a silent film. Then Grierson said that he could take me into the EMB, and so into the EMB I went. If I remember, I got £5 a week. That was regarded as fairly princely.

For some reason I was set to make a film on the plum harvest in the Vale of Evesham, at Pershore, particularly. This didn't go a bit well. The weather was lousy. I didn't understand about plums. I didn't like them very much, anyway. The rushes made Grierson sick, and the theatre reverberated with his curses. Finally I managed to get rid of it onto somebody else. I can't remember who it was, but somebody else who was working at the EMB took it over and finished it.

It obviously was a black mark against me, but Grierson was very good about that sort of thing, and he gave me a lot of material to cut which had been shot in coal mines. He asked me to make it into a two-reeler. And this was the beginning of *Coal Face,* because when it was cut, I somehow managed to make it look like a film. And then somebody had the idea of carrying it much farther, you know, and putting this whole interwoven sound track into it with Britten. Cavalcanti was in it by that time.

HARRY WATT *also joined the EMB in 1932.*

Watt: I came from a normal Scottish middle-class background. My father was a member of Parliament, an extrovert character who dressed like an Edwardian blood all his life, and I had an undistinguished career at Edinburgh University: I never went to any classes. Finally, when my father died, I sailed a sailing boat to Canada, bummed around Canada for a couple of years; then my mother was ill, so I came back.

I came to London with a patrimony of £3,000 and, in association with an Italian and a German refugee, started up a company in Slough Trading Estate to make rubber balls and sandals out of old inner tubes. This was a disaster and we went bankrupt, and I was broke in London. I had various jobs – looking after a midget golf course, demonstrating in Selfridges', storeman in British Home Stores – and gradually got more and more broke. I was sitting in a café in Soho wondering where the hell my next meal was coming from when I heard that a Scotsman was starting up a film unit. Now the

Scots are very like the Jews: they've always got relations somewhere. So I discovered that I had a cousin who'd married a relation of Grierson's and I wrote to Scotland and got an introduction. With this I went along to Oxford Street and got in to see Grierson.

There was this dynamic little grey-faced man sitting in his small office, with piercing eyes, and I was nervous. He said, "Well, tell me about yourself." So I laboriously told him about my various jobs, and I didn't even get a laugh when I told him about the rubber balls and sandals, and I thought, "Christ, I'm out." I then said, "But eighteen months ago I sailed across the Atlantic." He said, "Oh? Tell me about that." So it was quite an adventurous journey. Five of us had sailed a boat from Oban in Scotland to Newfoundland, and we got stuck in the ice and all sorts of things like that. For about half an hour I told him all the story of this, and he said, "Well, you'd better start Monday." I'd never have got the job, of course, if he hadn't been mad about the sea, which I didn't know. I think the salary was £2.10s. a week, because I remember I'd been getting £3 from British Home Stores, and I thought it was a bit bloody mean.

So on the Monday morning I arrived. We had two floors, and upstairs there was a storeroom. They used to call it the studio, but it was just a storeroom. And there in the storeroom was a harassed-looking bloke sucking on an empty pipe — thin, dark, very nervous — and he turned to me and through the pipe said, "Yes?" I can see it now. His name was J.D. Davidson. He was a cameraman, a professional cameraman, and he was the general dogsbody. I said, "Mr. Grierson told me to report." He said, "Christ, another!" Then he said, "What do you know about films?" And I said, "Nothing." I may say here and now — and this is one of the quotes I'm very proud of — I believe I'm the only one who went into the film business because I wanted to eat. I had no artistic bent whatsoever. All I wanted was a square meal. Anyway, I stood around, and he suddenly said, "Can you whitewash?" So I'd never whitewashed, but I said, "Yes, of course I can whitewash." So he said, "Well, there's some whitewash. Mix it with water and put it in that bucket over there. There's a brush. Go down to the end of the passage downstairs and start whitewashing." So down I go and start, and it looks jolly good when you put it on wet. It's when it dries that you realise your deficiencies. And I was whitewashing away there when Sid Cole (now a very well-known producer in feature films and television, Sidney Cole) wandered out of the cutting room, where he'd been on a short-term job. He was free-lancing then, and he'd come in to cut some film. He'd finished it because he was very efficient, and he'd nothing to do, so he started chatting, and he said, "Christ, you're bloody awful!" I said, "Well, can you do any better?" He said, "I'll bet you I can." So he started whitewashing. And that was my first day in films.

Then I remember being sent out on a film, to the aerodrome in the south of London where BOAC used to have those enormous trundling things to Paris. A boy called Clark — a bumptious youth who disappeared, presumably fired — was directing it. I was the assistant and, believe it or not, electrician. I made the most frightful cock of the electrics. I blew up lamps, which were very expensive. I gave myself a terrible shock. Finally the electrician from BOAC had to come in and help us, and I was taken off being electrician. This was the kind of job I did for a while.

Then suddenly I was summoned to Grierson's office — and I was really the lowest form of life there — and he said, "Bob Flaherty wants somebody in Ireland. He's making a film out there on a rock, and he wants a strong young fellow. Would you like to go?" I said, "Sure. Of course." I think it was five quid a week. He said, "It's going to be tough, you know." I said, "Right-o." He said, "All right, leave Monday." Now when he said a rock, I thought it was something like the Wolf Rock or the Eddystone Lighthouse, so I went out and bought myself oilskins and rubber boots.

I was met on the quay in Aran by the famous Pat Mullen, king of the island (who's still alive) who appeared in the film, and he says, "All the visitors always stop here at Murphy's Bar." So we stopped at Murphy's Bar, and they gave you dirty big shots, and I arrived paralysed for my introduction to Robert Flaherty.

The extraordinary thing was that Flaherty always lived like a king in these primitive places. You know, he took a grand piano to the South Seas. On Aran a rich woman had built a holiday house, and Flaherty had that. He'd imported a *cordon bleu* cook from the mainland, and he'd built a series of cottages for the youngsters and assistants — John Taylor, principally. And I never lived so well in my life. We had two grown men just to put the peat on the fire. I'd gone out a skinny youth, and they used to give me barrels and buckets of Guinness, and I had the easiest time of my life. I stayed there about a year, came back fat as a pig. I never got thin again. That made me fat.

I learnt a great deal, but I began to realise there, for the first time, that I had a journalistic capacity. You see, I had been very good at English; I was never beaten in English essays and stuff like that in school and university, and I had this capacity but nobody had brought it out. Flaherty, of course, was the most magnificent cameraman, but I began to feel that he wasn't a film maker. I began tentatively putting forward ideas, which were turned down flat. One of the ideas that was turned down flat, which put me off the whole thing, was that I discovered that on one of the three islands once a year they gathered the cattle on the beach, then forced them into the water and towed them behind these little currachs, fighting, and hoisted them aboard a steamer. It was like a rodeo, with these little currachs, and sometimes the weather was bad. I thought it was a wonderful scene, and the reason Flaherty turned it down was that he didn't want the public to know that the steamers came to the island, which meant that the film was a phoney. I mean, the whole thing was way back. They hadn't caught those sharks for seventy-five years. They hardly ever took the seaweed up, and they took it up on donkeys; they didn't carry it on their backs. I began to think a bit at Aran.

In 1932 Arthur Elton made Voice of the World, *which Paul Rotha described in his book* Documentary Film *(first published in 1936) as "I think the first documentary, at any rate in Britain, which used sound at all imaginatively." It was commissioned by New Era Films (the company which had acted as agent and distributor to the EMB since* Drifters) *but had an industrial sponsor, the gramophone company, His Master's Voice. Grierson's own association with the film as producer did not prevent him from reviewing it in* Cinema Quarterly *(Winter 1932) as follows: "Elton possibly unappreciative of radio's social significance and therefore lacking in proper (aesthetic) affection for subject. This point important, as affecting almost all the tyros of documentary. Too damned arty and post-war to get their noses into public issues. Miss accordingly the larger dramatic themes possible to the medium. The film, however, puts Elton first among industrial documentary directors in this country. Sound effects at all times intelligent, but a lack of finish in the cutting prevents some of them achieving full effect."*

Elton: I can't think it had anything very interesting in it, and now nobody can find it, so no one will ever know. It had, I think, a striking opening sequence in which we got a sound montage to give a particular effect of deprivation of people. I should think it's of no distinction at all, but, anyway, mercifully it vanished.

The next thing was an entirely new expedition which really shaped the thing up for me. I was asked to make a film on British craftsmanship, particularly in the aeroplane industry, so I made *Aero-Engine*, which took me at once into engineering. And my personal interest is in engineering — always has been — and the history of engineering and the history of technology. It changed my whole life, in a way, this particular film. I became fascinated with the processes and the people. I formed very good relations with the craftsmen themselves, and I never looked back. (I saw it about three months ago and was amazed. It now seems to me an astonishingly good film. I can say this because it is forty years old, and I couldn't remember it at all till I saw it, and it might just as well have been made by a stranger. So I am allowed to say I thought it was very good.)

But I think I'd always had these interests. I was brought up at Bradford-on-Avon, and my earliest recollection is of being left in my pram by the ground frame to the east of Bradford-on-Avon tunnel, where my nurse flirted with a signalman and I used to lie in my pram and watch the trains go by. Then, when I was a small boy, the Kennet and Avon canal was open, and I used to accompany the barge drivers, and finally, when asked where I wished to go, I always used to say I wished to go to the gasworks. And now my interest in technology, for no doubt obscure Freudian reasons, has been very much associated with the railways, canals, and coal gas. Well, this gave me the history of technology (which was latent in me all my life: my father had it, I think, though he never put it to any particular use) and this and *Aero-*

Engine fused together and gave me a new sort of perspective on films and on what I wanted to do. So far as I've contributed in films, it has perhaps been films on the history of technology. I think I must have been the first person to have attempted serious historical works on that kind of theme.

Aero-Engine *was a silent film, shot at silent speed. In the meantime, Basil Wright had gone off to the West Indies to film some material for the EMB and Orient Shipping Line, which resulted notably in* Cargo from Jamaica *and* Windmill in Barbados, *both shot at sound speed.*

Wright: *Cargo from Jamaica* was quite a considerable experiment in a type of film cutting at the time. I spent a long time on it. I'd got this material which I knew was going to lead up to this appalling scene on the dockside, with all these men being paid about a farthing a day for doing this tremendously hard work. I filmed it from every possible dynamic angle, because my desire was to show the toil and sweat involved in this particular work – and, indeed, the exploitation. Then it was Grierson who said, "Of course, we've got a lovely contrast," because when he was shooting some stuff preliminary to the film he never finished – the Port of London film – he'd done some of these very calm shots of the bananas in London coming along these endless belts with nobody touching them, nobody doing any hard work at all. He said, "You can have that. You can stick that on the end and make your contrast, so you can have your violence."

Cargo from Jamaica (1933).

Of course, this was all very influenced by the Russians — not merely by Eisenstein but by Vertov. I was trying to get a tremendous amount of dynamic clashing in the cutting without breaking up the actual movement, which was getting the stuff off the quayside and into the boats, and I think it works. Well, I don't know. I haven't seen it for years, but at least at the time I thought it worked. Then of course it just got dropped. It never had a sound track put on it. When the Empire Marketing Board was abolished, it got sort of lost in the limbo between EMB and GPO. It's a pity! It should be shown with some calypso records or something of that sort.

Windmill in Barbados does have a sound track which I didn't have anything to do with, either. This was put on by Cavalcanti and some of his assistants, because I was probably in Ceylon at the time. But I would always like to have had *Cargo from Jamaica* with a sound track, and I think its interest is slightly academic now.

After leaving the EMB, Paul Rotha worked on some "dreary scripts for feature films" until, as a result of meeting Jack Beddington (then assistant general manager and publicity manager for Shell Mex and British Petroleum — Shell International's marketing branch) he embarked on an independent career in film making that was to parallel and, to some extent precede developments under Grierson.

Rotha: I thought to myself, what Grierson has done — apart from making a remarkably interesting film in *Drifters* — is to find a different economic basis for film making. I realised that outside what Grierson had done, which was government money, we could try and get industrial money with which to make pictures. Beddington commissioned me to write a script for a possible, kind of avant-garde experimental film for Shell. Well, I'm no good at writing avant-garde experimental films, but anyway I wrote some sort of crap about the spirit of Shell or something, using animated cartoons, and, having no money whatsoever (I couldn't even pay the rent) I delivered this to Jack. Jack said, "Do you believe in this?" I said, "No." He said, "Nor do I." Then by an extraordinary chance (you won't believe this — it sounds like a Hollywood movie), the telephone rang. Jack answered it, and after a number of cryptic sentences, he suddenly put his hand over the instrument and said, "Paul, do you want to make a film about airways and air routes?" I said, "Sure. Of course I do." He said, "Well, that's Imperial Airways on the telephone." And that's how I made *Contact*.

The making of Contact *is described very fully in Rotha's own book,* Documentary Diary, *where Grierson's review of it in* Cinema Quarterly *(Autumn 1933) is also quoted. Grierson had many reservations, but he qualified them with the comment: "These criticisms are noted only because Rotha is coming into the first line of documentary and calls for all the heavy weather we can make for him. Even if the photography were not as beautiful as it is, the size and scope of* Contact *would make it of first importance in this year's documentary account."*

Paul Rotha making *Contact* (1932).

Watt: After Aran I went back to being an assistant at the EMB. We were still EMB, but by that time the Post Office was commissioning films, and *6.30 Collection* was mooted. I was made assistant to Anstey, and we went to the Western District Office and started shooting the film. I was *not* the electrician, but I was general assistant. Two-thirds of the way through — oh, more than two-thirds of the way through — Anstey got another job. I don't know what job it was, but he went somewhere else. And Grierson quite casually said, "Well, you'd better finish it off, Harry."

So, being kind of ambitious and young and bouncy and bumptious, I took over. It was just finishing it off: I knew what the film was going to be. It was a straightforward film following the sequence of the letters from the time they went in, to the time they went out, just following the process photographically. So I shot for about ten days with a cameraman; I think it was Onions, who was very good. We used free-lance cameramen then, and they helped an enormous amount. I don't think enough has been made of their contribution to the early days of documentary. Don't let's kid ourselves, the early days of documentary were basically an intellectual exercise carried out by a bunch of half-baked and inexperienced amateurs. The theory was right, but in practice we were just not skilled enough. And these free-lance cameramen — the people on the fringe of the film business who got a day's work with newsreels, small publicity films, and occasionally second-unit stuff with the feature boys — came in and photographed our films. About three guineas a day, I think, perhaps they would get, and they were very professional. They didn't know what the hell we were after and didn't care very much as long as they got their three quid. But being good technicians, they helped us, and those they liked they helped a great deal. Particularly one must remember the names of Onions and Bill Shenton and J. D. Davidson, who photographed a great deal. (He was not a free-lance. He took on a permanent job and lived in a state of permanent exasperation with us all, but he worked like hell.)

But the greatest character of them all was George Noble. George Noble was a short, fat, terribly scruffy Cockney, who winter and summer appeared in a dirty white shirt with a belt tightly round his enormous gut, pebble glasses, and a thick Cockney accent. And he was always laughing, always gay, and had an enormous success with women, which exasperated us. He thought we were just a lot of silly highbrows, and he'd come in and say, "All right, what've we got today? None of this arty-farty nonsense. You know George's motto 'Dead on and pin sharp.' None of these bloody low angles and high angles. I've got a hangover." But having said that, he'd go out and work like hell to get the stuff. There are many famous stories about George. He used to go off for a month's location with no luggage at all but with a spare thousand-foot magazine in which he had a pair of socks, a spare collar, and an extraordinary piece of fern, which we discovered was his idea of art. Whenever someone wanted a shot in the country this seedy bit of fern would be lugged out and stuck in front of the lens and he said "Well, you know, you want something in the foreground, boy. You want something in the foreground." Another person who was serious-minded was a man called Jeakins, and, as I say, Onions was serious-minded. But way back to the days of *Drifters,* that was photographed by professional cameramen.*

Anyway, then Grierson said, "You'd better edit it" [i.e., *6.30 Collection*]. Well, I had never hardly been in the cutting room at all. So I took all the stuff, Anstey's stuff and mine, and joined it together and ran it. It was, say, forty or fifty minutes, bloody awful. I tentatively took out some shots, and it still was terribly long and bloody awful, and I didn't know what to do. The strange thing was that you didn't go to anybody. You just went on by

*The professional cameraman in charge of photography on *Drifters* was Basil Emmott.

yourself. Then one of the tremendous pieces of luck that you have to have
in the film business happened to me. At that time the EMB had come under
the microscope of some committee or other. It was Depression times, and
the government was cutting down on little things like the Empire Marketing
Board, like when your profits are down you kick the office cat. They were
going to investigate what we were producing, so we get a memo from Grierson
that all films in progress had to show an extract, and I had to show seven or
eight minutes of *6.30 Collection*. So I was forced to be utterly ruthless and
show the process from the moment the letter is posted to the moment it goes
on the mail train in eight minutes. And I suddenly had a film. So then I was
more-or-less established as a junior director, though I think I went on as
assistant again for some time.

But there was very little instruction. And this is why, of course, I
latched on to Cavalcanti tremendously because I was desperately anxious to
learn my trade, and nobody was teaching me. Of course a great deal of talk
went on, and a great deal of reading of books and analysing of people's films,
and the influence of the Russians was enormous. But nobody really taught
you. Wright did try to help me a bit about editing at the very beginning.
Elton never helped me at all. Practically nobody helped me except these professionals who were around, like Sid Cole and the cameramen. And although
Grierson was a brilliant publicist, I didn't find him a good practical producer,
either in script or in rushes.

Elton: Grierson was very helpful when you were making films. He would
look at what you had done and would always be very revealing.

Legg: He was very much in on scripts. He saw nearly all the rushes,
and to some of us who were young and a bit nervous, this was a pretty terrifying process, because in those days Grierson was far from the relatively
mellow elder statesman he became. The theatre would reverberate with
curses at the slightest mistake in shooting. One learnt a lot at those rushes
sessions because he would dissect rushes and take them to pieces . . . . Hosts
of possibilities would be tossed out. Then he sat in very closely as films came
together on the cutting bench, full of ideas. And he was always there if you
got stuck and ran into difficulties. You'd take it to him and say, "I'm stuck.
These are the circumstances." And he would see it with you and see it
again and again, and then he would come through with an idea. I think this
was one of the things that inspired confidence in him: that he would never
leave you without some sort of lifeline to hold onto.

Anstey: We did a film about the making of the radio station in Droitwich, during the course of which I clambered four hundred and fifty feet hand
over hand up the mast. Fortunately it was only four hundred and fifty feet.
It was going to be six hundred, I think, but fortunately it had only arrived at four

hundred and fifty. There was no lift, so I went up. I wondered several times, but if you were trained by Grierson, there was no doubt. If you needed to get shots of the men putting the girders in positions and they were up there, well, you had to go up there. It took me between forty and forty-five minutes to get up. I was absolutely exhausted, of course, with the camera on my back, you see, and then I came down a bit faster. I think in thirty minutes I came down, but it had come on to rain, and the constantly pulling one's hands up and down this vertical ladder had taken the skin off. I remember a sort of mixture of water and blood coming down my shirt sleeves, and I felt very bedraggled and sorry for myself. In fact, it was worrying doing that kind of thing, but after a time you get so exhausted you feel perhaps any moment I won't care whether I fall off or not. I think if it hadn't been for Grierson, I would have questioned the wisdom of doing it.

Wright: You had to get used to doing without sleep and that sort of thing, but he was the most rewarding person to work with that I've ever met, because he was able to extract from you abilities which you didn't know you had but which he sensed. He never told you how to correct your mistakes. He simply told you how damned lazy – intellectually lazy – you were, not to develop the theme which you'd taken, in a proper manner. And you used to be sent back over and over again to reshoot a sequence because it wasn't good enough. Well, this really put you on your mettle. "Why isn't it good enough?" you said. "How can I make it better?" And you did. You did.

Anstey: I remember once (it was in the same Droitwich film) I needed a very simple shot of a stone being put onto a parapet, and I photographed it perhaps in a rather casual way. And Grierson said this laying of the stone meant nothing at all because it had no feeling of care and craftsmanship. The camera wasn't angled in such a way as to make it interesting. The shots weren't well composed. You didn't get nice shapes, and it wouldn't cut so as to get one shape moving against another shape, and so on. And so would I be so good as to (he didn't put it nearly as politely as that) go off and shoot it again.

Well, I didn't care to point out that the parapet, I knew, by this time was finished. I had to try to find another similar building where I could photograph the stone being laid, and I telephoned all around and went to various building contractors, and at last I found one and got these people to do it again – different people, of course. This didn't too much matter because it could be cut in; you wouldn't see in the long shots who the men were that were putting the stone down. I did it again, and I brought it back. And Grierson said, "Well, it still stinks. I suppose it's a bit better, but it's not good enough. It's just casually thrown in, becomes just a cutaway between two interesting sequences. It's no good at all. Every shot must stand on its own feet." He wouldn't use the phrase "work of art in its own right," but you knew it must have aesthetic quality. "You'd better have another go."

And I had to find another building because I knew that this other one had been done. And at last I got a shot which was acceptable. It was better, I think, than the other two. And this was really the way one worked. I mean that you didn't ever say, "Well, it can't be done" or "It's too late now," because the shot must always come first.

Watt: I believe Anstey had perhaps shot a little bit of *BBC Droitwich,* because it took a long time to make. It could only be done when the thing was being built, and therefore it spread over a year or eighteen months. He shot a little bit at the very beginning of it but practically nothing, because I claim this film, and the credits say that I directed it.

So I went off with a wonderful old cameraman, Bill Shenton. He was an old boy who drifted into the office asking for work, and he had been England's top cameraman in the Betty Balfour days, and he was a drunk. He taught me an enormous amount. I got to know that when the pubs opened at half-past eleven, we had to stop shooting, and he had to go up and have his stiffener — but he was very sympathetic to me because it was my first film. Anyway, we finally had to get the shots from the top of the mast, and old Bill refused point blank to go up. I mean, he couldn't. So I did it. The mast was about eight hundred feet high, and there was just a platform of wood on the top and it was blowing like hell. There was a lift up part of the way, but then I had to climb to the top, and I was very frightened, but one used to do extraordinary things. The shots weren't very effective. Bill had set the camera. (It was a Newman-Sinclair. Flaherty really popularised the Newman-Sinclairs; he got very long focus lenses made for the first time for them, because he had the money to have that done.) But of course in those days of reflex finders, you saw what you were looking for upside down, which was always difficult.

It was around this time that Grierson shot Granton Trawler.

Grierson: In the thirties we were all in together. We could all edit well. We could all write well. There was no part of it we couldn't do, even camerawork. The one credit I was absolutely insistent on was putting my name on as a cameraman on one picture, and it's still there. I'm very pleased with that, having my credit as a cameraman on *Granton Trawler.* I had to put my name on because there was nobody else on the picture except me. It was a solo effort. . . . It's a sweet little film. I've got a kind of funny feeling about it, a weird faraway feeling.

Anstey: It was a sort of holiday task because Grierson loved the sea and he loved fishing, and he went off and photographed a boat out of Granton. It was very, very rough, and he himself was very disappointed at the material when he got back — partly I think because he had been terribly sea-sick and he had miserable memories of the trip, although he was a very good sailor; he had some sailing blood in the family. But he saw nothing to be done with this film, and I left the Highlander in Dean Street, I think, or whichever pub we were drinking in at the time, went back into the unit (we were then at 37/39 Oxford Street), and proceeded to put this material together. It was an example of how one worked far into the night. I suppose by about three o'clock in the morning, I'd got the stuff in shape. What I found very exciting — it's still in the film — was that where, because of the rough seas, the camera had fallen over and Grierson was perhaps too sick to save it, you got absolute-ly wonderful shots for a storm sequence, whirling sky and sea. I chopped these up and used them to build the appearance of a much stronger and more violent storm than in fact had occurred. And this was the kind of editing we used to enjoy. One was synthesizing a storm on the bench.

Granton Trawler (1934).

Grierson was surprised and delighted because — it's very interesting — he'd never really seen the material. I think when you're photographing some-thing it's very subjective, and you see what you would have liked it to have been or what might have been. Only the editor starts with the material. He's not conscious of the circumstance in which it was photographed. It's one argument for not editing one's own film.

Anstey had no recollection of the sound track's being added to Granton Trawler, *but this is perhaps the most interesting aspect of what still stands as a successful small film. The sound track was added later by Cavalcanti and consisted of a few simple noises and the hum of conversation produced by Scots fisherman talking, in fact, about football.*

Watt: The atmosphere in the Empire Marketing Board, and later in the GPO was quite extraordinary in that Grierson was the god. He was the little dictator, and we all sat at his feet, and he was called by the majority of people "the Chief," and he played up to it. He was a great performer. The routine, say, of running the rushes, was quite fantastic. You got them back from the laboratory in the morning. You examined them and put leads on them and then went to the projectionist and had them threaded up. Then you went to this sweet little man, J.P.R. Golightly, who was Grierson's complete right-hand man and shadow and adored him, this little, quiet, *pince-nezed,* almost caricature of a civil servant with a very good English voice, and you said, "The rushes are ready." And he said, "Very well, Harry. I'll tell the Chief. Wait in the theatre." So you went back to the theatre and sat down and waited. And you just waited, and sometimes you waited quite a long time. Then you'd hear a crash and that would be Grierson's door being thrown open, and then another bang and that was him kicking the door into the passageway open, and the fast, fast steps coming down the passageway — then, crash, the door was kicked open again and in would come Grierson, followed by Golightly. He'd sit down and say, "Right. Shoot." And you ran your rushes. He would then go into a great deal of stuff which to me, who was the lowbrow of the unit (I didn't know any of the highbrow phrases or the social content stuff — I was always just making a picture to tell a story), seemed erudite and not necessarily practical.

The extraordinary thing about the whole atmosphere was that there was no discipline in the unit, although Grierson was this god. Everybody wandered in and out, and there were no hours. We worked every God's hour there was and wandered out to the pub and had a sandwich and a drink and came back and worked again and very often, if there was a rushed job, slept on the cutting room floor, all for a matter of two or three pounds a week.

The other extraordinary atmosphere about the office — and this is mainly in the EMB days — was the monasticism of it. We were all normal, pretty well, but we were absolutely forbidden to get married, and even the fact of having girl friends was rather kept in the background, even though one or two of us were living with girls at the time. And Grierson fell for this very charming Margaret Taylor, John Taylor's sister, and we knew all about it. She even came and worked there, and they got married while she was working there and Grierson didn't admit it for eighteen months. They didn't go out together or arrive together. I mean, you know, a definition of Grierson in many ways is a Presbyterian priest.

Elton: He is a philosopher, critic, inspirer, a revealer — prophet, if you like . . . . He looks at things from so many different facets always, peers at them from one side and then from another side, brings to bear so many other things which are in his mind in association, that his views on almost anything, as he talks, are always revealing. That, I think, is the most striking element about him, the fact that he can always take hold of factors most people have neglected, see things in things which other people can't or don't see. . . . He's a great man for revelation, and that, I think, is his most powerful feature.

The output of the British documentary movement between 1929 and 1933 is of mainly academic interest today. The merits and limitations of the two major films, Drifters *and* Industrial Britain, *have, I think, already emerged with sufficient clarity in the comments quoted on the preceding pages. Despite a good deal of enthusiasm — perhaps engendered as much by the memory of those pioneering days as by the films themselves — despite even the odd utterance of the word* masterpiece, *none of those interviewed would be likely to take serious offence at the allegation that none of the EMB films is actually a masterpiece. Certainly none is.*

A point of criticism which has not, and never would be raised by the film makers themselves because it is too fundamental to the whole development of British documentary, concerns the attitude displayed towards the workingman. While giving the documentary movement every credit for putting the workingman on the screen, I have to add that the fishermen in Drifters *and the various craftsmen and skilled workers in* Industrial Britain *are shown from what would today be regarded as a middle-class, Establishment viewpoint. (It would not have been so regarded at the time. Then it was obviously progressive to show working people at all, and the attitude would have been more apparently that of a Scottish Calvinist oriented slightly to the left.) The attitude in the films is that work is in itself ennobling, and hence it is no part of the general purpose to get too close to working people as people, to reveal their pay or their living conditions, the price paid to them or the price they paid. This outlook is nicely summed up by Edgar Anstey when he talks about his "belief that the workingman can only be an heroic figure. If he's not heroic, he can't be a workingman, almost." So the honest hands and honest faces said it all. But did they, in those Depression years?*

Most of the lesser films of this early period are simply lessons in film making, and not to be taken seriously in any wider context. The best of them are Granton Trawler *and* O'er Hill and Dale — *unpretentious, direct, and, each in its own way, charming.* Aero-Engine *is very long and very tedious, at least until the closing sequence, when the curious little antiquated aircraft, whose engine we now know so intimately, takes off on a rhapsodic, Dziga Vertov-type inaugural flight.*

King Log, *all that remains of Basil Wright's* Lumber, *looks a complete mess, mainly because the material used in it appears to have been shot at silent speed, then ruthlessly speeded up to match the tacked-on sound track.* Wright's Country Comes to Town *is equally impossible to judge, so naïve is its commentary.* Cargo from Jamaica *can now be regarded only as an uncompleted work, shot at sound speed but lacking sound.*

Many of the films, of course, no longer exist, notably Conquest, Uncharted Waters, Eskimo Village, Voice of the World. *Others, for one reason or another, were not available for viewing. But on the evidence of what I saw, I think it highly unlikely that any masterpieces have been forgotten or lost to posterity. It was apparent to me that the members of the documentary movement knew very well which were their best films, and have seen to it, rather more effectively than most commercial producers and distributors, that these survived. The importance of the first years of documentary, as most of the people concerned are ready enough to admit, was not the films but the creation of an environment in which experiment could begin.*

3

Innovations at the Post Office

When the Empire Marketing Board closed down in 1933, Sir Kingsley Wood (then postmaster general) appointed Sir Stephen Tallents to the new post of public-relations officer at the GPO. Tallents took the EMB film unit and library with him to the Post Office. The unit's offices from 1934 were at 21 Soho Square; they also acquired a small studio at Blackheath. For the first time they had their own sound-recording equipment. In an article, "The GPO Gets Sound" (Cinema Quarterly, *Summer 1934), Grierson reported:*

". . . the apparatus cost three thousand pounds or thereabouts; the re-recording apparatus is a luxury over and above that. This is the machine which orchestrates the different elements of sound – the natural sounds, the music, the dialogue – and, in effect, makes a considered sound strip possible. Add to these purely engineering costs the cost of your sound cameramen; add the cost of a created music. Access to the means of production is clearly not a simple matter. That we have found an economic basis for it in government propaganda and, with it, have retained the same freedom for directors we enjoyed with the EMB, represents a relief and thankfulness I leave to the imagination.

"We waited five years for sound at the EMB. We saw our first film fall in the gulf between silence and sound, and our subsequent films pile up in silence on a fading market. Our solitary access to sound last year was bound to be a disappointing one, for, selling some films to G-B, we were reduced to attendant orchestra and attendant commentator. Under such conditions responsibility passed out of our hands and experiment was plainly impossible. The result – in Industrial Britain, O'er Hill and Dale, Up Stream *and the others – was, I suppose, competent. From any considered point of view it represented no contribution whatever to the art and practice of sound.*

"By access to sound, I mean an intimate relation between the producer and his instruments. I mean a relationship as direct as we have established for him in the matter of camerawork. He is his own first cameraman and the silly mystery with which professional cameramen once surrounded their very simple box of tricks, is over and done with. With us, the producer is his own

sound man too, and in the same simple sense. In the studio the old camera nonsense has become attendant on the apparatus of sound. Mysterious bells are rung, and rung as for some great religious ceremony. High priests gabble in the same essential idiom as Thibetan priests over their prayer wheel, and a dozen perfectly unnecessary, or perfectly unimportant hangers-on, create atmosphere in the background. . . Other phalanxes of experts lie beyond: knowing exactly – on one showing of your film and a couple of rehearsals – what music you want. And with studio overheads – the hangers-on nursing their overtime as religiously as their machines – any variation from the routine job is too expensive anyway.

"By access to sound I mean the absolute elimination of these comic barriers between the producer and the result he wants. I mean the elimination of both economic and ideologic overheads. At the GPO we have established it from the beginning. We have one sound engineer, and a good one. For the rest, if we want music – and we do not want it much – we find it cheaper to have it written for us. If we want natural sound, the producer drives out and gets it. If we want to orchestrate sound we sit in the sound van and arrange the re-recording as we think best. If we want to play with sound images, or arrange choral effects, or in any way experiment, we have no one's permission to ask and no considerable overheads to worry about, because we do most of the work ourselves. We are even free, as on one occasion recently, to make our own orchestra. The instruments and players were as follows. One rewinder (Legg), one trumpet, two typewriters (office staff), one empty beer bottle (blown for a ship's siren), one projector (by the projectionist), some conversation, two pieces of sand paper (Elton), the studio silence bell (myself), cymbals and triangle (Wright). Walter Leigh arranged and conducted. The result was our title music for 6.30 Collection. *It cost us the hire of the trumpet.*

"Indeed it is remarkable that our experiments have all made for cheaper sound. It costs five pounds, I believe, to have a professional commentator, but we have never thought of spending so much on so little. We do the job ourselves if we want a commentary, and save both the five pounds and the quite unendurable detachment of the professional accent. Better still, if we are showing workmen at work, we get the workmen on the job to do their own commentary, with idiom and accent complete. It makes for intimacy and authenticity, and nothing we could do would be half so good. You will see the result in both Cable Ship *and* Under the City. . .

"These represent first variations and possibly not very important ones. 6.30 Collection *however, is probably the first documentary made entirely with authentic sound. . . I noticed when we showed the film at the Phoenix in London, that the natural noises and the overheard comments, orders, calls and conversations, created a new and curious relationship between the audience and the screen. The distance was broken down in a certain intimate delight – I presume – at seeing strangers so near. Eavesdropping, who knows,*

may yet be one of the pillars of our art. There was one superb sequence that we could not use. A dispatchman, edging unwittingly up to the microphone, loosed his more private opinion of some new and officious supervisor. The vocabulary was limited, but the variations were ingenious. . ."

Anstey: I used some of the first sound equipment the GPO film unit had. We went to the Central Telegraph Office, and what was very interesting was we recorded no dialogue at all, as I remember. We looked with contempt, really, on dialogue because of the kind of thing they had in Hollywood films. You know, it might as well be a stage play. All the time that I was in the Central Telegraph Office, we were recording the noises of the bits of equipment with the idea of using them (as we did eventually in a film on the CTO, the name of which I've forgotten) as a kind of musical score. Our first approach to sound was to use it in a kind of abstract way, in a mechanistic way, if you like, and try to take sounds and orchestrate them. Dialogue came much, much later, partly because we didn't have synchornous equipment but partly because we were terrified of getting close to the theatre or to literature.

Watt: All the best sound — RCA and all that — were American and tremendously expensive, and a British company called Visatone brought out what was basically a pirated system. They got round the patents, and they were so small I don't think the other big ones bothered about them. It was called an open track, and it was appallingly noisy — an acchh noise. And we had an Irish sound recorder, John Cox. He was very good, in the sense that he didn't give a damn. He thought we were all mad. He was a professional and a free-lance, again, and he thought, "the long-haired, stupid, left-wing bums!" He generally stank of beer, but if we said we wanted the sound of something or other very loud when it was very soft actually, he'd say, "You want it that way boy, you can have it. You can have what you bloody well like. It's terrible sound, boy, but that's what you want."

There was a certain amount of experimentation, but I can't remember very much about it, quite frankly, until Cavalcanti came in.

ALBERTO CAVALCANTI, *whose silent films with the French avant-garde* – Rien que les heures *(1926),* En Rade *(1928) – had been shown in Film Society programmes in the twenties, was already an influence on the British documentary movement before he joined it.*

Cavalcanti was born in 1897 in Brazil, where he began by studying law. He was "quite a wonder boy at the time," the youngest student in the university, but he was "expelled because of a quarrel with an old professor." His father sent him to Europe on condition that he "shouldn't study law and go into politics." He trained as an architect in Geneva and was working as a draughtsman in an architect's atelier in Paris by the age of eighteen. In order to earn more money, he went into interior decoration and from there

Cavalcanti (left) with Jean Genet, Paris, 1933.

to the film studios as art director. He quickly progressed from first assistant to assistant cutter, cutter, and finally director.

Cavalcanti: It was silent days, and all of a sudden sound came. I believed in sound, but sound at the time was only talk, and perhaps a door banging or a telephone ringing. It was very primitive to us. After passing two years in exile from the studios because the French, like the Americans, thought the silent film directors couldn't do sound pictures, I came back, and I did a lot of comedies. I did versions for Paramount of American films, in which I could learn the technique of the microphone. Then I started doing French comedies myself, which were terrifically successful commercially. But I was fed up with the talk, talk, talk, talk. And after four or five hits I was starting a sixth, and I really couldn't stand it, so I said I was sick. That is a trick I use quite a lot when I don't want to do something. I go sick. And yet I am as strong as a horse. Still, I couldn't do anything but try, and I came to London and met Grierson. It's very debatable who introduced me to Grierson. Dallas Bower says it was him, but as far as I can remember it was my old cameraman James Rogers who introduced me to Grierson.

Grierson told me to come to his place. I explained I couldn't stand the French comedies any more, and I wanted to experiment in sound. He said, "Oh well, come here for a month or two and amuse yourself at Blackheath." Then I installed myself in Blackheath, being very badly paid (I had, as far as I remember, seven pounds a week), and I started doing lots of things.

Watt: By the time *BBC Droitwich* was finished, Cavalcanti had come. I edited *Droitwich*. It was a very conventional film, starting with a hole in the ground, building the mast, and the final sequence was the start-up of Droitwich, which was the biggest radio station in Europe at that time I think . . . .

So the man pulled the switch, and the dials began to creep up. The enormous electric motors came on. The dials crept up a bit more. The man pulled another switch, and another dial came in. The camera panned to the window through which you could see the foot of the mast and changed focus to that. The change of focus dissolved to a pan shot right up to the top of the mast and then, from the top of the mast, right over Britain. Fade out.

I was rather pleased with this and showed it to Cavalcanti. Cav said, "It is a very nice little film, Harry, but I think the end is a bit dull." He said, "I think we could get some music perhaps."

Of course, we could only buy noncopyright stuff generally (you used to be able to get records with noncopyright stuff). But he took our sound system, and he recorded a vast number of things, mostly from radio. We just pinched it, but of course if you run . . . I think it's less than seven bars . . . you don't have to pay. So he ran opera and all the well-known voices of radio at that time, Priestley's voice, music, and so on. We only had two tracks, so we had to mix and mix and mix, and I remember thinking what a genius he was. He said, "That is an Italian tenor, and we want a German tenor." So he ran the Italian backwards (it was just on some high note) and, by Jesus, it turned him into a German tenor. This is pure professionalism – fascinating. So, instead of the whines of the machine, we had this montage of sound.

The film got a booking at the London Pavilion as a short – it was only fifteen minutes, I think. . . . So I let it go in on the Sunday, and I went down to the London Pavilion on the Monday, and it wasn't on. I said to the manager, "What happened to *BBC Droitwich?*" He said, "It got the bird, and we jerked it." I said, "What do you mean, it got the bird?" He said, "Well, that end bit when there was all that machinery and that music, nobody could understand what it was all about, and somebody started shouting. We can't have that kind of thing, you know. Might create trouble."

. . . So that was my first West End release. It lasted one day. . . .

Harry Watt's account of BBC Droitwich *went on a good deal longer: how he questioned the usherettes and others, and they assured him that it was a bunch of drunks who objected to the film; how C.A. Lejeune, on*

BBC radio, singled it out for special praise on account of its new and imaginative use of sound. From there, back to Watt:

Watt: I believe fundamentally that the arrival of Cavalcanti in the GPO film unit was the turning point of British documentary, because, as I say, we really were pretty amateur and a lot of the films were second-rate, don't let's kid ourselves. It was only the newness of the idea of showing workingmen and so on that was making them successful. But Cavalcanti was a great professional, and he arrived at the same time, more or less, as we had sound. None of us had any idea that cutting sound was so difficult. It's quite simple to juggle with a silent picture in twenty thousand different permutations and combinations of shots. . . . And our equipment was so poor, and our knowledge was so poor. Nobody had cut sound at all until Cavalcanti arrived. So he sat down, first of all, to teach us just the fundamentals, but his contribution was enormously more than that.

He was a professional, a man who had coped with all sorts of documentary films, semifeature films, highbrow films, and feature films. He was also enormously creative and sensitive and could look at a sequence, look at a shot (much more on the screen than in the script, because his English wasn't that good) and immediately put his finger, very practically, on a solution. Now this word "practically" is one I want to stress because there was far too much theorizing in documentary. There was far too much of the intellectual approach, when, as a struggling young director, you just wanted somebody to say, "Look, that sequence is two minutes too long, and you're hanging onto that long shot where you should move right bang into the close-ups." Nobody ever told you that. Then this wonderful, sensitive, charming, hard-working fellow arrived on the scene, and he was my saviour. I would say again and again, if I've had any success in films I put it down to my training from Cavalcanti, and I think a lot of other people should say the same thing.

Meanwhile Basil Wright had been in Ceylon, shooting material for four short films for the EMB and the Ceylon Tea Marketing Board.

Wright: In Ceylon I used to send my rushes back by sea, so I used to get a cable reporting on them six weeks after I'd shot them and moved on somewhere else. Grierson realised that nothing could put one down so much as to get an angry cable saying, "Your stuff is no good" when you are no longer on the spot, so his analyses were much more general. In any case, there was little anybody could do to control what we were shooting because of the long time lapse. I mean, I was back in England before they'd seen the rushes of my last fortnight's shooting. Anyhow, it so happened that he was more than delighted with the rushes.

Basil Wright making *Song of Ceylon* (1934).

*Wright wrote an article about his filming in Ceylon (*Cinema Quarterly, *Summer 1934) which included the following comments:*

"Production covered less than three months, of which seven weeks were devoted to almost continuous shooting. Final footage was 23,000 feet and about 1,000 stills were shot on a Leica by my assistant, John Taylor. . . .

"As we were shooting silent we have had to bring some of the dancers to England for synchronising purposes. . . .

"The film is now on the cutting bench, and it is interesting to note that material which, had we shot it last year in the West Indies, would have been a first choice, goes now straight into the waste bin, rejected purely for its externality, its superficiality – in fact, for its documentary remoteness.

"The synchronisation of the film will be a problem calling for very solid experimentation in sound technique. . . ."

Wright: When I came back from Ceylon, we were just moving into the sound studios at Blackheath, and all the experiments in sound really started then because Cavalcanti was there. I was enormously grateful to him and always shall be, apart from his friendship which I managed to obtain, for all the things he did on the films I was working on, like *Song of Ceylon* and *Night Mail.* His ideas about the use of sound were so liberating that they would liberate in you about a thousand other ideas.

Against that you've got to put the fact that he was, in a sense, a fish out of water. He was in a country in which he'd never worked before. He was in a milieu in which he'd not worked for the last four or five years — that is, a milieu of low-budget documentary people.

Then there came this idea, which he didn't just cook up — I mean, Grierson cooked it up, too — firstly, as we'd only just got sound-recording apparatus, to accustom ourselves to it by making a film for which we recorded all the sound first and put the picture in afterwards, and secondly, to make it a grotesque comedy, which must have been Cavalcanti's idea, because he'd been making these films with Catherine Hessling and others in France in previous years. And this was *Pett and Pott.*

Basil Wright and Stuart Legg were assistant directors on Pett and Pott. *John Taylor photographed it, and Humphrey Jennings, who had just joined the unit, designed the sets.*

Legg: So far as I know, the EMB/GPO thing had never attempted a comedy before. This was something quite new. The old sort of reactionaries among us thought, "Good God, what are we coming to — this lighthearted rubbish!" Others thought it was rather fun, and in fact it was very funny indeed — much funnier shooting it, of course, than the film when it was finished!

Cavalcanti: I never liked it, but it's not quite a film. It's a sound lesson, you know.

Wright: Well, I mean, we got away with *Pett and Pott* because Grierson was a great salesman, and he told everybody what a wonderful film it was and made sure that nobody ever saw it.

Taylor: That was the beginning of the division. I mean, looking back on it, it was a great mistake to have Cavalcanti, really, because he didn't understand what documentary was supposed to be doing.

Wright: Basically, the most wonderful thing was that Cavalcanti was, and is, a natural teacher, not by bullying but by example, by being there. He was wonderful for the editors. He was wonderful for the young camera boys, most of whom were telegraph messengers who'd come in and trained up. All these people like Jonah Jones and Chick Fowle, Fred Gamage, owe a lot to Cavalcanti.

Taylor: When Cav came, certainly that was when they started using sound imaginatively. There was a certain amateurishness in their technical approach to film making at the EMB. I mean, I'm sure you could have picked up a technician out of the studios who would have known far more than anyone there. Cav was much more of a technician, but he didn't have the approach to film making. Documentary was supposed to be for the service of people. It wasn't supposed to be in the entertainment industry — as far as I'm concerned, anyway.

Cavalcanti: I had always thought, as far as conception goes, that there is not such a big difference between documentary and feature. That is to say, to me, documentary should be scripted like a well-informed magazine article, and you can't improvise. I don't believe in *cinéma-vérité* at all. I think films must be thought out before you shoot them.

In fact, I hate the word "documentary." I think it smells of dust and boredom. I think "realist films" much, much the best. And it's funny because the first films I did, *Rien que les heures, En Rade,* although they had plots, were actually reconstructed documentaries.

I like Flaherty and admired him very much, not knowing him (I came to know him much later), and I think he was very important. He was one of the five geniuses of the cinema.* But I thought that documentary of faraway places, romantic documentary, was wrong. And I did *Rien que les heures* as a documentary of Paris town because, I said, it's just as interesting as Timbuktu or Peking or whatever it is. At the same time Dziga Vertov was doing the same thing in Moscow, and I didn't know about it. And Ruttmann was doing *Berlin.* Actually, Ruttmann came to Paris because he hadn't finished *Berlin,* saw *Rien que les heures,* and went back and worked a little more on it.

Pett and Pott is a type of *Rien que les heures,* isn't it? Jennings was very interested and very cooperative on it. I think there are bits that are quite successful: the robbery part in the suburban train is quite good, comes off, I think.†

HUMPHREY JENNINGS had known Stuart Legg, Basil Wright, and Arthur Elton at Cambridge, where he took a starred first in the English Tripos and did postgraduate research, preparing an edition of Shakespeare's Venus and Adonis *(published, 1930) and working on the poetry of Thomas Gray. Jennings was also a painter and by 1934 was concentrating almost exclusively on painting, with virtually no prospect of an income, until Gerald Noxon invited him to direct an advertising film for a large American oil company. The film concerned a mythical substance called SLUM, alleged to accumulate in car engines subjected to ordinary motor oils.*

Soon afterwards, Stuart Legg invited him to join the GPO.

Legg: Humphrey went in spirals. He had his literary research interests, Elizabethan drama and the nature of the image, the nature of the triumph and all that. He had his painting, a kind of pointillism. He had his theatre interests. He designed sets and costumes, that sort of thing. And he went into films to earn some money because he had a family. I think he was always

---

*Cavalcanti's other four "geniuses of the cinema" are Chaplin, Griffith, Eisenstein, and Stroheim. Fellini is "getting near to be the sixth."

†Poet and art historian Herbert Read particularly praised this sequence in the article "Experiments in Counterpoint" (*Cinema Quarterly,* Autumn 1934), in which he reviewed an early batch of GPO sound films (*6.30 Collection, Granton Trawler,* Evelyn Spice's *Weather Forecast*).

looking for his medium, and I'm not sure that his medium wasn't talk, because he was an exceptionally brilliant talker.

Cavalcanti: I got along very well with certain of the boys, which were brilliant boys. I still am great friends with Basil Wright, and there were many others of the young ones who were very good. But the two important boys were Humphrey Jennings and Len Lye. Those were my favourite boys.

LEN LYE joined the unit after making Colour Box *in 1935.*

Wright: Len Lye arrives with *Colour Box,* which is hand-painted on film to a rhumba or something of that sort. Grierson says, "It's marvellous. How can we use it?" He says, "Go away and paint the new rates for the parcel post on the last sequence of the film, and then we'll put it out as an advertising film."

Cavalcanti: It's funny that they both [Jennings and Lye] should have been painters to start with. I've seen very few of Jennings's painting, but I know that as soon as he touched films, he had a very acute sense, film sense. Len Lye was not exactly the same character, but he was very inspiring, a very adventurous kind of mind.

Pett and Pott (1934).

Wright: Nobody's ever defined the word "documentary" satisfactorily, because it's a certain approach to the use of the cinema on, shall we say, the social side of the community. That's all. I don't think it's ever possible to get clear about this. You can say that the documentary movement in the thirties was as free as anything you can think of. I mean, you had Cavalcanti making *Pett and Pott* and *The Glorious Sixth of June,* starring Humphrey Jennings as a telegraph boy, and I was producing Sir William Coldstream's (as he now is) *Fairy of the Phone.* These were all sort of filmic nonsenses and revues and so on, but it was all part of the rich pageant of life. Who gave Len Lye his first chance? Grierson. . . .

You see, it was a question of snatching at all the opportunities. Then, when Cavalcanti took over at the GPO, he had Richard Massingham working for him. He had Lotte Reiniger doing silhouette films. Norman McLaren had started there. Well, you may ask youself, what's this to do with documentary? And yet it is to do with documentary. These things only happen because of documentary. It's terribly important to remember that in the thirties documentary meant a chance for Len Lye, a chance for Norman McLaren, a chance for Richard Massingham.

Cavalcanti: Yes, well, it went very well. . . . It was a bit difficult to work with Grierson because he had a very confused way of administration. He had genius for certain things, for instance, for finding titles. He used to do some very sort of biting criticism when he saw rushes with me, which was not always the thing because he sometimes passed a very long time without bothering on these technical problems. But he used to come sometimes to Blackheath and, when a boy started cutting, quite rightly put him in projection and put the projectionist in the cutting room and mix everything up, mix it all up.

Watt: This very pukka young English boy arrived and was told that he was to be the projectionist. And this was absolutely typical. He'd never seen a projector in his life, and he was stuck in the projection box. I had rushes to run that morning, and the usual routine went through — bang, bang, crash, bang, "Shoot! Sit down!" and so the rushes start. And suddenly there's a most ghastly tearing noise, and you see the film tearing on the screen, and then there's a blank screen. Dead silence. And then the door opens from the projection box, and this little pink face comes round and says, "I say, sir. I'm damn sorry." And that was my introduction to Pat Jackson.

PAT JACKSON joined the GPO film unit on his seventeenth birthday, straight from public school.

Jackson: Sir Kingsley Wood was then postmaster general, and there was some distant friendship with my grandmother, who had known Kingsley Wood when they were young. So a discreet letter was sent to Kingsley Wood, and

Kingsley Wood sent an equally discreet letter to Grierson. . . . I got a messenger boy's job at seventeen and six a week. I think I was a messenger boy for six months, and then went into stills and the vaults, then into the cutting rooms, and that's where one began to learn a little bit through Cavalcanti.

I was a joiner on *Song of Ceylon* and made the cutter's mistake of joining some music for Basil Wright in a loop, so that, to his astonishment, instead of finishing at a certain spot, this piece of music ran on ten minutes into the bin. It went on and on and on. The join came on a perfect bar of music, so it was a perfect fit. We were about four hours trying to work this thing out, putting the Movieola forwards and backwards, and still the music went on and on, until it dawned on Basil, of course, that I'd joined it up in the wrong place and made an unending loop. God, the mistakes that we made! I look back on those early days with absolute shame because I was such a totally uncoordinated human being.

Wright: Grierson agreed to my suggestion that Walter Leigh should not only write the music but be in control, or work with me, on all the sound [for *Song of Ceylon*]. And the film quite quickly built up roughly to the shape it ended up with. Remember, it wasn't supposed to be this film at all. I was sent there to make four one-reel interest films about Ceylon (and we had to make four one-reel films, as well, in the end) but starting to cut it as four one-reelers, it came out roughly like what *Song of Ceylon* is today.

Song of Ceylon (1934).

Cavalcanti: Basil Wright knew very well what he wanted, and I gave a very few ideas, such as advancing the microphone while the vibrations were dying so that, instead of dying, they were deformed — small things that they used. But the whole construction of the sound of *Song of Ceylon* is Basil's and Walter Leigh's, of course, who was a very brilliant musician.

The part of the musician in documentary is very important, and we were very lucky at the GPO, a little because of me. We had Britten. We had Milhaud. We had Ernst Meyer. We had Jaubert. We had lots of very important musicians, and Walter Leigh was amongst them, with Rawsthorne and Britten. It's sad to say that both Jaubert and Leigh died in the war.

Wright: This film went on in its difficult and tortuous way until I felt that I had finalised the cut of the film. In fact, I said to Grierson, "Now can I show it to you before it goes in for negative cutting?" "OK," he said. So I showed him the film, and he said, "That is absolutely marvellous except that there's something so terrible at the end that you've got to put it right." He said, "You've got all this tremendous thing with the little man worshipping the Great Buddha and so on. He walks out of the picture, and bang, crash, without a moment at all, you have all these people doing this enormous dance, this violent dance." And he said, "It's a stupidity. It's a *bêtise*. It doesn't work. . . ."

I was by this time really rather exhausted. I'd been working on the film like a demon for months and months, and I couldn't see the point at all. And we had — the first time I ever had it with Grierson, in fact, really the only time — we had a real bang up and down row. I got into my car and went home. I remember I went back to my flat, and I sat down and started drinking. Then I went to bed. I got up next morning and had a large breakfast, and I paced up and down. Then I started drinking. I refused to answer the telephone. I refused to go to the studio.

Then on the second night I found myself thinking about the film and suddenly got an idea. I got into my car — I was living in Highgate at the time — and drove all the way down to the Blackheath studios, got into the studios soon after midnight, picked up a second take of the man reading that prayer on the mountain (which happens at the beginning of the film, in the first reel), chopped it up and related those phrases to the shots of the men dressing for the dance, which I hadn't used at all.

When Grierson arrived at the studio the next morning, I was still there. I hadn't bothered to go home, and I said "Would you mind coming to see the last reel again?" He sat and looked at it, and he said, "There, what did I tell you? There's absolute genius." But what you've got to notice is that he never said, "Why don't you do this or don't you do that?" He merely said, "You're traducing yourself. You're making a nonsense of the end of a very beautiful film." And he was right, and I was right because I found out how to do it. Because that sequence is vitally important to the end of the film. . . .

For a long time my life was dominated by working with Grierson, and, as the years went by and our difference in status, as it were, diminished, as it does with age (he was about five years older than I was and at that time that was terrific, just as when Benjamin Britten worked for us, as far as I was concerned he was a little boy and, you know, he used to get a bit ordered about), of course everything smoothed up. So Grierson and I ended up as very close personal friends and ditto with his wife, who's sort of my favourite woman in the world. I would say the most rewarding thing which ever happened to anybody in those days was to get a chance to work for Grierson for a long time — rewarding personally, psychologically, and rewarding in terms of work, of learning how to make films. He was a great, great teacher, and to have him and Cavalcanti in the same setup was absolutely magical. It was worth a million pounds to any young man to be there.

Meanwhile, Paul Rotha had made a second documentary, Rising Tide, *for Bruce Woolfe, head of the recently formed Gaumont-British Instructional, and was working on a third,* Shipyard, *for G-B Instructional and the Orient Shipping Line.*

Rotha: The Orient Line I think had in mind a film which would depict, stage by stage, the building of a new ship at their Barrow-in-Furness yards. This is all right — a descriptive, illustrative film — but, as you can imagine, did not interest me very much. When I went up to Barrow-in-Furness to do my research, it didn't take me very long to find out what the building of a new ship really meant in Barrow-in-Furness in a time of tremendous unemployment, 1934. The ship was a symbol of the fact that so many thousand men were going to be employed in the yard for a year. It could mean the opening of new shops. It could mean a boy and girl might become engaged to be married. In other words, it was the whole economic and social background resulting from the building of this ship which interested me, and this is what I tried to say in the film. I showed also, I hope, the craftsmanship and the skill and the design which went into the ship. But as a socialist, as I've been all my life, I tried to show the economic and social background. When the ship goes down into the sea at the end, there are the nabobs with their bowler hats and the champagne bottles being smashed and all that crap. And here are the men who were employed on that ship, hands in their empty pockets, all out of work again. In other words, the ending of the film was a tragedy for these men, who now go back on the dole, as it was called in those days. But it was also the triumph of the work of their hands which had built that ship. I believe, perhaps immodestly, that this was perhaps the first of the British documentary films with what I call a social implication.

Shipyard *was well received by the rest of the documentary group. Basil Wright wrote (*Cinema Quarterly, *Spring 1935): "Rotha has made an immense*

*step forward, and is now finally in control of his medium." Grierson wrote
(*Cinema Quarterly, *Summer 1935): "The most interesting event in recent
months was, for many of us, the arrival of Paul Rotha's* Shipyard. . . . *There is
something sufficiently distinct in Rotha's work to mark it as a separate tendency: distinct at once from the romanticism of Flaherty, which all the young
men have now respectfully discarded, and from the hard-boiled and certainly
more academic realism of the GPO group. . . ."*

*But it was for a quality which he called poetry, rather than for its social
implications, that Grierson seemed then to be commending Rotha's film.*

Shipyard (1935).

Rotha: The budget for *Shipyard* was fifteen hundred pounds. I myself
was being paid ten pounds a week. I wouldn't like to say a word against my
union, because I believe very much in unionism in our industry, but, of course,
I was able to work with only two people, myself and a cameraman. We hadn't

got sound, which made it much cheaper. All the sound was prefabricated afterwards. If you took out sound on location then, you had to take out a thing that looked like a London general omnibus, and it cost you about fifty pounds a day. You thought twice, on the limited budget of a documentary, of taking out a thing like this, and you were tremendously restricted in what you could do with it.

The Face of Britain (1935).

Rotha followed up Shipyard *with* The Face of Britain, *which consisted of material collected on his journeys to and from Barrow-in-Furness and showed some of the appalling living conditions in the industrial areas. This was also produced by Bruce Woolfe's G-B Instructional, as was a short road-safety film,* Death on the Road, *which Rotha directed for the* News of the World. *But it was not until he produced* Today We Live *in 1936-1937 that Rotha took a sound truck on location.*

Probably the first GPO film to use synchronised sound was BBC: The Voice of Britain *(1934-1935), which ran 56 minutes and included appearances by H. G. Wells, J. B. Priestley, G. K. Chesterton, George Bernard Shaw, and a brief performance by Humphrey Jennings as one of the witches in* Macbeth. *People are reticent about the trials and tribulations of this production, the most ambitious and expensive so far attempted at the GPO, but there seems little doubt that there were moments of crisis in its making. And, judging by a guide to documentary finances published in* World Film News *in May 1936, its probable cost was between £7,000 and £8,000.*

BBC: The Voice of Britain *was directed, scripted, and edited by Stuart Legg in collaboration with others. George Noble, J. D. Davidson, and Bill Shenton are credited with the photography. It may have been the last film Shenton worked on.*

Watt: Bill Shenton used to come in quite regularly to Soho Square, this pathetic little battered old man, and say, "Any work?" And we'd say, "No, Bill. Sorry, nothing." And he'd say, "Fine," and walk out again.

Suddenly Bill was found dead in some corner. He'd died of starvation, and we as the GPO film unit — because we were very elastic — could have taken him on, just given him a job for life because he was so good to train the boys. But he never said, "Look, I'm broke!" — never touched anybody for a quid, and this was a terrible shock. Grierson was very cut up about it.

Bill had been head cameraman at Gaumont-British, and sound had caught him out, and drink, of course. Younger fellows had come in, and he hadn't been able to cope, and presumably he'd let them down on the job through drink, and he'd just faded out. He became unfashionable. They said, "Oh, don't use Shenton. He's a drunk." And he was a sweet, sweet man.

It was slumming to come and work for us. You've now idea how looked-down-upon we were by the trade. The newsreels thought we were dreadful. The trade thought we were dreadful. We looked awful, you know. We were badly dressed and going about in a pretty amateur way. The trade, the whole of the film business, had no respect for documentary. There were certain highbrow magazines, and, of course, the film societies began to grow up. We all of us went round lecturing at film societies, raising enthusiasm for this type of film and running films. Grierson was very good at this. But we couldn't get to first base with the trade, and it was pretty exasperating. They despised us, and we despised them, and they never accepted us, really, until the war.

Grierson: Documentary was developed on the thought that it was not there necessarily for entertainment. Occasionally, it has been in the entertainment business but only incidentally. It's always been related to government sponsorship and to those sponsors who saw the value of using it to illustrate their interests or to create loyalties of one kind or another. The great example, of course, is Shell Oil. Shell Oil was the first and greatest of the sponsors because it saw the full implications of its international operation, its full implication in terms of instruction, in terms of social welfare and the preaching and teaching of social welfare. For example, one of the propositions that was first put to us in the early thirties was that they found in the Gulf of Persia that it took two men to lift a bag of cement. Therefore, they were in the nutrition business. So they were in the business not only of creating a new nutritional basis but of teaching nutrition, teaching sanitation, and so on. Well, they worked logically into all kinds of services of an educational or inspirational kind in the communities in which they operated, whether it was in Venezuela, whether it was in the Upper Persian Gulf, or whether it was in the Dutch East Indies. . . .

The Shell film unit was formed in 1934 as a result of a report written by Grierson for Shell International. The report was instigated by Jack Beddington of Shell Mex and BP (the marketing side of Shell International), who had already sponsored Rotha's Contact. *Grierson recommended Edgar Anstey for the job of running the new unit.*

Anstey: I found the premises in Shell Mex House, up on the first floor where they've still got part of their accommodation, and furnished it and got the staff together and started on a film called *Airport*. But I was young and impatient, I suppose, and the machinery is very difficult to arrange. We didn't seem to be able to get money actually to make films, and I finally fell out with them and resigned, to their astonishment, because nobody had ever resigned from Shell, it appeared.

We started on *Airport*, which is still to be seen, rather an interesting film about Croydon Airport, got that finished. But there was some kind of hold-up, and so I left in a huff. Afterwards Arthur Elton and I and Rotha and Donald Taylor started the thing called Associated Realist Film Producers, which became Film Centre, and Shell very generously invited Film Centre back to advise them on running the unit, although I had shaken the dust from my feet.

Arthur Elton later replaced Anstey at Shell. Meanwhile, in 1935 Elton made Workers and Jobs, *and Anstey and Elton made* Housing Problems. Workers and Jobs, *made for the Ministry of Labour, showed the inside of a Labour Exchange and was one of the earliest attempts to record natural dialogue with synchronised sound.* Housing Problems, *the first film from the Grierson school to carry serious social implications, was produced for the British Commercial Gas Association.*

Elton: By then Grierson was determined that we should apply the knowledge we had acquired in government service in the GPO film unit, to industry. Though I'm not sure that I particularly appreciated it at the time, I was thrown out to the cold world and made to apply our knowledge to industry. I worked with the gas industry, both the Gas, Light and Coke Company and the British Commercial Gas Association, jointly with Edgar Anstey, and we made a whole series of films, of which the famous one is *Housing Problems.* *

*According to *The Factual Film,* a survey sponsored by the Dartington Hall Trustees and published on behalf of the Arts Enquiry by Political and Economic Planning (Oxford University Press, 1947): "Early in 1935, the British Commercial Gas Association commissioned Elton and Anstey to produce a programme of five films, inviting their collaboration on the choice of subjects. This commissioning of a complete production pro-

Housing Problems was like a television presentation, only long before television.† It pioneered the interview. It pioneered all that kind of thing.

Anstey: This [i.e., *Housing Problems*] was a sort of political thing coming out which had been suppressed a bit, because we were all in a way politicians, but we were operating very indirectly. We were trying to show things as they were, people as they were, and there was a lot of indignation about unemployment, about malnutrition, about the bad housing at that time.

Arthur Elton and I succeeded in persuading the gas industry, who, after all, had a liberal tradition, a nonconformist tradition, that what you could do with film was to identify a big organization with social purpose, to the advantage of both. Perhaps this was the Grierson notion passed on by Elton and myself, that, in a way, no great corporation can dissociate itself from whatever the national social issues are at any given time — particularly if, like gas, you're in the field of housing, basically. You're providing a public service.

Anyway, we argued with them about this, and they agreed to do a film on slums and slum clearance and rehousing. We seized on this, because everybody had been told about the slums, but there was no direct communication about them. I mean, you could make still pictures and write articles in the press, but nobody had thought of the idea which we had of letting slum-dwellers simply talk for themselves, make their own film.

Rotha often criticised *Housing Problems* because he thought there wasn't enough directorial intervention and guidance and shaping of the material. Well, Arthur and I talked a lot about this, and we felt that the camera must remain sort of four feet above the ground and dead on, because it wasn't our film.

Wright: When Ruby Grierson and John Taylor and Anstey went down into the slums with their great, enormous sound truck and their microphone, they did *cinéma-vérité* interviews with the people who lived there. The circumstances were terribly difficult, but that's what they were doing.

John Taylor was cameraman on Housing Problems.

----

gramme was something new. Elton and Anstey hired studio facilities and assumed complete responsibility, finding this necessary since there was then no documentary company in existence. *Housing Problems* was one of this first series. From then until 1939 the Gas Industry sponsored an annual film programme, specialising particularly in sociological subjects such as *Enough to Eat?* (1936), *Children at School* (1937), *Smoke Menace* (1937) and *The Londoners* (1938)."

The titles of the other four films in the series with *Housing Problems* have not gone down in history, but, according to John Taylor (who photographed them), "they were all technical films about gas."

†BBC Television was officially inaugurated on 2 November 1936 but closed down during the war.

Housing Problems (1935).

Taylor: There was a British camera called a Vinton, which was a very cumbersome thing. The early models of it were very cumbersome. Most of it was shot on the Vinton. Some of it was shot on a Mitchell, which is an American camera and a very good one. We could shoot 1,000 feet (ten minutes) before reloading. We had to have a car full of batteries — twelve-volt car batteries — to do the lighting, and even then we could only have two 500-watt lamps, or something like that, and the stock was slow in those days. We had a vast sound truck outside, full of batteries and a big sound camera. It was terribly cumbersome equipment to try and do that stuff with.

Anstey: Nobody had been able to bring these poor, suffering characters to an audience before, and the woman in *Housing Problems,* the woman who jabs at the rat with a broom, was absolutely astonished. I got her to the Stepney Town Hall (I think it was) to see the film. They were all there, the people who appeared in the film, and you couldn't hear a word because of the roars and shouts as soon as a neighbour came on the screen. So we had to run it again, and this woman who killed the rat was absolutely astonished. I don't think she'd ever seen a photograph of herself before. She didn't recognize herself, didn't identify. She had to be told, and she gradually accepted it the second time through. But she had never been to the centre of London. She was a woman of, I suppose, forty-five or fifty, and she had never been further than this two and a half miles from her slum house.

The direction of Housing Problems *is credited jointly to Anstey and Elton, who obviously instigated the subject and in every sense produced it. Whether they really directed it, which meant, in this case, finding the people concerned and putting them so much at their ease that a sense of immediacy survives in the interviews even today, is another matter. In fact, this vital contribution was very likely made by Ruby Grierson. A sister of John Grierson, Ruby Grierson died in 1940 while making a film about British children being evacuated to Canada on the S. S.* City of Benares. *She was credited as assistant on* Housing Problems, *about which Rotha wrote in his book* Documentary Film, *"Ruby Grierson's ability to win people's confidence gave a spontaneity and an honesty to the 'interviews' that contrasted sharply with the previous, romantic method of handling people." Ruby Grierson later worked on Rotha's production,* Today We Live, *a film in which the human touch is again evident.*

After Housing Problems, *Edgar Anstey directed* Enough to Eat? *for the Gas, Light and Coke Company. Frank Sainsbury was his assistant. The subject was malnutrition.*

Anstey: Julian Huxley was the anchor man, as we would call him today. Boyd-Orr was in it, and Lord Astor, who was busy with malnutrition in the United Nations. We had people suffering from malnutrition, and mothers who couldn't feed their children, talking. It was very much like the contemporary television programme – but again, no attempt to dress it up, although I did start at that point to introduce animated diagrams to show what is meant by the importance of vitamins and proteins and so on. There was a bit of that kind of production value in it. Later on Rotha started doing films of this type, much more elaborately and with much more production finesse. *Enough to Eat?* was half-way between *Housing Problems* and these much more elaborate things which Rotha did, where you would introduce artists, as well, to play out scenes. It came also from the Living Newspaper technique, which developed in America, where you had these documentary things played out on the stage during the Depression. . . .

Those films [i.e., *Housing Problems* and *Enough to Eat?*] seemed so remarkable at the time to the press that they probably achieved more by the influence they had on journalists and public men, politicians and so on, than in their actual showings. Both *Enough to Eat?* and *Housing Problems* had whole pages in the *Daily Herald* and, I think, the *Daily News* as it then was. Ritchie-Calder [now Lord Ritchie-Calder] wrote the page in the *Herald*. I think the influence of those films through the press was much much greater than through the cinema screen, rather curiously. Suddenly a new thing had happened in the possibility of communication.

4

Night Mail

Back at the GPO, Coal Face *had been completed by Cavalcanti, and they were making* Night Mail. *It will be remembered that, before Cavalcanti came to the GPO, some material had been assembled by Stuart Legg for a film that afterwards became* Coal Face. *In the process of adding a sound track and making what he now describes as an "experiment in sound," Cavalcanti took over the final direction of this material, so to speak, on the cutting bench.* Coal Face *emerged in 1935.*

Wright: *Coal Face* began as a sort of compilation film; then we all went off and shot various bits of material for it. I seem to remember that Cavalcanti wanted some exteriors of coal mines, and I was going up to Scotland for some other reason and I shot some stuff up there on the side, some coal-mine stuff and some exteriors. In these sort of cases you have to remember that it was very much a question of teamwork. It's very difficult to pin anybody in particular down. . . . What *Coal Face* is famous for is the fact that Grierson managed to get together with Auden and Britten and produce a highly experimental film which was a sort of tryout, or a test-tube thing, if you like, which eventually came to true in *Night Mail* the following year.

W. H. AUDEN was for a short time a member of the GPO film unit.

W.H. Auden: I joined the GPO film unit through Basil Wright, whom I knew already. I think I was teaching then.

Wright: Auden wrote to me and said, was there a chance of him having a job in the GPO film unit, and I showed the letter to Grierson, and Grierson said, "Don't be a fool. Fetch him."

Auden: They'd made a movie about miners in the North of England, and I wrote a madrigal for it.* That was the first thing I did. I was with the

*Auden's madrigal for *Coal Face* was "O lurcher-loving collier, black as night."

unit for about three and a half months. I got £3 a week and was Bill Coldstream's lodger, so I got by.

Wright: Britten, I think, had turned up from elsewhere. He was a very
young man at the time. Cavalcanti and I went up to Malvern (where Auden
was a schoolmaster) with Britten, introduced them to each other. That's how
that collaboration first started. There's a bit about it in White's book on
Britten, which is actually based on the information I gave him.

Auden: I didn't see very much of Grierson. I worked regularly with
Cavalcanti, of course, and I saw a lot of Coldstream. . . . I wrote a commentary for a long film, which was never made, about the slave trade, and worked
on this with Benjamin Britten. It was entirely due to Grierson, I think, that
Britten was brought in. Grierson had this ability: he was able to recognise the
great composer that Britten would become.

Watt: Sometime after *Droitwich* — I can't remember the dates,
exactly — I was called into Grierson's office, with Wright, and they said they
had decided to make a film about the mail train that ran nightly from London
to Edinburgh and Glasgow. I knew nothing about it, and it wasn't my idea.
Wright had instigated it, and already I think some aerial shots, which were
unique for us (we'd never used an aeroplane before), had been made, looking
straight down on the train. I think I was shown them. For some reason or
other Wright was to do something else, and I was told I was going to take
over.

Wright: I wrote the script, and then a lot of things were happening, so I
had to become a sort of producer and look after all sorts of other things
which were going on at the time. The script I'd written, the shooting script,
was given to Harry, and he went off and shot the film. I was producer, the
immediate producer below Grierson and Cavalcanti, who of course were having
an overall look at it.

Watt: There was not a detailed shooting script, but there was a shape.
I then investigated the film in conjunction with the film Officer of the LMS
[London, Midland and Scottish], who called himself the film director and was
the only film director I ever knew who wore a bowler hat. He was a very
nice man, but he didn't know what hit him when we arrived. I travelled up
and down and finally got a script together.
    In those days we never had a complete word-by-word, shot-by-shot
script like one has in features. You shot basically in sequences, and you made
up your mind on the sequence and wrote out in detail for yourself, as the
director, what you wanted to shoot, more or less on the basis of how you
were going to cut it, because we generally edited our own films.

Wright: All the dialogue was in my original script because I picked that up with a stenographer actually travelling on the train, as today we would do with a tape recorder. But I think that Harry worked over the dialogue. I was not concerned with that. I mean, the film as it was finished (up to the Auden-Britten section, which was an afterthought, anyhow) more or less followed the shape of the script I'd written. But, obviously, if Harry was directing, he was going to direct it differently from me, certainly in a more human and down-to-earth way than I was probably capable of. I think this is the great thing he gave to the film. It was the way he worked with the Post Office workers and the locomotive workers and that sort of thing.

Watt: The unit consisted of Chick Fowle, Pat Jackson, and myself. Jonah Jones shot some of it; they alternated quite a lot, but Chick Fowle was the main cameraman. Then I was told that W. H. Auden would be attached to me as an assistant, as he wanted to learn about cinema. Again he didn't know what had hit him. Of course, I was a mad, keen young director, and I didn't give a damn if he'd written *The Ascent of F6,* or whatever the hell he'd written. He was just an assistant director, as far as I was concerned, and that meant humping the gear and walking miles, and he used to turn up late. Of course, he was an extraordinary looking young man. He turned up, and he looked exactly like a half-witted Swedish deckhand: his jacket was far too short in the sleeves, and he had huge, boney, red hands and big, lumpy wrists and dirty old flannel trousers and an old sports jacket and this blond towhead, and then the rather plumy, frightfully good accent, which was very surprising coming out of him. He just got kicked around like any young assistant would have got kicked around, and I don't think he liked it very much. But he didn't continue with us all the time.

Auden: I worked in various ways on *Night Mail.* I even did some of the direction myself. I remember this because we got a shot of a guard at Crewe, and he dropped dead about thirty seconds later.

Watt: I cannot remember the continuity of shooting, but we'd this tiny unit and we worked incredibly hard, very often practically night and day. The train stops for thirteen minutes at Crewe, and we had a sequence in Crewe Station. The railway was extremely cooperative, through the Post Office. We put up our scaffolding ourselves, put up the arc lamps (because we had arc lamps, which we'd hired), connected them up, lit them. The train arrived, and we shot for thirteen minutes. The train had to leave on time. We then unloaded the camera, and the reverse train was coming in. Pat Jackson would take the rushes under his arm, get into the mail van, go to sleep if he could on the mailbags, come down to Humphries Laboratory, hand them in by about half past two in the morning, go to sleep in an armchair, get them about five or six o'clock in the morning, go back to Euston and get on another mail train to Crewe. We would then go to the local cinema (the cinemas used to open at two o'clock in those days, so we had to get into the cinema before two), run the rushes, then start preparing the lights again for the next thirteen minutes.

Jackson: The first time I went out shooting was, I think, on *Night Mail*, and I still look back on that film with great affection because it was a landmark in documentary and it was a landmark for Harry, too. That was where he first showed his ability to handle people and get humanity on the screen, which until that time I don't think many documentary people had done.

Watt: Because we couldn't light it [the train], we decided to shoot the interior of the van — the sorting of the letters — in the studio. This was the first studio stuff I had ever done. We reconstructed the mail van, and, of course, we got the real sorters down. We couldn't afford what they have in feature films — that is, a rocker set, a set which can be rocked and moved. The studio was tiny. So all we could do was to move by hand, out of picture, certain things like balls of string hanging down, make them sway regularly to give the impression of the train moving, and get the chaps to sway a little bit. With the sound of the train, it gave absolute verisimilitude of the train moving along.

In the film there is a series of shots of the train going into the night, gradually getting darker. We'd finish shooting all day in the studio at Blackheath. We'd pile into a clapped-out car which we had, and we'd go all the way to Bletchley to get one shot of the train passing at sunset, which in the summer would be about half-past ten. We'd happily come all the way back to London and turn up again at eight o'clock in the morning and start shooting again. And my salary then was five pounds a week. Pat, I should think, would have been on about two, and Jonah on something in the region of six or maybe less. Less. And we never thought anything of it.

We shot the interior of the mailbag being put out, in the train itself. We had the doors open, and we had little lights, very little lights because we could only use batteries. We couldn't afford a generator or anything like that. There came the moment when we had to get a shot of the actual bag being whisked off the arm into the net, and we couldn't get it. The only way to do it was for Chick Fowle to hang out of the window about fifteen feet below where the arm came out and hold a hand camera and hope to God that the thing worked, because we were going at a hundred miles an hour and the bag hanging out gets caught by the net and at the same moment the arm swings back. So we held onto his legs, and he hung out of the window and got the shot.

Wright: A lot of the Crewe section was done in Broad Street Station

over a weekend, in the middle of the night, and of course I moved in then
and ran a second unit for Harry, with Auden as one of the assistants. . . .

Watt: We lit one platform, and we had the train coming into the station,
I think, for the departure. Everybody was helping, and Wright was there. . . .

I remember I had a shot noted down of the little man going along with
his hammer, tapping the wheels. At four o'clock in the morning, when everybody was looking at their watches and the stationmaster was saying, "You
must get away. There's a train coming in here," this little man came up and
said, "Do you still want me?" He'd been there since about eight o'clock the
night before, waiting with his bloody hammer. So we had to set up the lights
again and get him to tap. I said, "What are you listening for?" He said, "I
don't know." Anyway, we got the shot.

Night Mail (1936).

We were given an engine to ourselves going up Beattock. That was a lovely day. We could go up Beattock and down again, and up Beattock and down again with a lovely steam engine. Old Pat nearly got killed. He was sitting up top of the coal, holding a reflector down onto the firemen firing the engine, and he didn't see a bridge coming. The reflector suddenly went wham out of his hands, and the bridge must have missed his head by about an inch. This happened all the time. He was very nearly killed again at Crewe.

We got to Glasgow for the end of the film, those shots of the engine being put away into the engine shed. I got a telephone message from Grierson to say that they'd no more money. The film had to finish. The end. Well, I wanted more shots, so my mother lived in Edinburgh and had a large house in Edinburgh and we all — well, all four of us — moved over to Edinburgh and lived off my mother. We travelled by rail wherever we wanted to go, with sandwiches made by my mother, and we shot the extra shots we wanted. We went down to Dumfries, shot the shots of the rabbits running and the birds flying, things like that, on a wee farm in Dumfries.

By this time, during all the stuff in Scotland, Auden had disappeared. Auden had worked as an assistant down round London. But while I'd been shooting, Wright, who made an enormous contribution to the film, of course, because it was his conception, had been editing and assembling the stuff and working in conjunction on the film. Then Auden had to write the commentary. . . .

Wright: We'd seen the rough assembly of the film, Grierson, Cavalcanti and I, and somebody, probably Grierson, said, "There's something missing. . . ." He said in fact, "What we haven't got here is anything about the people who're going to get the letters. We've only had the machinery of getting letters from one point to the other. What about the people who write them and the people who get them?" I don't know how the conversation developed. Anyhow, the fact that we'd got Auden and Britten on our payroll was obviously significant and presumably somebody, probably me, said to Auden, "Look, write some verse for the end of the film. . . ."

From then on it sort of took off. With the verse in existence, Britten could put the rhythm to it.

Harry became aware of this idea as a result of a conference, I think, which took place between Grierson and Cavalcanti and myself, in which we felt that the film needed this coda, this end piece, and Harry didn't like it at all. He was very much against it, but he came round automatically without any pressure being brought on him. He came round in the most generous way. He suddenly turned up and said, "I was wrong. We'll put the sequence in, and I'll shoot the extra material," which he did extremely well.

If you ask me what material he had to shoot additionally, I can't remember because these sorts of films don't get made in a tidy way. . . . I've no doubt Harry had already shot shots of the train going up through Beattock, over the hills into Scotland, because you would if you were making a film of that sort, although not with the intention of them being used in the way they were. So there may have been all sorts of material lying around, and this may have influenced what Auden wrote. But when he'd written all he'd written, then clearly there were some other visuals needed. There are at least two shots in that sequence which I shot at least three years earlier in Scotland when I was doing some tests for another film which was never made. You see, this is a case where anybody's desire to pin it down to total accuracy is almost impossible. You'll get different stories from everybody. You'll only get the broad outline, and I can only give you my honest recollection, which was that Harry was very much against having the Auden and Britten sequence in the film and then, without pressure, by thinking about it, very generously (I remember it so well) came back and said, "I was wrong. . . ."

In fact, it is impossible to sort out precisely what happened at this stage on Night Mail. *At what seems to have been about the time that Watt remembers making the final shots on his own initiative, despite Grierson's telephone message to stop, Wright remembers Watt's going off in a huff because he disapproved of the Auden and Britten coda. Watt has no recollection of this disapproval, although he admits he might have had a row:*

Watt: I was a rower. I was very volatile, shall we say, which is a nice way of putting it. You see, I'm a kind of placid individual now, but I had a driving ambition, a tremendous ambition. I was going to be the greatest, and you have to have that, in a way.

Anyway, the bringing in of Auden and the idea of the commentary was not mine at all. It was either Wright's or Grierson's. Then we saw what enormous stature Auden had, because at the back, running parallel to the theatre at 21 Soho Square, there was a narrow passage, and we were provided by the Post Office at that time with Post Office messenger boys. They used to wear little pillbox hats, and they were fourteen-, fifteen-year-old Cockney kids, wild as hell, and they made their tea and whistled and played cards up at one end. The only place we could find for Auden was at the other end of this passage — say, twenty yards from them. There, on that old Post Office table, he wrote the most beautiful verse.

He kept bringing it, and — the cheek of us, in a way — we turned down so much. He'd say, "All right. That's quite all right. Just roll it up and throw it away." The most magnificent verse was thrown away, and in that situation, with all that noise going on and being harassed and used, he turned out the very, very famous lines of *Night Mail.*

Wright: Auden wrote one whole piece of poetry. It was too long, and we cut some of the stanzas from it, planning it with his agreement. He tended sometimes to make verbal images which were too violent for the pictorial content. He described the Cheviots as "uplands heaped like slaughtered horses"; no picture we put on the screen could be as strong as that, and therefore we felt it was going the wrong way around. I'm not sure that was right. I think we could have used it, but it was a very violent mental image to go against a visual image which was really a romantic landscape, taken from the train, of the Cheviots passing. It was what you might call a conceit, which we felt a bit difficult for a film like *Night Mail.*

Auden: It was a very professional job at the GPO, which I like; and it would vary from film to film. I learnt how films are cut, which is a useful thing to know. . . .

I suppose I left because I'd had enough. I found it tiring when I was hanging about the office with nothing to do at all. Of course, sometimes I was up all night working. But I like an organised life. I work very regular hours. I think I went back to teaching then. After 1937 I was able to support myself with my writing.

Cavalcanti introduced Benjamin Britten to Harry Watt.

Watt: I'd never heard of Benjamin Britten. Well, a lot of people hadn't in those days, but, as I say, I was a lowbrow, and I didn't know the arts circles at all. . . . So in comes this shy, blond, good-looking, very nice boy with blond, curly hair, aged about twenty or maybe younger. I, of course, by this time was getting a bit big for my breeches. I was the big director, so I more or less said to Britten, knowing nothing about him, "Now I don't want any bloody highbrow stuff, you know. I want stuff to go with the train. I'll show you the picture, and I've got a record here. I want not the same as this, but this kind of music." I ran him some American, shuffling-off-to-Buffalo kind of thing, with the train rhythm.

I can imagine what a yahoo he must have thought me, but he was terribly polite. I said, "Don't you think that's good? Don't you like jazz?" He said, "Yes, I like it very much. Yes, I think technically it's brilliant, but it's not quite what I would do." I said, "All right, Cav says you're very good. You go ahead."

We only provided him with, I think, seven or eight musicians — again, money; and he did lovely music, lovely music with that tiny little orchestra. . . .

Most of the sound on Night Mail *was added afterwards.*

Jackson: There wasn't a great deal of sync shooting while we were on location. Certain fragments we got, but we had to rely a good deal on post-sync, particularly when we were way down the main line, waiting for the up-fast to come or the down-fast to go by. That merely meant our being very careful to note what they said and revoice them. The scenes that were sync sound were shot as sync sound: all the mail sequence, of course, which was studio reproduction. For the scenes at Crewe and the tearoom and all the shouts there, we had the sound van taking endless sound effects, which we chose carefully and laid over various scenes.

Watt: Our sound system was exceedingly primitive, and the trouble with primitive sound is that it can't be selective. You got every conceivable extraneous noise. If you got any wind in the microphone at all out of doors, you just couldn't record. On the train we could get a kind of enormous roar, but the selective things were impossible. We wanted to get this clickety-clack, clickety-clack, clickety-clack, because this was an essential part of the sequence of the film, and we couldn't get it.

The first time we tried this, we did actually get the railway to put our van on a flat bogey, and we had the microphone in a carriage next door and we tried the microphone everywhere. We even put the microphone down the lavatory pan, hung it over the wheels that way. But there was so much other noise, the clickety-clack didn't come out clearly. Finally (I'm not sure that it wasn't Pat Jackson's idea), we got a scale model, the exact train, from Bassett Lowke the model makers, and we worked it out mathematically, made little grooves in the toy rails, and worked the little train back and forwards. We had to work out the speed mathematically, to make it the same approximately as the speed of the train because it had to fit in with the picture of the man counting. It was damn complicated.

Then there was the question of recording the commentary, and Legg was chosen. I'd nothing to do with it. Legg was suggested by Grierson or Wright to speak it. It had to be spoken at enormous speed — again, the speed of the train — and, of course, nobody could keep that up. So we had to work out a method. Legg would take an enormous breath and start off: "This is the night mail crossing the border bringing the cheque and the postal order letters for the rich. . . ." and so on, until he ran completely out of breath, went "Huh." We had to mark where he went "Huh," and then he had to start again further back.

Legg: A lot of these GPO films were made by teams of people, rather than individuals. I think it's fair to say, for instance, that *Night Mail* was a collaboration of almost everybody who happened to be available. This is not meant for one second to take away from Harry Watt, who directed the thing, very definitely. But a lot of people who were around went and helped whenever they could and did bits and things on it. I was caused to speak part of the Auden doggerel, and Grierson spoke the other part. It very much depended on who was around and who could do what.

Watt: There was, to my mind, one rather unfortunate anticlimax to the whole film, which was obviously successful. That was that when the credits came out (and the credits were chosen by Grierson), they said, "Produced by Basil Wright and Harry Watt."

Now, to my memory, ninety-nine percent of what was actually on the screen was directed by me; that is, I was behind the camera with the cameraman, telling him what to shoot, using the actors, casting the actors, all that kind of thing. I was, of course, a very ambitious young man and determined to be a "great director" (in quotes); and I was shocked when I did not get the straight directorial credit.

Grierson had a small farm down in Kent, where he went at weekends and generally got some unit members to go down there and work it for him, and I set out with my wife in an absolute blue, tearing fury, having talked about it all night and decided that if I didn't get the directorial credit I was going to resign. I went down there and said (I remember distinctly saying this) that Basil Wright had an enormous amount to do with the film (I'm not trying to take one iota from his contribution to the film) and his name could fill half the screen and my name could be in the most miniscule letters, but I wanted "Directed by Harry Watt" because this was my life to be a director, and this was the first biggish film that I'd directed on my own.

Grierson wouldn't give way and gave me the old spiel. The influence still of the maestro and the chief and all the rest of it, was too much for me, and he smooched me and talked to me, and I gave way. I've always regretted giving way. I didn't resign, partly because there was nowhere else to go. You see, we adored and believed in the GPO film unit. The other small units that were around, documentary units, we despised them. We were snobs about it, and I wanted to stay. So I gave way, but I've always wanted to say this, that I should have had the straight directorial credit, and I think this has been proved by the fact that I went on and directed many, many more films, which proves that I was a director.

Wright, as I say, was entitled, perhaps, to a bigger-size credit than I, because I imagine that it was Wright that brought in Auden, or had the idea of Auden doing the commentary, and all this contribution was extraordinarily valuable. The film would not have been anything like what it was if I had made it myself. It would have been just an ordinary documentary, and it became a rather extraordinary documentary, thanks to the contribution of Wright. But when you're young and you've got this drive and ambition, which God knows you have to have in this business, it was taking something terribly important away, and I've never forgiven Grierson for it. I believe it was politics that influenced him to do it. And I must say, we didn't have the guts, perhaps, to stand up to him enough.

Wright does not remember a credit that read, "Produced by Basil Wright and Harry Watt."

Wright: I will give you what I think is a fair statement about the credits on *Night Mail.* As I recollect, I didn't have anything to do with the drawing up of the credits. I didn't know there was any quarrel or fuss about them till I came back from a brief holiday. Certainly, what you see on the screen, amongst the other credits, is "Directed by Basil Wright and Harry Watt," and I can well appreciate that Harry Watt may have felt – and may feel – that this is a great telescoping of the actual process of the making of the film, which involved the fact that I found the shape of the film, wrote the script, including a lot of the dialogue (Harry, no doubt, adapted that, as I've said before, for his own purpose; being a good director, he couldn't take something without transmuting it in his own particular individuality), and that he indeed directed ninety-five percent of the film.

I came in on certain sequences (I mean second or third units and so on), and I did have a sort of overall supervision on the studio shooting but not on the location shooting. . . . I think that all that happened was that, as this was a film which was basically a film of teamwork and in that way difficult to divide all the responsibilities, Grierson perhaps mistakenly did not hive off the one highly creative thing which Harry Watt did. That was the actual, physical direction of the film in the studio and on location with the people. He attempted to cover the whole collaboration with the word "directed," when he should have separated off script, direction, production supervision, and supervisory editing.

Jackson: I was at the first showing of *Night Mail.* It was the first film shown at the Arts Theatre, Cambridge. There was enormous applause at the end, and laughs came where we hoped there would be laughs, and there were Harry Watt and Basil Wright. We were all sitting there, and we looked at each other with astonishment, thinking, "My God, it's coming off! It must be quite good! It's quite a good film! Good God, this thing we've been sitting on for four months, they're liking it!"

Documentary was considered a bit chi-chi, you know. You saw it before the newsreel or after the newsreel at the New Gallery, the audience thinking, "Oh God, here's a filler-out, and they're going to teach us something before we come to Ronald Colman or Madeleine Carroll." But suddenly you see they're laughing. They're enjoying it. They're taking this as entertainment, and that, of course, changed your ideas very much. It changed immediately the idea in which you would approach a subject. To hell with commentary and stuffy old information. This idea of disseminating facts, this became immediately old hat. No, don't let's disseminate facts. Let's disseminate situations. Let's get over what we're going to say in terms of feelings, expressions on people's faces, laughter, and so on. So an enormous amount comes from that effort of Harry Watt and Basil Wright, *Night Mail.* I name the two together because obviously it was both their creation, but it was Harry who got the humanity.

The early school of documentary was divorced from people. It showed people in a problem, but you never got to know them, and you never felt that they were talking to each other. You never heard how they felt and thought and spoke to each other, relaxed. You were looking from a high point of view at them. You were inclined to look at, instead of being with and part of — not, certainly, in Basil's *Song of Ceylon,* which was a poetic, beautiful thing, but unrelated to the Paul Rotha school of cinema which wanted to lay on what the problems were for Britain so that we should see and learn and do something about it. But you don't do something unless you feel some sort of empathy and concern with the problem, and the cold commentary voice doesn't really excite you very much. Documentary as an expositional statement with a commentary has never interested me one atom, and this was certainly the school of documentary that I, as an apprentice, joined, and always was terrified of, anyway, because these discussions seemed to me rather cerebral. What interested me was the thing that Harry Watt injected into documentary. For me, he showed the way.

Watt: To my mind, Grierson's tremendous function was in protecting us embryo film makers — because that's basically what we were — from the pressures of the sponsors. And he did this by his unending propaganda in writing and talking and also by "selling" the films. He had the ability to persuade people that our often pretty feeble efforts were works of art or moving towards a new art form. I remember, I think it was in *Coal Face* which was partly shot underground, the camerawork, to put it mildly, didn't come up to what was expected. It was bloody dark. Despite the efforts of the laboratory to get the brightest and clearest prints they could, in certain shots there was very little to be seen at all. And Grierson brilliantly converted this into a purposeful thing. As the film was being shown to the sponsors, he would explain that this is what we were trying to do, that in point of fact we wanted it to be as dark as this in order to give the impression of the dreadfulness and the difficulties of working underground. This was justifiable. . . .

The main thing to remember is not that all the films were gems. They were, many of them, amateur and second-rate, but they were revolutionary because they were putting on the screen for the first time in British films — and very nearly in world films — a workingman's face and workingman's hands and the way the worker lived and worked. It's very hard, with television nowadays and everything, to realise how revolutionary this was, that British films, as such, were photographed plays, that any working-class people in British films were the comics. There was the funny taxi driver or the butler who dropped the tureen or the comic waiter or the postman who got bitten by the dog. This was the workingman. But we, with *Coal Face* and little things like *Housing Problems* (a revolutionary thing, to get a woman to stand up and talk like that) and *Night Mail,* started to give the workingman, the real man who contributed to the country, a dignity. And *Drifters* — every credit to Grierson — was the first time. It was the hands, the hands of those fishermen doing intricate jobs with a net. It's extraordinary when you see a fisherman with hands like hams and great thumbs and he can tie the most beautiful little knot. And Flaherty, with his glassblowers in *Industrial Britain.* You've got to go back and get some of the propaganda films or the newsreels of the period to see the snobbism. Every film we made had this in it, that we were trying to give an image of the working-man, away from the Edwardian, Victorian, capitalist attitudes. And in this we were suspect. In this the Establishment didn't like us.

We were on a razor's edge. We were always financed by the Establishment, and the Establishment basically regretted that they'd started this thing. To start with, we were left-wing to a man. Not many of us were communists, but we were all socialists, and I'm sure we had dossiers because we demonstrated and worked for the Spanish War. As you know, in the EMB days, a detective was put in as a trainee editor, a man from the Special Branch. And we all knew who he was, and we made his life such hell by going behind the cutting room door and saying, "All right for tonight, Joe? Got the bomb? The job's on." He twigged, of course, immediately that he'd been spotted. . . . But there were always people until late in the thirties who were wanting to shut us down and cut us off. We weren't permanent civil servants or anything like that. Our life was really very precarious.

Between 1934 and 1936, Grierson's documentary movement produced practically all its most interesting work, revealing talent that in some cases became submerged again (Basil Wright never made a better film than Song of Ceylon*) and raising hopes that to a fair extent failed to be realised. (The poetic experiment of* Coal Face *and* Night Mail *was never developed further except in a new direction in the work of Humphrey Jennings during the war, but Grierson never liked Jennings and never claimed him as one of his protégés.)*

The setup during this brief period at the GPO was brilliant. Grierson and Cavalcanti were both great inspirers, yet what each had to offer was completely different. Perhaps because of this, there was an atmosphere in which even potentially incompatible personalities could pull together to possibly greater effect than if they had depended on their individual talents. Night Mail *is still a fine example of that rarity, a truly collaborative work of art. It is so obviously not the work of any one man that, however misguided Grierson's ordering of the credits may have been (and Grierson's ordering of credits was sometimes a bit strange), it must be admitted that he had a problem here.*

Outside the GPO the school of Grierson, during this same period, largely overcame its inhibitions in its approach to the working classes with Housing Problems, *a film of which Grierson remained justifiably proud until his dying day. But, just as there were no more poetic documentaries like* Night Mail,

Housing Problems *and* Enough to Eat? *stand out now as comparatively rare examples of a wholly successful kind of simplicity and directness.*

Looking at all these films today is an extraordinary experience of promise somehow later unfulfilled. By 1936 the documentary movement had made it. All the doors were open to them, and the future seemed bright indeed. Ironically, the only limitations were technical ones — poor equipment, inadequate funds. The fascinating experiments with sound in Coal Face *and* Night Mail *were marred by inferior recording apparatus, so that we now hear these sound tracks with our imagination, rather than our ears. The fact that this imaginative leap is necessary seems today almost symbolic, because it is less for its actual achievements than for what it attempted and what it stood for, that the British documentary movement is remembered.*

5

The Movement Divides

Grierson: Documentary has explored very, very well, but there is one weakness. It ceased exploring into the poetic use of the documentary approach, with us in the thirties. I think we represented the top in Britain — people like Basil Wright, Stuart Legg, Arthur Elton, myself, Cavalcanti, Benjamin Britten (music), Auden (poetry).

Auden: We were experimenting to see whether poetry could be used in films, and I think we showed it could. I agree with Grierson that this hasn't been developed. I did write a poetic commentary for a film about long-distance runners for the National Film Board of Canada about three years ago. Unfortunately it required two speakers and only had one; it wasn't very well spoken either. I should have been there to direct it. But I am interested in the possibility of the use of poetry in the cinema. I would always be prepared to undertake a commission of this kind. I am a great believer in commissioned work. I love command performances, like the United Nations hymn which I have just been writing.

Grierson: We worked together and produced a kind of film that gave great promise of very high development of the poetic documentary. But for some reason or another, there has been no great development of that in recent times. I think it's partly because we ourselves got caught up in social propaganda. We ourselves got caught up with the problems of housing and health, the question of pollution (we were onto that long ago). We got on to the social problems of the world, and we ourselves deviated from the poetic line.

Although this shift in emphasis from aesthetic to social purpose had been developing gradually in the early thirties, it was only after Night Mail *that it began to have an obvious effect on the careers of all Grierson's closest adherents. At the same time the independent Paul Rotha definitively linked social purpose with the documentary idea in his book* Documentary Film *(1936), the first full-scale study of the subject to be published in Britain. On the front page he quoted Grierson: "I look upon cinema as a pulpit, and use it as a propagandist;*

and this I put unashamedly because, in the still unshaven philosophies of cinema, broad distinctions are necessary."

Rotha: I think that the interest of those of us who first became involved in British documentary, who joined Grierson after the making of *Drifters,* was at the time an aesthetic one. It was only later, through the thirties, because of the whole economic and social background of this country plus the rest of the world as a result of the Wall Street crash, the fantastic growth of unemployment, the Spanish Civil War, and so on, that we grew alive to the political significance of what was happening in the world. I think we tried then to express our point of view towards what was happening.

Now Grierson, as head of the EMB and GPO film units, was in a very hand-cuffed situation. After all, he was using government money, and obviously he could not make films which would in any way express a, shall we say, socially progressive outlook. I mean, take *Night Mail.* It has no social purpose whatsoever. It's a wonderful film. It's beautifully made, superbly made, but what does it do in the end? It merely tells you how the postal special gets from Kings Cross to Edinburgh. It cannot possibly tell you about the conditions of postal workers or anything of that sort. That was outside Grierson's brief. I can't criticise him for that, and anyway I wouldn't. He made a wonderful film out of it. A little later on, Harry Watt made a film *North Sea.* Again, I think that's a wonderful film, but again he couldn't with the finance. . . . I mean, finance always conditions what you say in a film.

Finance for the documentary with a social purpose was to come largely from industry. Housing Problems *had demonstrated that an industrial sponsor, unlike the government, might enhance its own image by exposing bad social conditions. The development of industrial sponsorship seemed to offer, not just a new basis of finance but also greater freedom. This field was now to be explored.*

Already Rotha's Contact *(for which Shell put up the money) had led to Grierson's preparing a report for Shell and the formation in 1934 of the Shell film unit. In 1935 Donald Taylor, who had worked for a short time under Grierson, set up Strand Films, the first company to undertake the production of documentaries exclusively on a sponsored basis. Rotha joined Strand as its director of productions, taking with him three contracts he already had to make films for London Transport, the National Book Council, and the National Council of Social Services.*

Legg: In the early thirties you had in this country what was virtually a pre-revolutionary situation, owing to the Depression. There was need on the part of governments for communication, and a little later, industries too. And I think it's true that under the sponsorship formula, which was devised by Grierson, documentary has always flourished in times of trouble and not when things are going smoothly. I think this was one of the reasons why it got going at all.

Now it is possible, I think, to accuse the documentary movement of, in principal at least, being prepared to sell itself to the wishes of the government, of the major industries, the Establishment, the capitalists, whatever you like. And a great deal of philosophical effort, and in fact argument with sponsors, was devoted to pointing out that you cannot exact a total control. You can only exact control to the point where minds meet. And, of course, several people went out of it because they wouldn't collaborate to the point which was necessary to ensure money. Then people went out and came back again. Given a certain film, they would say, "No, I don't like this. It's too close to the needs of the government of the day" or something like that. Then they would just resign, but a year later they might be back. I can't remember who they were, but I do remember it happening quite definitely.

But perhaps because there was an art of sponsorship and perhaps because Tallents understood it so well, we in the GPO who were making the films, I think, were not awfully aware of this. Later on, of course, when one became a producer, it was sometimes absolute agony because if this delicate balance of understanding between the sponsor and the film maker went wrong on either side – if the sponsor became too insistent on his managerial needs and his sponsorial dictate, or if the film makers became ballerinas and started talking about their souls and how frustrated they were becoming – then the thing went haywire. It was no longer viable when that began to happen. Sometimes it happened, and sometimes it didn't.

Watt: When we began to make some successful films for the Post Office, other government departments got jealous and began to approach us to have films made. But, of course, the Post Office, with the help of Tallents, was so elastic-minded and allowed us to choose our own subjects, and these people expected to come in rather like you'd hire a company to make a film and the public-relations department would tell you what to do, what they wanted to show. You know, the managing director driving up in his Rolls Royce and being saluted by the commissionaire. This is what they loved in company films, and when we started making our own type of film, they got cold feet pretty often.

There was one film the Ministry of Housing approached us about. The flats they wanted shown were the ones at White City, near White City Stadium, which were then the best council flats that had ever been built. We naturally got out some kind of script and shot the dreadful slums which these people had been moved from in Fulham, or wherever it was (they were knocked down). Immediately they said, "Well, we love the pictures of the flats at White City, but we don't see any need to have these at all." We said, "What's the good of showing these flats unless you show what you're bringing them from? That's the story." And they couldn't see it. Whether it stayed in or not, I don't remember, but that kind of vetting, that kind of censorship, was always present. This was long after *Housing Problems*.

Legg: The whole problem of the purpose of sponsored documentary, the relationship between film maker and sponsor, is at the root of everything we've done for the last forty years. I think in the GPO one wasn't terribly conscious of it. Grierson looked after all that and, of course, Tallents; and the great thing about Tallents was that he understood how to use creative people. This was the whole art of sponsorship all the way through, not only in the GPO but with the gas people. The British Commercial Gas Association had Clem Leslie as their PRO who again understood this thing. Imperial Airways had Snowden Gamble, who was of the same mental makeup. Shell had Alex Wolcough, who was wonderful at that. We always said there was an art of sponsorship, and there was very definitely.

In December 1935 an organisation called Associated Realist Film Producers was set up to liaise between documentary film makers and potential sponsors. Its executive directors in 1936 were Arthur Elton, Marion Grierson, J. B. Holmes, and Stuart Legg.

Legg: When the GPO film unit began to get a reputation for its films, industry got interested. . . . I think it's worth putting in an aside, at the risk of contradiction, that its reputation rested quite largely on Grierson's flair for publicity. This may be heretical. There were certainly some remarkable films. There was *Night Mail.* There was *Song of Ceylon.* There was this and that. But if you look at the vast body of the films that the GPO film unit made, they're bloody dreary. They're bad films. They were films largely made by people who were learning their trade. There were the rather major films, and then all the bits and pieces and definitely advertising films like *Post Early* and, of course, the films that Len Lye made, which were only two or three minutes but were very special. But Grierson was really training people, and, obviously, in the training process a lot of the films weren't very good.

However, when the GPO began to get a reputation, industry got interested in the use of this new medium of public relations, and began first to ask the GPO film unit to do it. Well, being a government body, the GPO couldn't oblige. Its terms of reference were government, and it couldn't undertake outside work — or only under very exceptional circumstances. Therefore, some of us went out and formed Associated Realist Film Producers, and I think that a lot of the industrial sponsorship was born out of the ARFP thing.

An advertisement in World Film News *(August 1936) described Associated Realist Film Producers as "an independent group of directors who have established themselves among the leading documentary film makers" and listed its members as Edgar Anstey, William Coldstream, Arthur Elton, Marion Grierson, J. B. Holmes, Stuart Legg, Paul Rotha, Alex Shaw, Evelyn Spice, Donald Taylor, Harry Watt, and Basil Wright.*

Grierson was not a member of ARFP. He was, however, one of its consultants, along with Andrew Buchanan, Alberto Cavalcanti, Professor J. B. S. Haldane, Professor Lancelot Hogben, Julian Huxley, E. McKnight Kauffer, Walter Leigh, and Basil Ward.

ARFP had an office at 33 Soho Square and offered the following services:
1. *Advice to bodies desiring to have films made.*
2. *Preparation of scenarios.*
3. *Drawing up of complete production programmes.*
4. *Provision of Film Directors to handle complete production programmes.*
5. *Arrangement for all types of distribution.*
6. *The taking of the responsibility for the production of films by qualified units.*

Anstey: We sent our prospectus to Shell, not knowing how it would be received, but we had reason, I suppose, to think they might be ready to consider using us because, although I walked out on them (which was perhaps an intemperate thing to do), they had had difficulty subsequently with the unit, and we thought they might need some help. Alexander Wolcough, who was then in charge, I think perhaps indicated to us that they wouldn't be averse to hearing.

So they invited us to a meeting, and actually we took over the Shell film unit again. Arthur and I both thought it would be a bit more tactful not to rub their noses in the fact that they'd brought us back in again to tidy things up, so Arthur took over, to begin with.

Arthur Elton became producer in charge of the Shell film unit in 1936. In the same year Basil Wright turned from directing to producing.

Wright: The idea was to form firstly an advisory body, to which potential sponsors should come and get advice, and secondly the units which could provide the actual service of making the films. Donald Taylor and Paul Rotha formed Strand Films to try to take up some of this leeway, and then shortly after that Grierson impelled me to start Realist film unit on a rather limited scale: I think when we started we said we would only make six quality films a year. That was formed by myself, John Taylor, Cavalcanti — the three sort of main people — and one of the first films we made was called *The League at Work*, which Stuart Legg directed for us.

Meanwhile, in 1936 and 1937 a great deal was happening at the GPO. Len Lye was making Rainbow Dance *(produced by Wright)*, Trade Tattoo *(produced by Grierson), and* N. *or* N.W. *(produced by Cavalcanti):*

Cavalcanti: It was not in colour. It is one of the few black-and-white films Len Lye did. It was very, very good. In fact, I felt I could work with him very well. It was a very good time at the GPO in those days. Things like *N. or N. W.* are very important.

Wright: I loved Len Lye's films. I produced one of them (*Rainbow Dance*) without knowing what the hell it was all about. It was like producing *Diary for Timothy*. I must say, seeing it again, it was very interesting. They had a retrospective in Canada, and I saw it there. I hadn't thought much of it in retrospect, but I was frightfully impressed when I saw it again.

Cavalcanti: I regret he [Len Lye] left films, but he's now doing very extraordinary sculptures in America.

Grierson: He's making five-, seven-, nine-dimensional sculpture, sculpture that plays tunes and sculpture that turns itself upside down and bares its breast to the skies.

He still makes films. I saw one of his, not so long ago. No, Len Lye, he's essentially a flaneur; he's a tinkerer; he goes from one thing to another. An amazing man — one of the happiest circumstances of our lives was when Len Lye came in, because it was he who taught Norman McLaren.* Norman McLaren learned all this business of painting onto the films from Len Lye. Len Lye's *Colour Box* was the beginning of that process. *Colour Box* is Len Lye. It's not Norman McLaren, and it predates Norman McLaren. Norman comes from my home town. He comes from Stirling, and I brought him down from the College of Art in Glasgow and put him with Len Lye to learn, as an apprentice.

Then, of course, he got lost. When I was over at the beginning of the war in Canada, I found that he was lost in New York somewhere, making advertising films — some dreadful thing. So I bought him out of that and got him up to Canada.†

For the GPO and the telephone company in Zurich, Cavalcanti spent a period in Switzerland directing three films, photographed by John Taylor, which emerged in 1937. Of these, Line to Tschierva Hut *and* We Live in Two Worlds *had music by Maurice Jaubert, and the latter was scripted and narrated by J. B.*

---

*Grierson's memory seems to be not quite accurate on this point. Interviewed for the BBC Omnibus film about Grierson (first shown in 1973), Norman McLaren said: "We had Len Lye, who, though I never worked with him, had a terrific influence on me because I saw his *Colour Box* and he pioneered a new type of film, painting directly on film. And again he experimented in other films such as *Rainbow Dance*. . . ."

McLaren's first films for the GPO were *Book Bargain* and *News for the Navy* (1937) in black and white. His *Love on the Wing* (1938), produced by Cavalcanti, was in colour.

†The opportunity given to Norman McLaren to develop his individual style, untroubled by pressures, financial or otherwise, over a period of more than thirty years at the National Film Board of Canada, is almost unique for a film artist and can be attributed entirely to Grierson.

Priestley. In Documentary Film *Paul Rotha wrote: "Of all the films of this period, Cavalcanti's film-talk with Mr. J. B. Priestley, the novelist,* We Live in Two Worlds, *was perhaps the most technically mature. With its by-product,* Line to Tschierva Hut, *it was a model of shooting, editing and imaginative use of sound. Both films require several viewings to appreciate their subtle technique, which, at first sight, appears so simple."*

Cavalcanti: I am not at all like my colleagues. I think it is one of the many differences between us, that I am like certain mothers who prefer the ill-formed children to the strong and beautiful ones. So I, in general, prefer films of mine that haven't been as successful or haven't been well understood, perhaps. . . . I don't like, for instance, something as well made as the Priestley film, *We Live in Two Worlds*. I prefer things like *Line to Tschierva Hut* or quite unimportant ones.

Today, We Live in Two Worlds, *with its impressive sound and image montage, still seems the better of these two films.* Line to Tschierva Hut, *at least on a single viewing, fails to live up to the hopes raised by Cavalcanti's own enthusiasm about it. Both films, however, show a developed style which could seem unremarkable in the 1970s simply because so much of it has passed into the everyday language of the documentary film.*

In the same year at the GPO, Harry Watt, with Cavalcanti as associate producer, was directing The Saving of Bill Blewitt:

Watt: I was suddenly summoned in and told that a film had to be made about saving. Well, this was anathema to me. I'd never saved a bob in my life, and making a film about the savings bank was rather like being asked to make a film about the Salvation Army. But the excellent thing was that you always had to go out and find an angle. It wasn't a question of just shooting a lot of scenes in the savings bank.

I had acquired — no doubt, by saving — a very large, noisy, and huge semi-sports car for £50. I had also acquired through the family a huge overcoat, and I set off in my sports car with my huge overcoat to go round the coasts of Britain, because I had decided on making a story in a fishing village, being mad about fishing.

Back I go to Scotland, to a little fishing village called Pittenweem, and there I am playing the big film director in my great big Ulster coat, walking around holding my hands up as though it were the frame of a camera, and a wee boy in a tattered jersey is gowping at me. I patronisingly look down and say, "Hello, son!" And he says, "Hello, fatty!" That punctured me, being the big film director in Scotland!

Eventually, stretching it out as well as I could to get away from Grierson, I got to a place called Mousehole in Cornwall, and it is pouring with rain. I go into the pub, and there's one man in the pub at the bar. So I say, "Have a drink," and he has a drink. He asks me to have a drink, and we're drinking double rums. By lunchtime I'm stewed, and he's stewed. We're absolutely paralytic. I stand up and say, "Well, I must find the postmaster." He says, "I am the postmaster." And this was Bill Blewitt, one of the greatest characters that ever was in British films. He became quite a well-known character actor in British films.

Well, I'd written a story, and it was, I think, the first story documentary, a breakaway. And Grierson agreed to it. It was basically the story of two fishermen who had a fishing boat that was wrecked. . . The only way they can get another boat is to save up, and Bill Blewitt, who was a drunken old bloke in the film, just as he was in life, gets horsed into a local meeting of the savings department by mistake. When he comes out of the pub and sees his wife, who's going to hit him over the head if she finds him drinking again, he jumps into the first doorway and finds it's the savings office. They get ten bob out of him to start his savings. . . .

I shot it like a story film, and Pat Jackson was the assistant, and we had no money as usual: God knows how little, I suppose a couple of thousand pounds, maybe. And we had to have an actor to play the young man. I couldn't find a local boy, so I employed a boy called Joe Jago, who became a very well-known feature cameraman in the end. But I brought him in from the outside. He was brother-in-law of that fat cameraman I was talking about, George Noble. Onions was the cameraman, and also Jonah Jones. And my wife was down there, working like hell with me and this tiny unit. I'd been married fairly recently. I suddenly get a phone call from Grierson to say, "I understand your wife's down there." "Yes." "She's got to leave immediately." Now this was years on, and he still had this monastic thing. He insisted, and I was still so much under the extraordinary, dymanic influence he had over us, that I sent her away. She was a tough cookie, and she went back and gave Grierson hell. I mean, it was one of the few times he really got balled out. But she left, and it was a tremendous loss to us.

We made the film, and Grierson was very bewildered by the film. He didn't know whether to like it or not.

Cavalcanti again helped me enormously with advice. We couldn't afford sets, and we found a ruined cottage without a roof. We painted the walls and put furniture inside this ruined cottage and, just using the ordinary sunlight, got some lovely effects, because you could look through the window onto the harbour. It looked like a most beautiful set with back projection, but it was real. Of course, it was an enormous advance for me. I was learning an awful lot. Cavalcanti found me battling to get close-ups against the cottage, and he said, "Don't you realise, Harry, that a wall's a wall. . . . You don't need to shoot Bill here. Take him into the sun over there, and put him against any cottage, and then you can cut back to the long shot outside this cottage." Of course, this is such a simple thing for features, but it was a revelation to me.

The documentary thing was so ingrained that you would insist on shooting somebody outside the real cottage.

I shot a love scene in it, which Grierson cut out. It wasn't a very good love scene, but I actually had a love scene. And the little film, I think, had a lot of atmosphere. I was always pleased with it. I haven't seen it for twenty, thirty years, and it could be terribly naïve, terribly poor when you see it now. But it was a tiny stepping-stone, and it's the kind of thing that I was the only one to try and do.

The Saving of Bill Blewitt (1937).

Although the performances in The Saving of Bill Blewitt *do seem rather naïve now, the film points in an interesting direction that it is surprising none of the Grierson group pursued.*

At the time, of course, there was something different for everyone.

The March of Time Series, which had been running in America under Louis de Rochemont since 1935, had just set up a London office. Grierson greatly admired the March of Time: "The world, our world, appears suddenly and brightly as an oyster for the opening: for film people — how strangely — worth living in, fighting in and making drama about. And more important still is the thought of a revitalised citizenship and of a democracy at long last in contact with itself." Now he became a consultant to the series, and a few of the documentary people worked on it in Britain.

Anstey: All my movements are in a way due to Grierson — well, a number of them, the early ones — although why I went to March of Time was, I suppose, because they were interested in *Enough to Eat?* They asked me if I would direct a film about malnutrition in this country, with particular reference to anxieties which were felt about the quality of manpower here because of malnutrition and underfeeding. This had come up, I think, in relation to army recruitment. There had been some army investigation, and it had been found that the quality of manpower was not what was called for in a modern army. They asked me if I would do a sort of version of *Enough to Eat?,* which I did.

Then I stayed with them, and I did a number of films in this country, including one which I was rather pleased with, called *Black Areas,* about the hideous conditions in coal-mining, which had always interested me. It was shot partly in South Wales, and we also did a sequence of a famous strike at Harworth Colliery, where the new breakaway Spencer Union was eventually formed. There were fights between blacklegs [scabs] and the striking miners which we tried to photograph by eluding the police (who were staying in the same hotel that we were) and photographing what the local miners called the chain gang (that's the blacklegs) going to work on the night shift. They were taken secretly by back ways to the mine. So we got out a lot of torches and people to hold them, and we tried to photograph this chain gang passing along a road at the back of the colliery, by lighting up these torches at the crucial moment and rushing madly alongside. The blacklegs sort of broke away. They didn't much care for this. The police seemed rather impotent and stood back, and then the blacklegs attacked the crew. Nobody got hurt, but I do remember a boot being thrown. . . .

It all finished fairly quietly, and we were very excited by this material we'd got because it was very much in the news, this particular strike. I think there were one or two shots of this in the finished film, but they were virtually invisible because there wasn't nearly enough light from these flaming brands, and the stock wasn't very fast in those days. A number of the miners' leaders appeared in the film, and I think also the breakaway union leader may have appeared in it and made a speech.

Doing one or two of these things gave me a chance to be more directly political because, whatever the politics of *Time-Life* may have been, the March of Time was very militant in social causes in those days.

Watt: At some time or other — and chronologically I'm not sure when — I was loaned to the March of Time, which had started up a European office headed by Dick de Rochemont [Louis de Rochemont's brother] . I was getting, I think, eight pounds a week, which was an enormous salary from what I was getting at the GPO, something in the region of three or four pounds then. I found working with them fascinating because there was a lot more money available, and you could actually stay in decent hotels and things like that. (One thing about the Post Office was that we weren't permanent civil servants, so we were graded as something like first-class postmen or second-class line men, something like that. We got seven and sixpence a day, or five shillings a day, and therefore we stayed in the cheapest possible places, like seaside digs. We never got any transport. If you had your own car, you didn't get milage, but you got a little money for the petrol, and we used to get Post Office vans sometimes. Cavalcanti and I once created a considerable sensation by driving up to Claridge's in a Post Office van and parking it outside and going into a cocktail party. Anyway, that's by the way.)

The March of Time was very good to work for, but it was a trick. The March of Time had developed this *Timese* way of writing, in which short, sharp, inverted sentences were blared out by a man with a voice like a megaphone. The way you made a March of Time was you wrote, to the best of your ability, the commentary. You then shot to the commentary. You were never allowed to pan the camera. Every shot had to be static. That was because they cut it in such short little bits. Instead of a sentence like, "In Britain today the arms are beginning to pour from the factories again," they would say, "The factories. Are pouring. Arms." So you had to have about six shots to cover that little sentence.

I was given the job first of all to make a film on tithes. Now there was a big controversy going on in the press at the time because the church had the right of a tenth of all the produce of a farmer. This became very considerable, and the farmers refused to pay it. The church commissioners had the right to go in and have a forced sale, and they started doing this, the fools, because the farmers got together and when the auctioneer arrived for a sudden forced sale, the buzz went round. They had boys on motorcycles who tore around the neighbourhood, and all the farmers chucked everything in the fields and rushed to the sale. The prize bull, worth, say £500, would be put up, and they'd bid a halfpenny, then they'd bid a penny. Anybody who tried to bid properly got done. They just kind of kicked the feet from under him. So no professional buyers would dare go to these sales.

I reconstructed a sale down in Kent, and it was reasonably successful. Being film people, we'd take advantage. We used to go to sweet vicars living in a twenty-room house and with a congregation of ten, mostly old women. And I'd say, "What a beautiful house and beautiful church. May I photograph?" Of course, I was showing that he was living in this enormous house and having ten parishioners. The church was very annoyed about the whole thing, but it was just what the March of Time wanted.

I made a second one on football pools, which had just arrived, and that was absolutely banned by the football-pool people. It was fun to make because we did it in the American concealed-camera style, waiting outside people's houses in the early morning for them to come out and get into their Rolls Royces. Of course, they'd run past and try to get out the back way, and we'd tear round with hand cameras and stand in their way, and there were always rows. It was rather newsreely kind of stuff. That, I believe, was the first one of the European productions to be shown on the American circuit. They had enormous success at that time in America. I realised, after doing two, that it was a trick and you'd never get any further. You could go on making March of Times till the cows came home, but once you'd mastered the trick you weren't really teaching yourself any more.

In 1936 and 1937 British documentary was widening its horizons in many directions, experimenting in terms of technique and subject matter, increasing output by the formation of new units. Yet it was still a closely-knit group of people – basically the twelve members of ARFP and those who worked with one or more of them – and it still shared a common allegiance, varying only in degree, to John Grierson. Those years can be seen now as the heyday of the movement as a movement.

Rotha: Social relationship was a very vital part of the British documentary movement of that particular period. Right from the earliest 1929, 1930 days, it was encouraged for us all as we grew in size, to meet in the evenings and to talk and, of course, obviously to drink, within reasonable limits. I can remember in the thirties, at a time when there were certainly three units working round Soho Square (there was the GPO film unit, Basil Wright's Realist film unit, and my own film unit, Strand), every night at about half-past six or seven, if we weren't working, we all met in a local pub. We talked about the films which were being shown in London – I mean the entertainment films – and we discussed politics. We talked of everything you can think of for about an hour, an hour and a half, then drifted off home. And this, I believe – and I've thought a great deal about this in later years – was one of the raisons d'être, one of the reasons for the success of that period of the British documentary film.

Wright: the local pub was very important. We used to go there every evening, and we'd go to one pub for two years and then suddenly, like lemmings, we would desert it and move to another one. . . . We played shove-half-penny and darts and drank bitter, and we talked and we talked. All sorts of people used to drift in. Grierson had a marvellous sort of magnetism, you know. If any eminent film person was in London, Grierson would find him and bring him around and, as often as not, to the pub in the evening.

Rotha: It was in a way like an English equivalent of café life in Paris. Instead of foregathering at the Deux Magots or the Dôme or whatever, we used the local pub in Soho. . . . I remember D. W. Griffith, the great Griffith, coming there one evening, and we almost knelt at his feet in memory of *Intolerance, Birth of a Nation, Broken Blossoms* (there was to be a remake of that, but it never came off). Josef von Sternberg came one evening. Al Lewin came one evening, and of course Flaherty spent a lot of his time with us. . . .

Legg: In the sort of early, historical days, he [Flaherty] was always a kind of semimythical figure over the horizon, a friend of Grierson's and therefore probably someone of significance. Then, one day he turned up, and one began to get to know him. He was a beautiful man, great big, half-burly, half-obese figure, with a hat on his head and piercing blue eyes and this great rugged face. . . . He was an explorer in his earlier life, I think in the service of the Hudson Bay Company, and in the southerly indent of Hudson Bay there is a group of islands called the Flaherty Islands; you'll find that on any large-scale map now. . . .

When he was in England, he would sit in the Café Royal, the old Café Royal, of an evening, and he would start telling a story, probably about a couple of Eskimos in the Arctic. And this story might go on for three or four hours, and one just sat enthralled. He was such a marvellous storyteller. He was in the tradition of the bards, the verbal poets, the saga narrators. . . .

Wright: Also, of course, there were the Friday night shows, which were awfully important. The offices in 21 Soho Square had quite a large cinema — I forget how many it would seat, but maybe eighty. And the tradition sprang up — it was started by Grierson — of having what was called a Friday night show. . . . New GPO films, when they were finished, got their first showing there. . . . And then if anybody was around, they came along. If Moholy-Nagy was in London with a new abstract film, somehow he'd turn up there with the film. Even if they hadn't got films they'd turn up. Carl Theodor Dreyer turned up, and he was in a terrible state. He was very nervous, and that sort of thing. At the end of the evening Grierson got hold of me and said, "Come on, Bas. You live down in the country. Your parents won't mind. Take him down for a quiet weekend." So I found myself saddled with Dreyer, who was on the edge of a nervous breakdown. . . . Paul Hindemith came for one whole evening and saw films, talked about film music. The Friday night shows were very exciting because anything could happen, and did.

Rotha: This disappeared, of course, in later years completely. But like all movements in other arts — the post-impressionists in Paris and so on — this movement grew up in London round Soho Square, and I feel when that died (I don't wish in any way to be nostalgic about this), but I feel something moved out of the sort of inspiration behind our group. The war inevitably was partly responsible for this, because when the GPO became the Crown film unit and as such moved from its modest premises in London out to the larger facilities of Pinewood Studios, the whole of that section moved away down to Buckinghamshire and became remote from us. Grierson himself, always of course a very central figure — Grierson was in Canada, in America, later in Australia, but only on spasmodic visits to England. And the whole movement, as a movement, just sort of disintegrated.

In June 1937 John Grierson resigned from the GPO film unit.

The official explanation was that he wanted to work independently in a wider sphere. None of the press reports was specific about this.

The News Chronicle *quoted him as saying, "I am not going over to Mr. Korda or Mr. Goldwyn or anybody like that. But the documentary film has been doing pretty well for some time in a limited field. I am going to have a shot at extending it. . ."*

The Daily Telegraph *said he was "going to try to start a new profession – that of film consultant."*

A few papers were aware that his first move in practical terms was the setting up of Film Centre with Arthur Elton and J. P. R. Golightly.

Wright: You want to know why Grierson at that stage resigned from the GPO and set up an independent organisation, separately financed and not sponsored in any way. Well, really it's a success story. The success of the EMB and GPO led to other big organisations (monopoly capital organisations and so on) realising that it was good public relations to set up their own use of film. (I'm thinking particularly of the Shell film unit, which eventually grew into one of the most important documentary units ever.) Well, a lot of other things were happening. All sorts of outside organisations wanted to use the documentary film.

Noting that the world was expanding and that international organisations like the ILO [International Labour Office] were looking in this direction (Grierson and I wrote what is now a classical report for the ILO, a sort of basic report as to how any international organisation should use film), Grierson saw that the point had been reached in which there should be an outside advisory and promotional body which would also guarantee to look after the interests of the sponsors. When he formed Film Centre, he formed an organisation which would advise any potential sponsor as to how they should go about making a programme of films, would act as a middleman between that sponsor and the film production companies. Film Centre would see that the production company didn't swindle the sponsor and also would guarantee to the production company that it wouldn't be swindled by the sponsor. Film Centre was specifically for long-term planning for the sponsor.

This was the first stage towards what we hoped would be an international system of distribution which, in fact, got switched into the war, in which Grierson went to Canada and started the National Film Board, and documentary remained in England through the Crown film unit and an immense development of Film Centre. Film Centre was as big and as powerful as the Crown film unit in relation to the Ministry of Information during the war. It was this which Grierson was foreseeing, and all these things I've mentioned which made it essential that he should leave the GPO, which had really become one small section in the whole vast world of documentary and nontheatrical.

Anstey: Film Centre was the direct successor of Associated Realist Film Producers. It was in 34 Soho Square: the same place and virtually the same function. We just changed its name (I don't know why; it was a clumsy name, Associated Realist Film Producers), and Grierson came into it. It must have been while I was with March of Time that this transition into Film Centre took place, I think.

Legg: Film Centre, as I remember, emerged out of ARFP. ARFP was a temporary measure in many ways. It was people graduating, as it were, from the GPO into the industrial field before the industrial field began to take its own shape. Of course, it had taken shape in so far as Strand existed and Rotha had developed it on his side already. But when particularly the Shell operation started, it was clear that something more definite than a loose association of film makers was needed, and Film Centre emerged to form this liaison with Shell and look after Shell's film work and to do other work, as well, other industrial work, and indeed other governmental work with our government and international agencies and so on.

Wright: ARFP gradually switched into Film Centre, which was a very formally organised body. And it worked an absolute dream, because Film Centre protected everybody.

Another possible way of putting all this is that Film Centre simply usurped the function of the democratically organised Associated Realist Film Producers. And certainly, ill-feeling seems to have developed between Grierson's closest associates and some of the other documentary people at this time. Understandably, nobody cares to make a statement about this now. Nobody outside Film Centre seems, in any case, to have sufficient facts. It should be said, however, that ARFP, which was conceivably always an ineffectual organisation, did not disappear when Film Centre started. On the contrary, ARFP continued to exist until 1940. In its last years the membership was watered down to include not just director/producers but almost everyone who worked in documentary films.

From the beginning Film Centre had some kind of formal link with Shell.

Legg: Film Centre was one of these wonderful English formulae that mystify everybody. In fact, it was perfectly simple. Film Centre was not a film-producing body, it was a planning body and a supervisory body. This was the Shell formula. Shell have always had their own film unit, on their own staff, paid by them, on their own premises. It's in Shell House now, and it was always under their roof. But Shell said, "We do not want an entirely Shell operation because if that is done then it will obviously become a house operation. It will become an ordinary piece of Shell public relations from the inside. We want it to be of the outside world as well as of the Shell world." So this curious arrangement came into being that, while Shell had their film unit under their own roof, the planning of the films and the supervision of them was done from outside by Film Centre. I think there's no doubt that this arrangement gave the Shell films their detached, objective sense, which made them so well known. They were not house films. They were not Shell films in the sense of being limited to Shell. They were universal in their application.

Wright: Of course, Film Centre still exists. They're still doing the similar sort of job.

Legg: I'm still a director of it, but I'm dormant. In principle its function never changed. That is, if, let us say, a foreign government wishes to make a film in this country, it may go to Film Centre (it may go anywhere else, but it may go to Film Centre), in which case Film Centre will look at the problem and, having assessed what this government or international agency or industry or company wants to do, will say, "We think the best thing to do is this; make this sort of film or that sort of film, or don't make a film at all. If you think our advice is right, we can arrange to have this done." Usually Film Centre will then employ an outside agency to do it.

Certain things happened that did alter that to some extent, but they were things connected with Shell. Shell, at one stage of its career, wanted to concentrate its work more in the oil business (which, after all, is its business) and sought to shed some of its more ancillary operations, not only in film but in road tankers, all that sort of thing, and they asked Film Centre to undertake certain physical operations in connection with films. For a period Film Centre housed the Shell film unit under its roof. It inspected all their prints, did this and that. And Film Centre certainly now and then engaged in production itself, on special films where it was difficult for one reason or another to contract a film out, either because very specialist personnel were needed or because it was secret or something. But on the whole Film Centre was not a producing organisation. It was consultant.

Grierson was a director of Film Centre until his death in 1972. Arthur Elton was active as a director of Film Centre and also adviser to Shell until he died in 1973. His association with Shell had lasted, with occasional breaks, since 1936.

Elton: I've had already two leaving presents from Shell. I go in and out. It's a curious relationship.

Shell started on a policy of excellence: we will present in the best possible way aspects of the work we do, never put our name on the films. And we practically never do from that day to this. You'll very rarely find the word *Shell* inside a Shell film. There are no advertisements. (I know sometimes there are specific advertising films, which we're not speaking of). And this presentation of its own world has been made year after year from 1936 till today.

It was when he left the GPO in 1937 that Grierson's interest in developing the nontheatrical field first became apparent.
When the EMB film unit was set up, educational and instructional films were already being distributed nontheatrically on both 35 millimetre and 16 millimetre (which was known as substandard because of the unavoidably inferior quality of the prints). Bruce Woolfe and Percy Smith's Secrets of Nature *series began in 1919. But the intention was to show EMB films in the theatres, and it was certainly in part due to a lack of success in achieving this that the policy changed. Exhibitors were reluctant to take these films and paid very low rentals for them. Consequently, even those that were commercially successful had small chance of recovering their costs.*

Wright: What I think Grierson seized on when he found it difficult to get theatrical distribution on a proper scale for our documentaries was the fact that this nontheatrical market could be enormously expanded through governmental and other sponsorship, and that there was in fact a latent demand for it: that people wanted the film — the visual aid — in the classroom, in the club, in the college, in the hospital, or wherever. And then he said, "Now I realise there are more seats outside the cinemas than in them, which meant, in fact, the gradual switch of the whole documentary production towards nontheatrical distribution, the theatrical film being the exception and not the rule.

There were a few symptoms of nontheatrical distribution in the EMB days: regular film shows in the cinema hall of the Imperial Institute, and a library of EMB films being offered to schools and approved societies on free loan.

Elton: I think that the technical developments of the 16 millimetre projector were absolutely crucial and, in fact, the rise of the 16 millimetre projector made possible a new kind of communication. We were essentially people outside the public cinemas.

According to The Factual Film: *"In 1935, as an experiment, GPO vans were sent out to give film shows on the road. The idea began to have effect and the makers of 16 millimetre projection apparatus . . . offered to provide their sponsors with mobile projectors to give road shows. The British Commercial Gas Association tried the same method of distributing the films it had sponsored. . . ."*
By 1937, in its report of Grierson's resignation, Sight and Sound, *which at that time concerned itself primarily with the educational use of the film, mentioned the contribution already made to education by "the travelling pro-*

*jection units which have taken GPO films to schools and educational institutions
throughout the country."*

*It should be noted that the nontheatrical distribution of government- or
industrially-sponsored documentaries was free of charge. Consequently, the situation of the independent documentary producer hoping to recover his costs
and if possible make a profit, could only have been worsened by this development. The documentary movement never found a way of making documentary
films pay. On the contrary, they established the tradition whereby audiences
expect to get such films for nothing, or next to nothing, to this day.*

Anstey: I suppose you could say that Grierson was basically a teacher,
an educator, and this is what we all are in some sense, although he was also
sort of schizophrenic in the sense of the split between the social purpose and a
passionate feeling about art, a word which we were never allowed to breath. On
the other hand, if you did anything which could be regarded as inartistic,
either in your writing or in the composition of a shot or in editing, he was down
on you like a ton of bricks because he believed, and I still believe, that you can
only communicate with art. That's to say, communication and art are insepar-
able. . . . This would be true, I think, of all the early people, that they were
artists, really, who had come to see, as was common in the thirties, that it was
a very dilettante position to take up, to be simply an artist, that there were
social issues which couldn't wait while the artists built the world in their way.
The artist had a primary duty to do something about society.

Elton: Grierson was a propagandist. He wished to project points of view,
to influence people's thoughts, ideas, and views. We all did. I'm interested, I
was interested and always have been interested, in making people understand
things, in explaining things and to hell with the aesthetics. I wish the films I
make to be exceedingly well made in their way, but the primary thing for me
is the message, and the art comes afterwards.

Legg: He [Grierson] made certain contributions which were decisive at
a certain moment. He developed the sponsorship formula which generated
millions of money, not only in this country but in Canada, Australia, America,
everywhere else. Enormous sums came, one way or another, out of this formula. The other thing was that he developed a school of film making in which, as
I say, in bringing on young people, he would never fail them for support, for
an idea. He could have blazing rows with them. He could fire them from his
presence, and forever, and did on certain occasions — not very many, but now
and then.

Now why? Why did this happen? And why did they all take certain lines
of their own, I mean Basil his in the poetic field, Arthur his in the scientific
thing, and so on? I think because Grierson had a certain kind of personality.
He was never interested in money. He never earned any serious money. He was

interested in power: schools, continuity, strength, development not of one
person but of many. And he believed that power lay along this sort of road
and not along an individual road.

Watt: After *Night Mail* the split took place in which Grierson and his
closest associates — that is, Wright, Elton, Legg, and John Taylor — left the
GPO film unit. Now, strangely enough, I don't remember a great deal about it.
I wasn't in the debates about it, but my understanding of it was this: we had
enormous difficulty in getting our films shown in the cinema. I think *Night
Mail,* when it came out first, got three days in a newsreel cinema in Charing Cross
Road; I don't remember what distribution it got, but it gradually got better
known. . . .

Wright: It got very good release in the theatres, profitable release. It was
taken by ABFD, distributors who were very much more sympathetically concerned towards documentary than a lot of the other ones. They'd taken some of
our films which they couldn't make much money off, but with *Night Mail* they
did very well indeed. It got a wide release, made them money, was a popular box-
office film.

Watt: The people who appreciated us, of course, most were the film societies and basically the more intellectual people. We were sneered at by the trade
and basically disliked by most people.

Grierson, who was a tremendous public-relations man and operator, may
have felt that his influence in the civil service was waning. . . . but theoretically
he is supposed to have suddenly had the great revelation that outside the cinemas altogether, which, as I say, were practically cut off from us, there were
twenty or thirty million people in Britain who never went to the cinema, who
lived in the country or for other reasons didn't go. And these were a vast potential, what was called the nontheatrical audience, and there was the future of
documentary.

Well, I don't quite believe that this was the only reason, but I really don't
know. Anyway, there might have been lots of politics behind the scenes.

Now this idea of Grierson's didn't appeal to Cavalcanti and me at all. We
believed — and we had these enormous conceits — that we still could influence
the cinema as a whole, that anybody who goes to see a film at an exhibition to
rest their feet is no catch at all, that we would have been a failure unless we
could make films that sold and competed with commercial films, and we were
determined to go on until we bust to prove this. So we refused to go with Grierson. I think Cavalcanti didn't like Grierson. He had been, to my mind, tremendously exploited by Grierson. His contribution had never been sufficiently
recognized in the way of credits, which is the most important thing in films,

and I think he was quite happy to see Grierson go.* I also was not unhappy to see Grierson go, and I wasn't very intimate with the others in any case. So we stayed on.

You see, Grierson, as I say, was an operator, and he had the idea that if he went out, he could place his people in key positions in the documentary film, because at that time the idea of big companies and government departments making films on their own had gradually seeped through because of the comparative success of us. There was a certain amount of jealousy, and the Post Office were getting prestige, for they had been the first people to have a unit. So he was going to cash in on this. And then there was this interest from Canada and Australia. In Australia he went over and he did enormous reports, and Stanley Hawes was put into Australia. He finally went to Canada himself, but he went all over the world propagandising this idea.† We just went on making films.

I do believe — and this is my personal point — that Grierson's decision then was a disaster, an enormous mistake, because I don't think that the films they made ever advanced very much after they left the shelter, the umbrella, if you like, of the wonderful sponsors of the British government. Once they were then free-lancing and they couldn't experiment, really, they settled into a way of making films for different people, and when you get a first sponsor for a film, very often he wants to play safe. It was much easier to play safe and continue making the kind of films that were acceptable and that they were accustomed to making.

*There was argument about Cavalcanti's credits around this time. His name was probably not on *Coal Face* when it first came out. According to Paul Rotha, this was because Cavalcanti himself did not want to be publicly associated with such avant-garde work, in case it had an adverse effect on his reputation with the industry. Grierson's final comments gave nothing away. "The selflessness of some of the documentary people was a very remarkable thing," he said. "They didn't put their names on pictures. People finally had to try and discover where the credits lay, and the poor old Film Institute's never quite discovered how the credits of documentary lie even today, because we kept on putting on the names of the young people, not the names of the people who were concerned. There were years when Cavalcanti's name never went on a picture. It was because we weren't concerned with names. We weren't concerned with that aspect of things, with credits. It was only latterly that credits became important to the documentary people."

When questioned further about the accuracy of the records, Grierson said: "We're getting them more and more correct. I think Paul Rotha's memory has been pretty good. Oh, I'm quite sure that some of them are totally wrong, but I'm never going to change the record. It's of no interest, but I merely cite it to say that one of the aspects of the documentary movement, of its difficulties over the thirties, and one of the signs and symbols of its engagement with the larger purpose was that it did not concern itself with personal publicity."

†Grierson went to Canada, New Zealand, and Australia as film consultant to the Imperial Relations Trust, which was set up by the government in 1937. Sir Stephen Tallents was an active member of the trust.

One of the first films produced by Wright and Grierson for Realist was Children at School, *which Wright himself directed. It was made for the British Commercial Gas Association.*

Wright: There are two films that I've made which I like very much. One of them is *Children at School,* which was, I suppose, apart from *World Without End,* my most committed, social-political film, and the other nonsocial film which I made for the Festival of Britain called *Waters of Time,* which I'm frightfully fond of and nobody else likes at all except the Italians, who adore it. (I don't know why, but everybody in Italy seems to know it as my best film.) Everything I'm saying is outside *Song of Ceylon,* which is the film I've made which I really like best.

Children at School (1937).

But I feel much more proud of *Children at School* than anybody would believe. About ten years ago they had one of those obituary programmes at the National Film Theatre, at which somebody like myself is dredged up as though from the grave and they run through some of the films you've made. They showed not all, but a bit, of *Children at School,* and I was absolutely thrilled by it. I thought, "My goodness, what genius I had then!" And, incidentally, I'm particularly proud that it won a prize in Venice last year, in competition — and you know this film was made in 1937. The other thing is that this film shows up appalling conditions in the schools in Britain in 1937 which are identical with the ones which came out on the television the night before last: overcrowded classes, schoolrooms falling down, and so on. It's the same story. That is really terrible, isn't it?

But going back to that film, it was the point at which we switched very much from the aesthetic and the formal shaping of films into the reportage film and, after all, the beginnings of *cinéma-vérité*. *Children at School* was made as a reportage film, although I did have some aesthetic sequences in it. I used James Elroy Flecker's poem *The Golden Road to Samarkand* as an ironic overtone.

But this was all very important to me, and one was socially and politically conscious, if only because one was in the face of the coming war and was living through the occupation of Manchuria, the attack on Abyssinia, and, of course, the Spanish Civil War, which was for my generation perhaps the crucial turning point. We could all see, if this one wasn't stamped on, then the great holocaust was bound to come. It was obviously, without anybody attempting to disguise it, the rehearsal. Guernica was the Luftwaffe's rehearsal for mass bombing and so on.

Some of my generation went and fought in Spain. Others didn't. I didn't. I didn't think I would do much good fighting in Spain. What we did at Realist was that we made an appeal film for the Basque refugee children, all the children from the Basque area in Spain, including Guernica. A lot of them were brought over to England to be looked after because of the chaos there, and we made a film about them, to be shown for charity — I forget, some adoption schemes. We made it in conjunction with one of the big film units at Denham, who had the same idea simultaneously. We went down to somewhere near Portsmouth, I think, where the camp was, and shot this film.* We made everybody give everything free. We got the stock free from Kodak. I think the labs processed it free, and that sort of thing.

But that was a critical moment. It was the turning point. That was followed by Munich, and there we are.

Rotha: A number of younger writers, poets particularly, felt very frustrated about the whole political scene in England and in Europe, and they saw in Spain an opportunity for a release of their frustrations. People like Orwell and Spender and Auden went into the International Brigade and various other sections of the Republican army and took an active part in the Spanish endeavour. Well, we in British documentary knew these people. We were friends with them. We knew their work, and we knew them personally, and we felt, "Should we go to Spain? Should we drop what we were doing?"

Each person individually came to a conclusion, and the general conclusion was no, because we thought we were doing a more important job here, staying in our own country, safer though it might be. We at least were making films about the social abuses of our own country, like the slums and education,

*It was called *Modern Orphans of the Storm*.

and we thought it more important we should make these films than go to
Spain to make newsreels on the battle front. This, in a summary, was the general opinion. There are exceptions. Thorold Dickinson and, I think, Sidney
Cole went to Spain and made three — well, not very good films — but they
made the films, anyway, under very difficult conditions, to show at the Film
Society; they had no other showing at all. And Basil Wright, in England, made
a film about the Basque refugee children, which he did for free and gratis.
But that's about all. The only reason I mention it is because a younger generation coming up, reading or looking at British documentary in the thirties,
might say, "Why didn't they take part in the Spanish activities?"

Among the films Rotha had produced for Strand by 1937 were Alexan-
der Shaw's Cover to Cover *(1936) and* The Future's in the Air *(1937), and*
Ruby Grierson and Ralph Bond's Today We Live *(1937).*
    Cover to Cover, *which was about books and included appearances by*
many leading writers, was the first film, apart from newsreels, to be transmit-
ted by BBC Television in 1936 — a fact not regarded as sufficiently important
at the time, or even ten years later, to be included in the main histories of
documentary, although Rotha mentions it in his Documentary Diary *of 1973.*
The film itself is now lost.
    Today We Live *fortunately survives. Shot partly in a village in the Cots-*
wolds (where Ruby Grierson's direction had humour as well as warmth) and
partly in the Rhondda valley (where Ralph Bond directed), it presents a very
affecting picture of people struggling against the demoralizing effects of un-
employment and stands today as one of the documentary movement's most
convincing examples of genuine social concern.

    Rotha: When I started up the Strand Film Company, I had as a result of
my journeys into the Midlands and into Scotland, seen so much of the unemployment and the ghastly state that people were in, that I was determined to
make films about these things. . . .
    Take a film like *Night Mail,* for which I have obviously an enormous ad-
miration. . . . The hero of the film, if you have a hero, is the train, not the
people in the train. I mean, one remembers their faces, of course. . . . But by
and large, when the film is finished and over and in your memory after years,
the real thing, the hangover, if you like, in your mind, is the train itself. It's
not the human beings. Now, if you take a film like *Today We Live,* I suggest —
I don't "say," I suggest — that you remember the out-of-work miners in
South Wales, and you remember the women in the Cotswolds. . . . You don't
remember any single thing like a train. You don't remember the village hall
or the hall they were trying to build in the Rhondda Valley. You do, I hope,
remember the people. This is what I tried to do in this film. It's a question of
purpose.

For Strand and the Anglo-Iranian Oil Company, John Taylor was sent off to Persia on Dawn of Iran, *which he directed, photographed, and edited. Arthur Elton produced the film, which was completed in 1938. On returning to England in 1937, Taylor joined Realist and directed* The Smoke Menace *(1938), about pollution, produced by Grierson and Wright.*

In the second edition of Documentary Film *(1939), Rotha wrote perceptively about the films of this period: "The fast-moving tempo of the March of Time, with its anxiety to find an edge to every item, was now to influence the technique of the British documentary film. Trying to put across facts in journalistic style, a film like* The Smoke Menace *showed small care for the visual importance of the medium. It used the screen as an illustration to its commentary, broken up here and there by a personal interview. It had nothing of the pictorial beauty of photography which was usually associated with documentary films. The formula, because that was all it was, succeeded in restraining the individual style of the director. It was difficult, for example, to recognise that the director who made* Song of Ceylon, *with all its sensitive beauty and inherent film qualities, could later make* Children at School. *Yet the latter became reckoned a more important film than the former. In actual fact, the British documentary people were finding that the making of films about the task of social reconstruction was a great deal harder than the dramatisation of the steel-worker and the fisherman as symbols of labour. . . ."*

But the movement was never more active in the task of widening all its spheres of influence.

Legg: I did one or two films with ARFP. I was then set the very odd job, which I wasn't very good at, of developing the sales side, sort of sales management, of *World Film News,* which I did for six months or so.

Wright: Right from the start — and I mean from about 1930 — nobody in documentary ever turned down an invitation to go and lecture. Even if you weren't getting paid, you did it for your expenses. And it was terribly useful because we'd got the film societies interested in us, and the informed criticism of film-society audiences was the only chance we got of finding out what people thought about the experiments we were making.

In the same way, writing — we took any opportunity to write an article or anything of that sort, not merely about documentary but about the cinema as a whole from our particular documentary or sociological point of view. The Edinburgh Film Guild was publishing this excellent paper called *Cinema Quarterly,* which is a great mine of information of that period, really took over where *Close-Up* left off, and at one point we succeeded (partly through putting the bite on my aged grandfather) in getting a bit of money, and we managed to take over *Cinema Quarterly* and we turned it into a glossy paper, which wasn't a documentary paper at all, called *World Film News**, which I find one of the most indispensable of all reference books. (If anybody will do an index to it, I would be prepared to subscribe at least ten guineas towards it.) This was to me a marvellous paper because it was about the cinema in general, every aspect of it. It had a lot of influence. It started the great British film crisis at the end of the Korda era, because we published the true facts about British film finance. It caused the censor a tremendous amount of embarrass-ment and difficulty, I'm delighted to say. If you look at it, you'll see that there was no aspect of cinema which it didn't cover. It was merely an attempt to look at the world of cinema from an intelligent and slightly more socially oriented point of view. It lost money because we would not accept advertise-ments in return for editorial, and we therefore never got enough advertisements. We ran at a loss. We were helped tremendously by all sorts of people: Sidney Bernstein, now Lord Bernstein, at one of the most critical moments just came to our rescue like that. He said, "I hate the paper. There you are. There's the money to keep it going."

In September 1937 Rotha left Strand to visit the United States at the joint invitation of the Rockefeller Foundation and the Museum of Modern Art film library.

Stuart Legg replaced him as Strand's producer, taking over a series of twelve films on aspects of animal evolution, in collaboration with Julian Huxley, then secretary of the London Zoo.

In 1937 Edgar Anstey also went to New York, as a foreign editor on March of Time. Returning to Britain in 1938, he continued with March of Time until 1939.

Anstey: They wanted me to stay [in the United States] , and there was some talk of my taking over the March of Time eventually, but my mother was here, and it looked as if the war was going to start. I wanted to get back, much as I loved America. I lost my heart completely to America.

The March of Time was very militant about racialism in the South, very strongly pro-Roosevelt, and very anti-Nazi. Their film *Inside Nazi Germany* (which I had nothing to do with, although I was working for them) was, I suppose, the first of the antifascist films. They made a number of others in-cluding one which I did after I got back to London. During the later part of 1938 and early 1939 I did a film about the League of Nations and particularly Anthony Eden's association with the League of Nations, because he had gone very much against the government at this time, and he was pleading . . . for

*Cinema Quarterly was published from 1932 to 1935 and *World Film News* from 1936 to 1938.

antifascist policies to be pursued, for resistance to Nazi Germany and Mussolini's Italy.

This item, which was exposing what we saw as Nazi Germany's intentions so far as Western Europe was concerned, was the centre of a great deal of commotion. During the making of it, I was arrested in Whitehall and appeared in court accused of conduct calculated to cause a breach of the peace: we were out with the unit in and around Downing Street, photographing the anti-Chamberlain crowds and the protests against Munich and things of that kind. The film was never shown in this country because, when we got it back, the British Board of Film Censors refused it a certificate. We at last managed to extract from them a reason: it was said to be unfriendly to a friendly power, which, of course, was Nazi Germany. We were never able to prove that they had shown it to the Foreign Office, but there was obviously no doubt that the Foreign Office had seen it and had banned it, this and another film that was made in New York. This was one of the first cases of political censorship. There has not been much, really, in the cinema. Anyhow, that all came right in a sense, I suppose, and Eden's view prevailed.

I appealed to Churchill at this time. Through his son, Randolph, I managed to see Winston. This is interesting only because Winston, who tottered in, looking very old and lame and using a stick, said, "Well, Mr. Anstey, I've every sympathy with you. I'm entirely on your side, but there's nothing I can do to help you to get these films shown because I am a very old man now, and I'm long past the point where I can be of any help." And he looked it. He really believed it. Absolutely extraordinary, you know. It was partly because he was very demoralized at that time. He was making propaganda with Eden and seeming to get nowhere, and they were both terribly dispirited.

After he came back from America in 1938, Paul Rotha joined Film Centre, directing New Worlds for Old *for the Gas Council. That summer Basil Wright also joined Film Centre.*

Taylor: Grierson was always ordering people around. He'd say, "You go here. You go there," and he took Bas off to Film Centre, and Bas left me to run Realist. I made *The Londoners.*

The Londoners *(1939), made for the British Commercial Gas Association, is still a very interesting film. Philip Leacock assisted on it, and it had verse by W. H. Auden. It included reconstructed historical scenes, which were very well done, showing London a hundred years back.*

Taylor: People had used reconstructions long before that. I'm thinking of films like *Potemkin,* and Dovzhenko and so on. Nothing in films is ever new. This is the thing you notice as the years go by — in techniques, I mean. Techniques are used and forgotten, and then someone thinks what an exciting technique this would be, like Orson Welles in *Citizen Kane:* all this business of using a one-inch lens with great depth of focus and ceilings on the sets and so on, it had been done before. It's a very good film, *Citizen Kane,* but the technique wasn't the important thing about it. It was how he used the technique.

After *The Londoners* we had a film, which was finally made during the war, called *Goodbye Yesterday.* It was about problems of people living in cities. That was 1939, and it was cancelled before it was made. The war started. It was finally made for the Ministry of Information, but the script was altered.

Stuart Legg meanwhile joined Grierson in Canada.

Legg: Grierson in the meantime had been in Canada developing the whole National Films Act, but before that came into being, the Department of Labour in Ottawa had asked him if he could provide someone to make two films for them. I went to Canada to do this, and I never came back, so to speak, because that was 1938 or very early 1939. The Films Act came on to the statute book early in 1939, and after a good deal of to and fro Grierson became the first film commissioner, just about the time the war broke out. I was finishing these two films, and he asked me to stay with him as a producer, get the thing going.

During these years Arthur Elton was developing the Shell film unit, under Alexander Wolcough. In 1939 he produced Transfer of Power, *directed by Geoffrey Bell.*

Elton: The first films we made were simple ones about the oil industry, as such — how the motor car works, things of that sort, basic principles of drilling for oil — simple, informational films which went all over the world. There were no films like them at the time. They look quite crude now. We started a complete programme of films of this kind.

We then went on to a more elaborate kind, and we tumbled on *Transfer of Power,* the history of the toothed wheel. This was an entirely new departure, coincided with my own personal interests, so I was allowed to ventilate my hobby, which was history of technology. It fitted what they wanted. It gave them an historic past, which Shell perhaps would like to have had but hadn't. There was scholarship in the film, so they became scholars in a technology. And Shell has never looked back from that day to this.

Wright: It was the first great expositional film, in which Geoffrey Bell used (Arthur Elton produced) this tremendously imaginative concept for its time of turning a dry-as-dust lecture on what is a gear wheel into something which is still quite fascinating. It's a very, very important film. I always show it when I lecture at universities and that sort of thing.

Transfer of Power *is simply a very lucid exposition of the development
of the toothed wheel. The subject of the film is the wheel itself and not the
way in which wheels have affected human lives or human thought. Consequently, it is successful within a rather limited field, but there can be no denying
its excellence as an example of the use of the film as a teaching aid.*

*Activities at the GPO around the same time show documentary moving
in almost the opposite direction from this.*

Watt: After the split, Cavalcanti and I immediately set out to prove our
point by finding a subject which came under the umbrella of the Post Office
and would be a box-office film to go into the cinemas and be paid for.

The subject we found was ship-to-shore radio.*

Away up north of Aberdeen there was this radio station which kept in
contact with the fishing boats out of Aberdeen. I went up to Aberdeen and
hunted around and wrote the story. I wrote it as a feature film. We, of course,
had very little money, perhaps £3,000. I cast the film in the Labour Exchange.
. . . I cast the whole of the crew there, but I couldn't get a skipper. We found
that in casting these nonactors, the higher you went up the social scale the
more self-conscious they became. The fisherman and the shepherd were marvellous natural actors; the bank clerk and people like that were frightened of
making fools of themselves. I had to have a qualified skipper, or at least somebody with a ticket of sorts. Then they said there was a man called Mattie
Mair. He proved to be colour-blind and never could be a skipper, but he was
a mate and had done a lot of public speaking.

He was coming back from a three-week trip at six o'clock in the morning. I went down to the harbour. The boat was pulling alongside, and there,
working on the deck, was this tough little man with about two-weeks' growth
of beard, in a dirty old sweater. I said, "Are you Mattie Mair?" He said, "Aye."
I said, "I'm thinking of making a film. Would you be interested?" He said,
"Oh well, I don't know." He wasn't put out at all. So I said, "Would you
come up to the hotel tonight, and we'll have a yarn about it?" I was sitting
at the bar, and this character came in in a blue suit with a bowler hat, believe
it or not, and an overcoat, looking very much like a bank manager. Thank
God, I'd seen him on the deck, or I never would have cast him!

We started shooting in Aberdeen in the winter. When the unit came up,
we moved into digs to save money. We had a very good little unit: Jonah
Jones and Chick Fowle, Pat Jackson and Ralph Elton, Arthur Elton's young
brother. We hired an old trawler and went to sea with our acting crew running
it. We didn't have anybody else running it. They had to run the boat and act
in the film at the same time, and we trawled, as well, to make a bit of money
towards the film. The fish we caught we sold.

The only outside person was Bill Blewitt, who was a professional fisher-

*This was *North Sea* (1938).

man. He was the postmaster in Mousehole, but he had been a fisherman all his life. We brought him up just to mix in with the others and show what film acting was. . . .

We wanted it stormy, of course. It was about a fishing boat in distress. So, when all the other fishing boats were running for harbour, we would plough out in our awful old boat and carry on filming. They were so beautifully built, those trawlers, that they couldn't take sea over the bows. We put sixty gallons of water in the bows to make her put her head into the water, and the trouble we ran into! We would set the camera up (we were working with Newman-Sinclair cameras), and, just as we were going to shoot, an enormous wave would come over the bows and drown us and drown the camera Then down below we had to take all the film out and dry it out and start again. Poor Ralph Elton was seasick practically all the time but ploughed on, soldiered on.

We shot some interiors up there, and we had an extraordinary experience of the kind that happens to you in documentary. We were to have a scene of the skipper leaving to go on the fishing trip and saying goodbye to his wife. Somehow or other, I found a very handsome woman about the right age. She was an unmarried woman, living with her skipper father, and I persuaded her to play the part. All she had to do was to come to the door and say, "Well cheerio!" — no kissing or any non-Scottish thing, just "Cheerio! See you in three weeks. Aye. Take care, Mattie." The morning we'd to shoot this, it had snowed in the night, just a little snow. This didn't fit into the other scenes, so we spent the whole morning removing all the snow from the garden and from the cottage roof and door. Then I sent Elton off to get the woman. He came back and said, "She's not coming." I said, "Don't be a bloody idiot, go and get her." And he said, "She's not coming." So I get in the car and rush off. Her father, whom she lived with, had come back from the sea and he was Salvation Army. He wouldn't allow her in a film. I sat with this dour old man, and she took me aside and said, "He'll throw me out if I do this. I want to do it more than anything I've ever done in my life, but he'll throw me out and I've nowhere to go. . . ." She was in tears, poor soul. I had to chuck it and get somebody else.

We decided to do the interiors at Blackheath. We had to have a moving set — that is, moving because it was on a boat. In big studios they have hydraulic jacks and springs and all sorts of things like that. A Scots art director, who was also stills man, called Jack Bryson, who was a very ingenious fellow because he'd had no training in films at all but he just used his nut, built a set on a thing like a wooden saucer. You just had to press on each side of the saucer, and it moved like a ship. It was so big that you couldn't move the camera round the set, so we moved the set round the camera. We just pushed the saucer round, and we kept the camera set in one place. By that you got superb angles, because you could move your set three inches just to get the absolute right angle. To see *North Sea* you'll not realise that it wasn't shot on

North Sea (1938) — the studio set.

some of the best sets, and Bryson needs an enormous amount of credit for thinking that out.* After it, I was summoned down to Denham and offered the second unit of *Goodbye Mr. Chips* (the first *Goodbye Mr. Chips*), and the American producer said, "I saw your picture and liked it very much, but the trouble is you haven't had any studio experience." I said, "Yes I have. I shot the interiors of *North Sea* in the studio." He said, "I don't believe it. Those were shot on board a ship."

One problem we had, of course, was the Aberdeen accent. We decided to keep the accent, and that was absolutely necessary. This dialect business

*In charge of the design for *North Sea* was Edward Carrick, who was art director on many subsequent documentaries, including *Target for Tonight, Merchant Seamen, Coastal Command, Fires Were Started, Western Approaches,* and *Children on Trial.*

has always been an enormous problem if you're trying for box office, unless the visuals are very good. A great deal of the dialogue in *North Sea* was, I think, incomprehensible to people in the south, but the dialogue wasn't all that important.

Anyway, the film did what we intended it to do. It got excellent notices and a theatrical distribution. Admittedly, it was an enormous success in Scotland . . . but I think it was a good film. It had great atmosphere, and I think it came off. It was right in the tradition of documentary, but it was sold and people paid to see it. This was our final triumph, that people were happy to pay to see it. It wasn't forced down their necks like some handout.

I was enormously helped by having a practical and sympathetic producer with me all the time. Cavalcanti wasn't in Aberdeen during the shooting (I think he came up just to have a look around), but he was on the telephone all the time, seeing the rushes and advising me, and he was editing the film with McNaughton. I believe very much in the function of the producer, of a director having a producer (I fight with my producers continuously) as a catalyst – and particularly a practical producer. The trouble is the word "producer" is such a prostituted word. Anybody who can raise a few thousand pounds and get a film made calls himself a producer, and they're just financiers. Korda was a great producer because he was an ex-director. Very few of the producers were practical men.

North Sea, *which is an excellent film, got slightly grudging praise from the Grierson school when it first came out in 1938.*

Watt: We were completely divorced from Grierson and the other crowd. We really didn't see them much at all.

Pat Jackson made his directorial debut with Men in Danger, *a film Harry Watt had started about industrial disease. Watt made* Big Money, *about Post Office finance, and also did some work as second-unit director on Hitchcock's* Jamaica Inn *(1939).*

Watt: Of course, as I said, we were contemptuous of features, and I'd no ambition to go into features, but Hitchcock was one of our considerable gods, in a sense. The early Hitchcocks were the only British pictures worth a damn: *The Lady Vanishes* and things like that. Therefore, to work with Hitchcock was a tremendous challenge, and I was also to get thirty quid a week. I got leave of absence to go and do six weeks or so, I think it was supposed to be. And the extraordinary thing, typically of features, I had made a film of a storm in a real boat in a real storm off Aberdeen, and my main job was to make a storm in a tank. I'd never seen a tank. I didn't even know they used tanks. It was all artificial wind machines, artificial waves, and great cascades of water coming down, and unfortunately I didn't work with Hitchcock at all. I worked separately, and I did all sorts of little shots. I worked in a big studio and I suppose it gave me a certain amount of experience of shooting with big units and seeing big studio stuff shot. In my conceits, I wasn't impressed. I wasn't in the least bit fascinated, and I happily returned to documentary, I suppose having picked up things. . . .

With Cavalcanti as producer, Humphrey Jennings did his first significant job of direction in Spare Time *(1939).*

Cavalcanti: I think that things Jennings did with me, like *Spring Offensive,* like *Spare Time,* are perhaps the best jobs that were done at the GPO. Yes, because things like *Coal Face* and *Night Mail* were experiments in sound, but *Spare Time* is very, very important — a very important document. I think it's moving; it's a very moving film. I think it's one of the films which stay.

Jennings was very quick, and he had a big heart. He was a film poet, I think. He understood about film. He had in film possibilities quite, quite huge.

Cavalcanti's view of Humphrey Jennings is now widely held. But in 1939 Spare Time *came in for a good deal of criticism from the Grierson school.*

Wright: I don't think too much should be made of this, but the general feeling when the film first came out — and I remember there was a showing of it to all of us at 21 Soho Square — was that Humphrey seemed to show, in our opinion, a patronizing, sometimes almost sneering attitude towards the efforts of the lower-income groups to entertain themselves. I'm thinking particularly of the kazoo band sequence in which these poor freezing girls and boys in their flimsy dresses in an industrial landscape were trying to do some sort of a procession in imitation of those great big ones they do down Broadway in New York. As I've written since, I've revised my opinion on that. I think we were a bit too doctrinaire in our attitude in those days and, looking at the film again today and remembering that it was made for Mass Observation, which was a particular organisation with a particular purpose, I think that perhaps we may have missed the point. Certainly, in relation to the corpus of Humphrey Jennings's work — I think the film today stands out in a very much better position.

But Grierson was always critical of Jennings's talent.

Grierson: Jennings was a minor poet. I don't think he was a great poet. He was a minor poet. How do I feel about his work? I'll tell you how I feel about his work. Jennings was a very stilted person. He was not a very coordinated person physically, and I find his films reflect that. They're not very coordinated physically. He's not a beautiful woman walking with a sari; he just doesn't know what walking on the high hills of Poona is like. That to me, of course, is the image of all beauty: a woman walking on the high hills of Poona. But he hasn't got this inner feeling for movement that Basil Wright has and lots of the other first-class documentary people have, a sort of inner gift of movement.

He was certainly, certainly a very considerable talent — stilted, I think, a little literary. He was fearfully sorry for the working class, which is a kind of limited position to be in, you know. Yes, he was safely, safely sorry for the working class, which did credit not just to his liberal spirit but to his lack of relationship with the living thing, sometimes. I think the word is that he didn't have a sense of smell. There's no question he had good taste, visual good taste.

Spare Time (1939).

6

War and the Peak of Achievement

When war broke out in 1939, the British documentary movement was divided,
and its founder, John Grierson, was working for the Canadian government.

Legg: The Films Act, which Grierson had drafted with the aid of Canadian departments who were interested, with the aid of the Parliamentary drafts-
men and so on, came on to the statute book. It became a law of the land in
Canada: there shall be a National Film Board.

Nothing like this had ever been contemplated anywhere else, I think. In
a way, it was kind of model of what Grierson believed was the answer to this
whole experience of film, of visual information and education over the previous
ten, twenty years, the model of how it should be used.

He had worked very hard, indeed, to design the whole Films Act and to
see that it was going to work in Canada. And it became necessary to implement
it extremely quickly, partly because the war was getting going and partly because many departments of the Canadian government wanted to use it. Grierson's job was to create a body of people who could serve all these different
needs of information, instruction, wartime propaganda, and so on, on the screen.
It was a tremendous job.

Grierson: As a politician, I think the best operation, the neatest operation,
I've ever been associated with was the founding of the National Film Board of
Canada. That was a tidy operation, and I had the great advantage of having the
sympathy and support of the prime minister there, but it was in every way a
well-done thing. It was very difficult because it meant liquidating many vested
interests, and it meant a good deal of cruelty in the liquidation of vested
interests, so don't think it was an innocent affair. But as a piece of public service, rather progressive creative public service, so far as the use of the film in
the public interest is concerned, that was a very tidy job.

The setting up of the National Film Board of Canada was a prodigious
achievement, probably the greatest thing Grierson ever did, but surely he would

have preferred to work for the British government at this crucial time. Could it be that the British government failed to ask him? Maybe this whole puzzle will be solved some day.

Rotha: He came back, I remember, three times during the war, just for very short visits, and I arranged for him to meet various documentary people, particularly the young people who hadn't ever known him. They knew his name; they'd seen his films; they knew his myth and his legend, but had never met him. And on each occasion John always refused to say anything. Now I don't know psychologically why this was. I think perhaps it was because he was in Canada all during the war. He'd missed the blitz. He'd missed everything that we were undergoing during the war. He'd missed the deprivation our units had suffered, with no cameras, practically no film stock. Of course, in Canada they'd had everything, you know. I think perhaps John felt this, and that's why he could not — after lots of liquor had gone around and so on — he still could not get up and talk.

Anstey: I've always been told by my wife, who was with Grierson from fairly early days in Canada, that they were required to begin absolutely from scratch with him. He was very anxious that they shouldn't be influenced by the work which he and other people had done in Britain because he believed that the wartime situation made its special demands, was a more compelling one than we had perhaps been faced with here, always of a different nature anyway. So he set a ban on the screening of the early British documentaries, so that they could concentrate their attention on a series like the World in Action and Canada Carries On and the various series which they were preparing mainly for nontheatrical distribution, which were calculated to make Canada become quickly aware of itself and mobilise itself for the necessary war effort.

Legg: Within two years or so, the film board was five hundred people, many, many of whom had never handled film before. . . .

We had been making from the beginning of the war in Ottawa a national editorial, a one-reeler which appeared once a month under the rather old-fashioned title of Canada Carries On. This was about what was going on on the Canadian war front and why and who and all the rest of it. But when it became clear that America was shortly going to get involved in the war, we set our sights higher. We made one two-reel film about what was going on in the Pacific — this was before Pearl Harbour — and what appeared to be the implications of the Japanese presence. This was called *War Clouds in the Pacific,* and it predicted war between America and Japan. By the grace of God, rather than good management, this film was finished about a month before Pearl Harbour. Everyone said we were mad, that there was not going to be a war between America and Japan and of course, the Japanese negotiators were still in Washington. About a fortnight before Pearl Harbour, United Artists in New York saw this film and said, "This is our meat; when can you produce the next one?" And by the time *War Clouds* was on the screen in the States, Pearl Harbour was just about happening. Well, this was one of those pieces of incredible luck that occur now and then.

United Artists said, "You people seem to know what's happening, or perhaps you have a private line to God or something, but continue to make these things, and we will distribute them not only in Canada but in the States as well." So we went ahead with the World in Action series, and we made these films from the end of 1942 until 1945, once a month. I don't think I've ever enjoyed anything so much. . . .

All the time we were concerned in making these films, not with the surface events of reporting but with why things were happening, what was likely to result from things which were going on in the world. In that way we tried to foresee what would happen in this country after the war, and I think we did, with some accuracy. We foresaw the Labour government, and the end of it and so on. We foresaw the whole coming of the Arctic air routes, because it seemed obvious from what was taking place during the war, with the increasing use of northerly latitudes, of Atlantic ferries, and so on, that soon it would be the polar thing; and we made a film on the global air routes of the postwar world. We looked into the whole question of the German interest in geopolitics and made a film on that. I suppose there were about twenty or thirty of these things.

Now we hardly ever shot a foot [of film] for them. The reason was that, obviously, during the war you got every country producing officially an enormous amount of footage which was made remarkably available everywhere. Much of the American stuff came to us, much of the British, a good deal of stuff from occupied Europe, and very much captured material (German, Japanese, Italian, and so on). One could sit in the theatre in Ottawa sometimes and run, let's say, forty or fifty thousand feet all day, of a Tolstoian panorama of what was going on in the world. It was incredible. I've never seen anything like it before. You had this vast sense of global upheaval, in which millions and millions of people were involved, and you would be trying to take hold of the growing points around a given subject or given theme, and organise it. It was a remarkable operation, and I think that was probably the thing I most enjoyed in my film career. I was never any good as a director, but I did love editing other people's material, not mine, because it seemed to me always that other people could shoot so much better than I could.

The World in Action was basically a monthly series of two-reel film editorials, reports, not in the ordinary reporting sense of simply telling what has happened, but of editorial comment, of taking events and relating them to each other in juxtapositions which perhaps were not completely obvious. . . . In that sense I think it was not related to any previous effort in the British documentary thing. There had been, of course, a strong reporting tradition growing up in films like *Housing Problems, Enough to Eat?, The Smoke Menace,* but those were sort of social propagandist things. The World in Action was an international canvas of strategy, of politics, of international affairs, which sought to get at the truth. I'd gone into films, into documentary, but I don't think I was ever very good at it, really. In the more aesthetic sense, the actual film movie sense, I don't think I was ever really completely interested in films. I was interested in history. I was interested in international affairs, and I was interested a little later, as came out during the war, in the birth and emergence of the underdeveloped countries. I was interested in strategy and the meaning of strategy. That is, I was exceedingly interested in the whole world scene which began to unfold with the onset of the war.

Stuart Legg in the cutting room.

Added to that, I think possibly one of the more exciting moments of my life was when I saw the first issues of the March of Time. . . . I think that perhaps some of the earlier issues of the March of Time were the best they ever made, particularly when they had two, and even three, stories in one issue of two reels, because then they really had to concentrate, and some of the things that came out were remarkable pieces not only of reporting but of film making I think perhaps they never mastered the two-reel shape. It began to get a bit diffuse . . . but even so, they had something that interested me very much indeed, and the debt of World in Action to the March of Time I certainly acknowledge every time and in every way.

Anstey: Not everybody realised it at the time, but he [Grierson] was putting Canada into a rather unique position, involved in the battles but also perhaps sufficiently on the sidelines to be able to look objectively at the conflict from several thousand miles away. So he felt a new type of film was required, and he didn't hesitate to use the material which we were making for different purposes here and convert it to his own needs in Canada. We had mixed feelings about this because he and his editors would take something which had been a carefully considered — perhaps he may have felt rather discursive — treatment of a subject, and then reduce it by about two-thirds in length and put it out as a very fast, quick, hard-hitting thing using mainly our material.

When he appeared, I remember, from Canada during the war with Pamela Wilcox, a young woman who was working closely with him at that time, and Herbert Spencer, I think it was, who is now looking after the Film Finance Corporation in Canada, who was also a young trainee of his, we felt that these two youngsters, aided, abetted, encouraged by Grierson, were looking rather askance at the old gentlemen sort of plodding along in the middle of the war, as we felt we were. Grierson was very inclined, for the morale, no doubt, of his own youngsters, to try and inject a sort of spirit of greater drive and urgency and so on into their attitude, as compared with what they found amongst the plodders here. This didn't make him awfully popular, or at least we were so devoted to him that we tended to turn our criticism against these two poor young people, who really had rather a rough passage, but it was probably very healthy for everybody. I think he was also very anxious that they shouldn't feel any inferiority because they'd come to where the war was from a place where really it wasn't. . . .

But there were a lot of fairly lively discussions about the use which was being made of the local films which, as I say, were being sort of dismembered to produce something which we sometimes thought was a bit over-direct, even to the point of vulgarity, perhaps.

At the outbreak of war Cavalcanti, Harry Watt, and Pat Jackson were at the GPO film unit.

Watt: When it became obvious that war was coming, we were approached very, very secretly to make an instructional film about radar, then in its infancy. We did certain shots for it, but it never came off, for some reason.

About a month before war broke out we were again approached and asked to make a film about how to act in an air raid. It wasn't very secretly made. Of course, air-raid shelters had been built. But it was a very simple film. A thousand copies were printed, and on the outbreak of war these were to be distributed all over Britain and shown in the cinemas. . . . Well, war broke out and immediately after there was the first air-raid warning, and the public did everything differently to what the government expected. They all went into the streets and gowped into the sky. Nobody went near an air-raid shelter. So this film was never shown.

Immediately war broke out the Ministry of Information was formed. We, the GPO film unit, were moved from 21 Soho Square, which was supposed to be an old building, to Savile Row, where a company called Spectator Films had a brand-new office in a great, enormous concrete building.

Nothing happened for six weeks, not a thing. We sat on our backside looking out at the window, watching the tarts. It was absolutely stiff with tarts in Savile Row, and we used to run a book on how many men certain tarts would have in an afternoon. Then Cavalcanti took it upon himself to send us out. This is where Cavalcanti was great. He said, "History is being made. We can't sit here."

The First Days (1939).

We photographed them filling sandbags and drilling with broomsticks and men in plus-fours and monocles directing traffic, any old thing we could find. A film was made. It was called *The First Days*. Marvellous material was in it. Humphrey Jennings got some excellent stuff, and there was an enormous amount of other material which I've no doubt was lost. But there was no script. There was no shape. It wasn't a good film.

We turned up at the Ministry of Information films department — Bernstein and Beddington hadn't got there yet — and we said, "Here's a picture." They said, "God, what are we going to do with it?" So Cavalcanti and I went down Wardour Street with this film under our arm, and some dreadful distributor took the film. He didn't like the film, but he took it because he thought, as a businessman, that there'd be lots of other government films coming out and he'd get the in on government films.

Soon afterwards the unit went back to Soho Square, and, as a result of a request for a film about balloon barrage, Watt directed Squadron 992.

Watt: Balloon barrage was manned by Air Force territorials, old chaps, the local butcher and the local gardener, who liked swanking around in the little towns in their Air Force uniform in peacetime. But when war broke out, they were all hoicked from their jobs and stuck in a field with a bloody balloon which went up and down, and nothing happened, and it was cold as hell. It was a very cold winter, and they were deserting by the thousand and just going home. So this very intelligent air,marshal or air vice-marshal came along and said, "I want a film made to show the real value of balloon barrage."

This was just after Christmas of the first year, and the only thing that had happened was the raid on the Forth Bridge. They weren't trying for the bridge; they were trying for some ships lying round there, and it was an unsuccessful raid, the first time the Hurricanes and Spitfires shot down the Germans. They didn't have a balloon barrage there, strangely enough. They had them stuck all over the docks — Liverpool and places like that. But immediately it happened, they moved balloon barrage from all over Britain up to the Forth. So I took this episode, and I reconstructed the raid on the Forth Bridge.

I was arrested twice as a spy because film making was absolutely unknown, and anybody with a camera was a spy. And we did some fantastic things. We got the Air Force to put German markings on their aeroplanes, and we had German planes scooting all over the Forth to the absolute consternation of the multitude, I may say. And we moved huge convoys of balloons all over Britain. It wasn't a bad film. It had one sequence in it which I'm very proud of.

Cavalcanti: Some of the films were sort of documents, and those have not been resuscitated yet, for instance *The First Days, Squadron 992*. They were some of the war pictures, and even some of the films prior to the war will, I think, be considered as very important later. But, of course, people are still impressed by these experiments in sound, colour, etcetera, and I think it is less important. The social side is to me much, much more.

Watt: *Squadron 992* had one showing at the Leicester Square Cinema, and it got some jolly good write-ups. Then, just when it was due to go out in the cinemas, the real war started — Dunkirk and all the rest of it. So the film never got shown. Some Americans saw it, I think, and said, "It's very funny, these balloons. Can we have the film?" And I believe the Ministry of Information gave it to them, and it got some showing in America. They called it *Elephants in the Sky* or something like that [it was *Flying Elephants*], and it was a very truncated version I think.

In the early months of the war the Ministry of Information seems to have had no clear policy on how to use even the GPO film unit, which was the official government unit. The other documentary units were threatened with extinction.

Taylor: We kind of hung on, and Realist almost closed down. We made a few odds and ends: a film for the British Council and another for the oil company.

Elton: The directors of Shell decided to close the film unit, but Alexander Wolcough, who was a very far-seeing man (he's still alive, and he's the most important man we've got, after Grierson) said that films would be needed in the war. He said to them that they'd better finish the present films, because this was very valuable for instructional purposes. Then we worked on the British Council like mad, and they finally commissioned a series of Spanish versions of the films. So that kept the place open for the time being, our premises intact and our cameras. All the film was hurried to the country to be kept in a pigsty on Grierson's farm in Kent because it was very dangerous. I mean, it was inflammable, and they were frightened of a bomb falling on Shell Mex House and it setting everything on fire.

Anstey: The March of Time gave up because the war was coming. They closed down their London unit. . . . The documentary people, all of us, were left in the wilderness. We weren't used because the Chamberlain government was very much opposed to everything that we stood for, and they had their own film people, who moved into the Ministry of Information and were powerful in other quarters. The documentary group were left in a way high and dry — although I was a member of the Officers' Emergency Reserve, I think it was called, and, rather to my indignation at the time, they refused to call me up because somebody, perhaps wisely, said that he was quite sure that the documentary film people would be wanted in the war effort. So I couldn't even join up.

Elton: Meanwhile, in the Ministry of Information a tremendous war was raging between the old-fashioned people, who would still have liked to fight the war in terms of society ladies dressed as Britannia, and some of the rest of us who believed the only way to fight the war was to be very realistic about it. The public, if they were going to fight at all, had better know what they were fighting about. We were not here political, at least not overtly political, but we wanted them to know the facts and factors that were involved, and there was a tremendous row. You see, it really is much easier and much nicer to make films about Britannia with society ladies in them. Korda made a film — bless him, I like Korda very much — but he made a film called *The Lion Has Wings.* That alone is enough, I think, to tell you everything.

The Lion Has Wings *was the first war propaganda film.*

Watt: It was a ghastly, bloody film. There was Ralph Richardson in beautiful clean overalls, white, and everybody else in black overalls, so that the star would stand out, you know.

Cavalcanti: I couldn't stand Korda more than a month. I was working for him on a thing about the story of the aeroplane; it became *The Lion Has Wings.* And he called me in and said, "Well, Cav! (as he called me) I hope you don't mind when you're shooting if I, as your producer, come to your floor and do some things." I immediately was very quick and said, "Oh yes, yes," like I don't mind at all. "It is your right as producer to do it, and besides, you know, between ourselves, I think you are a much better director than producer." He didn't like it, so he added immediately, "Do you mind if my little brother Zoltan comes too and does some things?" I said, "No, Alex, You yes, but your brother no." And then that same night I got my blue ticket. I was thrown out.

Grierson: I knew Korda personally all through the years, and my dealings were entirely personal. I used to dine with him a few times a year. Of course he was marvellous to dine with, and he was good on painting. I shared a certain pleasure with him in one or two of his purchases, paintings. I liked Korda very much personally, but he was the sort of person I would have discussed the whole world with but never worked with.

Elton: Korda, who was a wonderful man, didn't finally come into the battle, which was the battle between the old and the new. The attack was to get the Ministry of Information to base its policies on realism rather than 1914 romance.

In January 1940 Film Centre brought out the first issue of Documentary News Letter.

Wright: By this time *World Film News* was folded because, as I said, Grierson and I were, between us, sort of paying off the losses — oh, slowly, thanks to extremely sympathetic publishers who'd helped us a lot. Then we started a little sort of Roneoed thing called *Documentary News Letter.* After one issue there was such a demand for it we went into print. That was given to one person each month, who was responsible for getting the stuff, all the layout, paste-up, everything of that sort, and on top of everything else, that took a bit of time.

It became a very, very influential journal throughout the war. It had an enormous influence on government thinking in the information services. This is no joking at all: many the time I went into a government office to see somebody and there would be a file marked "priority," which would be a clipping from *Documentary News Letter* with a notice from the minister asking what was the answer to this question. I believe it was tremendously useful, actually.

Elton: *Documentary News Letter* was under attack by the government. We were investigated by Scotland Yard as dangerously disruptive elements but were given, so far as I know, a clean bill. We were attacked, documentary was attacked, the whole time.

The battle between the old and the new was won, of course, decisively. When I joined the Ministry of Information in January 1941, it was already won. The realist school then prevailed and has influenced film making to an extent ever since. In the war it made the very tinselly kind of film more difficult to sell, so that there was an enormous influx of feature films from people like Anthony Asquith and others. The Pressburger pictures were deeply influenced by our realist techniques, and lots of other directors of every kind moved into a realistic phase.

Some of the films now look pretty extraordinary when you see them, but this had a profound effect on films and, in my opinion, led progressively to the whole European movement of realism. Grierson, of course, carried his theories to Canada. A different version of his theories grew up in Australia under Stanley Hawes. So this fertile thinking of Britain had a very powerful effect all over the Commonwealth — all over the world, I think it's fair to say.

In April 1940 Jack Beddington was appointed head of the films division in the Ministry of Information, and the documentary movement got the kind of leadership it wanted.

This was just before the country, as a whole, got the change of leadership that carried it through the war, for on 10 May 1940, Neville Chamberlain resigned as prime minister and Winston Churchill formed his coalition government.

Anstey: When Churchill came to power, there was a great clean-out of all the Chamberlainites in the Ministry of Information, and they started using films properly as part of the war effort, or to hold a mirror up to the country, to try and articulate some of the things that were happening. Shell put their unit at the disposal of this new, revivified Ministry of Information and also the [armed] services, and I took that over again, following the time I started it in 1934.

For the British the war now began in earnest. The Germans invaded Holland, Belgium, and Luxembourg and swept across France. The British army fought a retreat to Dunkirk, from where it was brought home between 29 May and 3 June 1940.

Harry Watt was making Dover Front Line.

Watt: There was only one hotel left in existence in Dover, and stationed at that hotel were the vultures of Europe: the American correspondents who had seen Czechoslovakia fall, Poland fall, Belgium fall, Holland fall. And they were there to see the fall of Britain.

I was at the receiving end of Dunkirk. Jonah Jones and I had camera and lots of film, and we begged to be sent to Dunkirk. Some bloody officer would say, "Do you realise, old boy, that you going over there might mean the lives of two British soldiers?" This was because of the two places we'd take on a boat. Four years later, when they realised what propaganda was, they would have sent a battalion into action just to get one shot. The Germans were covering Dunkirk, marvellous stuff; they were sending all over the world these hundred thousand British prisoners trudging away. And the only shots we've got of Dunkirk were by a newsreel man with a hand-held, small camera, who was being evacuated. Of course we, being professional propagandists, would have seen the discipline of the Guards and we'd have shown that. Oh, what propaganda we could have made! And I was begging the bastards to let me go. I was the only man there, of the government. I shot a lot of stuff of men coming ashore, but that was bad propaganda — the poor, beaten devils coming ashore with no arms, just in rags.

There was one episode which started my dislike for Jack Beddington, who was then in charge with Bernstein. We were down on the beach, Jonah Jones and I — and Jonah Jones, when he was on *Bill Blewitt* had practiced following seagulls with long-focus lenses for hours and hours, and he was a dab hand at picking something up quickly with a long-focus lens. We were shooting a convoy being shelled in the Channel — we bloody near copped it there — and suddenly I heard the sound which tells you a plane is being shot down. . . . There coming right down towards us was a plane. I said, "Look Jonah!" We had the longest-focus lens, about a seventeen-inch lens on. So he whipped up the lens, and he picked this thing up and he followed it right down. It hit the water a few hundred yards in front of us and bounced, and then hit the water again and disappeared. And you actually saw the body come out of the cockpit, if you looked closely as it hit. It was a fantastic shot, and I thought, "That's the climax of the film. We'll finish it on that."

All the stuff you sent to London was censored at the War Office. When the newsreels were having their stuff censored at the same time as ours (we were sitting there with Jack Beddington), they saw this shot and they said, "Jesus Christ, what a shot! Can we have it? Can we have it?" And he gave it away. He gave it away to the newsreels. He wanted to be in with the newsreels. Oh, he gave great explanations: the newsreels were very important for propaganda and so on. But this was the climax of my film.

I put it in the film, but it had been seen in all the newsreels, and everybody thought it was a newsreel shot. It's been used again and again. It's one of the great shots of the war.

In the summer of 1940 Cavalcanti left the GPO to join Ealing Studios as director and associate producer. He was succeeded, as head of production at the GPO, by IAN DALRYMPLE.

Dalrymple: Cavalcanti was a very brilliant bloke, who did simply marvellous work at bringing on young people, but he was a Brazilian, and as there was a state of war it was considered that they couldn't very well have an official government unit, which the GPO became under the Ministry of Information, run by a Brazilian.

Wright: I think that when Grierson left and Cavalcanti almost automatically became the producer in charge of the GPO film unit, that was not his métier. He was not good at dealing with the higher-ups at the Post Office, and he was not, perhaps, good at dealing with the unit as a unit, as opposed to the unit as a collection of individuals whom he could deal with each one, person-to-person. I think that probably, after a bit, he was glad to get out of that and move into his extremely distinguished career in feature films with Michael Balcon at Ealing. But in the historical perspective I would say that, whatever other people may think, his period with the GPO was very, very important to us.

Taylor: Cav certainly had tremendous influence on Ealing. I mean, the important man at Ealing wasn't Balcon, it was Calvalcanti, who was a wonderful teacher and who made Ealing Studios, without any question of a doubt.

Ian Dalrymple's appointment was decided not just by the Ministry of Information but by the GPO film unit itself, whose representatives were consulted.

Watt: Jack Holmes and I were left in charge, and both of us were absolutely incapable, really, of doing the day-to-day routine, the civil service work that was necessary. After great discussion, it was decided to try and allow them to bring in an outside producer, and we played with a lot of names. Somehow Ian Dalrymple, who had been an editor and who had done some writing (I forget his record), was invited to join us.

We thought he had the realistic approach, but he hadn't, and particularly I didn't get on with him at all, and I'm quite willing to say that.

Dalrymple: On the eve of the war, I had two offers to go to Hollywood, one for one picture at £300 a week, and one long-term arrangement with MGM at £180 a week, or something like that. Come the war, of course, all that fell through, in any case. Nothing would have induced me to go out of the country. I made one film in the "phoney war" period which was a phoney film, then went into the government service and dropped to £13.10s. a week. Two top cameramen were getting £6 a week, marvellous photographers, so one couldn't complain. Anyway, one was occupied in a very interesting fashion and hoping one was doing something towards the general effort. It would have been dreary otherwise, because, you see, in the war you don't want people like me at all — quite the wrong time. . . .

At the beginning of the war, Alexander Korda had made almost overnight (the whole thing took about five weeks) a picture called *The Lion Has Wings* about the Royal Air Force, to reassure the British public they weren't all going to be blown to pieces in five minutes: the Royal Air Force would prevent it. I'd acted as producer for Alex on that film. As we made the film, of course, we realised that some defences were pretty slim, and we were wondering whether we should ever finish it before the holocaust started. Owing to the "phoney war", we sold it in America, and it was well received and all that. I may say that Alex really paid for it by pawning his last insurance policy at the time, because he'd been caught at the beginning of the war with a great mass of product which he couldn't immediately show. . . .

The Lion Has Wings was the first production work I'd done. Before that I was a scenarist, a screenplay writer with Alex, and before that my first eight years in pictures were in the cutting room.

Well anyway, I'd done that, and I'd also at the beginning of the war sent in a memo on what I thought the official unit should be doing, because we'd studied a little bit what the Nazis had been doing before in their great films. No notice was taken of this, whatsoever, needless to say. But in the summer before the fall of France I'd made two little pictures, one about a thing called Seaforth, the other about the pioneer soldiers. That was really a stopgap, and (I think it was in June) I was approached by both sides, by both the Ministry and the principal boys who were in the GPO film unit, "Would I go and be producer?" Well, I was supposed to go into the army, but I wasn't very much good as a soldier, and I thought, "I'd better do this, because I do know something about this."

The boys had me to lunch at the Café Royal in June or the beginning of July 1940. We then went to that little place they had then in Soho Square and ran some of their pictures. I saw first of all Harry's *North Sea* and *Night Mail*, before-the-war pictures, and I saw part of Jack Holmes's *Merchant Seamen* film, which he was then working on, and something by Pat Jackson on industry which I was very impressed with. Humphrey was there all the time, and Humphrey was the most modest man alive; he never by any chance sold himself at all; he was quite wonderful. So everybody else's films were shown, then sort of as an afterthought Harry said, "Well now," (because Harry always felt a little bit, you see, that Humphrey was a highbrow), "Humphrey, let's see one or two of yours." Well, they showed me one or two pictures he'd made before the war. I can't remember exactly which they were now. Then I saw this film called *Spring Offensive* which he'd just made, and I was tremendously impressed. I thought that Harry was marvellous for the action films, and so were some of the others, but Humphrey had something special of a quite different kind, to be used in quite a different way.

By August 1940 Dalrymple had taken over the GPO film unit, then renamed the Crown film unit.

Dalrymple: I found this brilliant band of young enthusiasts, fervent enthusiasts, all living on nothing and being paid nothing, dying to do something for the war effort, because they'd been more-or-less frozen since the beginning of the war, although they had, off their own bat, made one or two films. *The First Days . . .* was a very fine record of that moment.

When I got in with this lot, Harry Watt and Jennings and Jack Holmes, Jack Lee, Arthur Elton's brother Ralph Elton (now, alas, no longer with us), and one or two others, I felt their brilliance and their terrific devotion to their craft. All that tied up with the fact that we were dealing with the [armed] services very largely and some of the ministries, made you feel that you were doing something about things. To work with them was an honour, and in fact was the best time of my life, really.

The Battle of Britain was now at its height, and an all-night raid on London on 23 August marked the beginning of the blitz.

With Harry Watt as supervisory director, the Crown film unit made London Can Take It *in two weeks during the blitz.*

Watt: Cavalcanti, Jennings, Jack Lee, Pat Jackson, and I had often discussed the film we would like to make about London, and Humphrey Jennings was the other operative one with me, but the film was a collaboration by the whole unit. Everything else stopped for it. I think I wrote the script. At least I wrote it down, but let us say it was a communal script. It was one night of the blitz, from sunset to sunrise. The whole theme was how extraordinary it was that London went back to normality so quickly.

We worked, literally, night and day. We shot in the underground shelters during the night. We shot all sorts of things during the day. We had an arrangement with the Ministry of Defence, or something like that, to keep posting us where the blitz was worst, and off people would go into the heart of it to get fantastic shots and to be there, of course, as dawn came up, before all the real damage was cleared up. Everybody was sent round looking for people just carrying on. We reconstructed quite a bit. We wanted a bit of humour in it, and I got the shot of the civil servant with the Anthony Eden hat and the little attaché case and the umbrella getting a lift from the East End in a donkey cart going to Covent Garden. That was a fake, but it was true, you see.

Dalrymple: Humphrey did a lot of the shooting on *London Can Take It*, which Harry was in charge of, but Humphrey did some marvellous stuff about evacuees . . . pictures of the blitz actually at night and so forth.

Ian Dalrymple.

Watt: The famous last shot of a little Cockney workingman lighting a fag was one of Humphrey Jennings's touches of genius. He shot that.

McAllister was editing the film down at Denham, and we were pouring the stuff into him. I was never at Denham. I was liaising with the ministry.

Jackson: Everybody in the crowd was shooting for *London Can Take It*, but, of course, it was Harry who found the American journalist, Quentin Reynolds, that remarkable voice.

Watt asked Reynolds to write the commentary first.

London Can Take It (1940).

Watt: He wrote reams and reams, and I would pick out the stuff that fitted, and we finally got a good commentary out of it.

Then we got Quentin Reynolds down to Denham. Ken Cameron, who was the sound man, put old Quent up in front of the mike, and the first line is, "I'm speaking from London." So he stands up, and he says, "I'm speaking from London." We said, "That's great. That's marvellous, Quent, but hold on a sec. There's just a technical problem." We go in the back and say, "Christ, he's awful! Jesus, what are we going to do with this ham?" We have another go. "Quieten down a bit, Quent," and he is just about as bad. We go in the back and say, "God, we'll have to get somebody else for this commentary."

Then Ken Cameron said, "Look, he's a great big bugger. It's a huge diaphragm. Why don't we sit him in an armchair and nearly put the microphone down his throat and let him whisper." And suddenly this magnificent voice came out, a great, deep voice. Of course, the technique is well known now, but it wasn't then.

According to Watt, the ministry's first reaction to the film was unfavourable.

Watt: Arthur Christiansen of the *Express,* who was the great top editor of Fleet Street, came to the press show. He was a friend of mine. He just turned around and said, "That's the greatest war film that's ever been made." All the boys took it up. Christiansen said it, you see. So it got marvellous write-ups.

Chris said, "Come and have lunch with me and Quent." I had three days' growth of beard, and old McAllister, this very broad Scot from Glasgow, was with me. I said, "Can I bring Mac along?"

We went to a very posh restaurant, somewhere like Simpsons in the Strand, and Chris said, "What'll you have, Mac?" Mac looked at the menu: "Oh lobster soup, *bisque d'homard*! Oh, great! I've never had that. Can I have that?" They'd just brought the *bisque d'homard* and stuck it in front of him when he fainted right off with fatigue. He hadn't slept for forty-six or sixty hours.

Jackson: Quentin Reynolds put the film in his briefcase and flew straight to America, to the White House, where he had an audience with Roosevelt. And it's apparently well authenticated that it was an enormous help to the cause that Roosevelt saw that film almost within forty-eight hours of the unit having finished it. It confirmed Roosevelt's feelings, and he had a document that he could show, something with visual impact to help him in his battle to get Congress behind him for lease-lend and this sort of thing.

Humphrey Jennings is often credited as codirector with Harry Watt on London Can Take It, *but there seems to be no doubt that Watt was in charge of production. Moreover, I have found no direct evidence that Jennings worked with the editor, Stewart McAllister, in the cutting room in this instance; it is hard to see how physically he could have managed it, when he shot a good deal of the material and much of the editing was simultaneous and the film was completed in two weeks. Of course, he may have had a strong influence on the script, but the codirector credit is probably inaccurate and the result of a later feeling that anything good with which Jennings was associated could safely be attributed to Jennings. I would rather regard* London Can Take It, *which was an excellent film, as part of the invaluable background experience that enabled Jennings to arrive at his personal style. I think it should always be remembered that, for Jennings, this formative experience went back to the work of the GPO film unit.*

But, certainly, London Can Take It *had things in it that could not be attributed to the action director Harry Watt, now set firmly on his own predestined path. His* Target for Tonight *(1941), although not a film that stands up too well to the passage of time, was a landmark as the first of the feature-length documentaries made during the war.*

Watt: *Target for Tonight* was produced by Ian Dalrymple, but it came about through discussions at the unit before Ian Dalrymple joined us. We were getting very tired of the "taking it" angle, and so it was decided that we would try and make a film about bombing them, about Bomber Command. The initiative came from us at Crown film unit, not from the air force. . . .

I had to write the script, and I was taken all round Bomber Command, including very secretly into the headquarters of Bomber Command. It was finally decided to make the film at Mildenhall in Suffolk, and I started researching. The skipper of each bomb mission had to write a report, and I went through about three thousand reports. I also lived at Mildenhall for about three weeks with the station commander — again, of course, as a civilian, which was a great advantage. I could go and drink with the airmen and hang around in the dispersal huts and chat. . . .

So the script came out as a conglomerate of a great deal of experience, and it was a very exciting but horrifying experience. . . . The new crews would go with the experienced pilot for the first few flights; then came the night when they would go off by themselves. They'd have these seven or eight blokes lined up in the CO's office — so young, averaging about eighteen, nineteen. Maybe the captain would be twenty-one, or something like that. Lovely kids from all over the world, Australians, New Zealanders. And so often it was those ones that didn't come back. Very often on their first solo flight they copped it. We cast the film out of the squadron there. Practically two-thirds of them were killed later on. . . .

It was a lovely summer. We were getting on fine, shooting away, and I suddenly get a phone message from Wing-Commander Williams [head of the Royal Air Force public-relations department] to report in Whitehall tomorrow. It was an awful job getting from Mildenhall to London in the blitz because the trains were all blacked out, and I had to go by train. I couldn't go by car. It took hours and hours. I got to London and reported next morning. He said,

Edward Carrick's original design for the big set in *Target for Tonight* (1941).

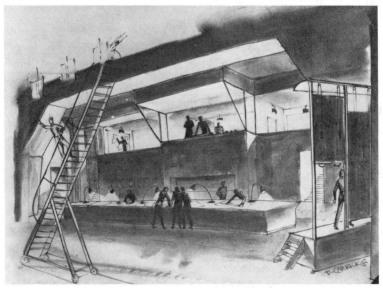

"Something rather serious has happened, old boy." He said, "You and your cameraman, the other day, went into the officers' mess in only a shirt and trousers. This is not right, this kind of discipline, and I must ask you always to wear a tie and a jacket, or you will be refused the courtesy of the officers' mess."

So we went on and finished all the stuff up there. We desperately tried to get shots of bombing, but the stock wasn't fast enough. We put cameras on bombers time and again, but they flew too high and we couldn't get it. We got perhaps a newsreel shot or faked something. I think we faked some stuff, but we did a lot of flying, of course.

All the interiors were shot in studios. The changing room was shot in a little subsidiary studio at Elstree. The big set — and it was the biggest set we'd ever had in documentary — which was the Bomber Command, was at Denham. Round the walls they had the squadrons, and we cheated, in the sense that we doubled the number of squadrons that the British had. The C.-in-C., Bomber Command, was to appear in the film. We persuaded him, although he was fighting the Battle of Britain, the bombing of Germany. He said, "We'll give you an hour." So we lit the whole set and rehearsed the scene with assistant directors. Every shot was worked out. We had spies up the road, waiting for the convoy to come, because he arrived with all his aides-de-camp, his navy liaison who was an admiral, his army liaison, and his adjutants and seconds-in-command, a whole bloody bunch of brass you never saw! I was waiting, shaking them by the hand, "Come in, sir. We're all ready. Won't take a minute. You sit down in this chair and you turn around like that and you say to Wing-Commander So-and-so, 'What's on tonight, old boy'." (or some remark like this). So he sat down in the chair and turned round, and from the chair came a most ghastly squeak. It was a revolving chair.

"Hey, props. Something wrong with the chair. Fix the chair for Christ's sake." So they start, and they cannot get this squeak out of the chair. They take it to bits, saying, "All right, guv! Don't trouble! Don't worry!" Worse than ever. To cut a long story short, he was about four hours on the set. They got fascinated and wanted to be in on the act by that time, so the war stopped for four hours till we got this shot.

We asked Williams for the fuselage of a bomber to shoot the interior of the aircraft. Well, there were wrecked Wellingtons all over Britain. In every airfield they'd been pranged and practiced on. So we wait three weeks. "Oh yes, old boy. Any day now." Three weeks.

It was disposable, in the sense we could cut it up, so we cut holes in it to get the camera through. We were shooting away quite happily, and on to the set came an RAF type who was interested in having a look inside the bomber. He said, "God God, have you seen that?" There on the side by the instruments was a little box, and he said, "Do you know what that is?" I said, "I don't know what it is, some equipment I suppose, something to do with the controls." He said, "Well, if I were you I'd ask somebody to unscrew it very quickly and

put it in the safe." In point of fact, it was one of the most secret new pieces
of equipment that had just been brought out to beat radar, their radar, and it
had a charge in it to destroy it if the aircraft was coming down. It was of in-
estimable value, and it had been in the studio with a hundred technicians mess-
ing around with it for a week.

Dalrymple: I was producer, but I was really, in my view, merely running
the show. I saw rushes, of course; I saw the film as it was gradually cut, but I
kept muffled down as long as I thought things were going fine, and *Target for
Tonight* was a terrific success. Harry was greatly helped on that by another
young man called Julian Spiro* .... He did the second-unit work and some
of the shooting, I think, the landing of the Wellington. He also worked with
Harry on a picture called *Christmas Under Fire,* which Harry made as a sort of
follow-up to *London Can Take It,* and it was a very nice job indeed. It included the first time ever that Kings College Chapel had been recorded and
photographed for the choir service, because we thought this might be the last
chance. It might be blown to bits, and indeed all the time we were trying to
make the film in Kings Chapel, the Spitfires were practising, zooming over the
whole time, and at last we got them to stop because we couldn't record.

Harry thought that the producer should be on the spot with the film as
it was being made. I didn't think that was my job at all because (a) all these
boys knew their kind of work much better than I did and (b) a lot of films had
to be organised and somebody had to be at base. Somebody had to do that. So
Harry criticised me quite a lot. Anyway, he went and saw Jack Beddington,
who was the head of the division, and Sidney Bernstein, who was Jack Beddington's sort of trade assistant, in the sense that Sidney did all the selling of the
films in the most marvellous way, distributed them all over the place and was
the character who knew all about the distribution and exhibition side. Beddington was really a public-relations man with a wonderful discernment for artists.
Well, Harry went to them and said, "Dal's going on like this," and they took
my part. They said, "Well, that's what he's there for. He's there to push you all
around and not actually sit in the field producing. . . ." So Harry said he didn't
want to work that way, and at that moment the Americans wanted him to do
Eagle Squadron. So he went off to that.

Watt: I got £100 a week and free accommodation at the Savoy and I
went on a gigantic piss-up, the only time I really became a nightclubber. The
whole thing lasted six weeks.

They hadn't got a script, and they wanted to start shooting right away.
So we started shooting background with the real boys and at the same time tried
to write a script, working day and night but also drinking heavily. It was the
time that the fighters started escorting our bombers over, the daylight raids,

*Harry Watt also gave credit to Julian Spiro, with whom he had worked on
Jamaica Inn.

Harry Watt — film studio portrait, circa 1941.

and we'd shoot with a boy in the morning and he'd be dead by the afternoon. Of the twenty-four, eventually nineteen were killed, and it was utterly hopeless because there was no continuity. After six weeks I chucked my hand in and went back to ten quid happily.

But I had this, and this was the impact of *Target for Tonight.* I used to go into a nightclub and suddenly the spotlight would be put on me, and the compère would say, "Ladies and gentlemen, tonight we have the honour to have the man who made that film *Target for Tonight,* Harry Watt! Three bottles of champagne on it!" It was the only time I had this because Ealing was a homely place, but the first thing I did after I went back, I found myself hanging onto the side of a quarry, making some shot or other with Jonah Jones, and I suddenly thought, "I'm happy again. This is me."

Meanwhile all the other documentary units had got going.

Taylor: After the fall of France there was tremendous demand for this kind of film, and we made dozens and dozens of them, hundreds maybe, I don't know: instructionals, propaganda films, agricultural instructional films, medical instructional films. I mean, there's a long list of Realist films. Realist, during the war, was a very big unit indeed. At one time we had about fifteen directors there, which really was bigger, I think, than any other unit in the country, including Crown. You know, we didn't make *Gone With the Wind,* or whatever Crown were making at the time, but as far as we were concerned, they were important films, important to us.

Wright: The bulk of the war I was working at Film Centre, producing any and every sort of film in the national effort, as we used to call it. A lot of them weren't worth seeing, but, I mean, Edgar Anstey and I were both at Film Centre and I think at one point in the war we totted it up and we were each of us producing about eighteen films at that very moment.

It's never been particularly my wish to be a producer. My work as a producer was done, well, more from a sense of duty to begin with. Grierson said, "You'd better produce some films." When I set up Realist film unit in 1937, I directed films, as well, at that time. During the war I had to give up all thought of direction because I was sufficiently senior to presumably have the experience which the youngsters would need if we were going to have this tremendous output of films on how to boil potatoes and how to dig a ditch, quite apart from the ones we all remember like *Fires Were Started.* So this was it, as far as I was concerned. "What did you do in the great war, Daddy?" I gave up directing films and became a producer. Grierson made me do it before the war, in a sense. Still, there are rewards from producing.

Edgar Anstey was also, from then on, a producer rather than a director.

Anstey: In certain ways, the least interesting films I made then, but looking back now perhaps amongst the most useful, were the agricultural ones. There must have been anything up to a hundred films we made during the war addressed to farmers, to young farmers clubs, to people with gardens, people with allotments, to try and stimulate production of more efficient methods. I was the producer on that series for the Ministry of Agriculture, so I wasn't able to give much time to any one of them, but I kept the programme going.

Then we did — and these were partly through Shell — a lot of films for the Ministry of Home Security, which were to do with the technique of survival. They were films for the Fire Service, films for the rescue squads (civil defence groups who tunnelled in buildings to get out bombed people), films on new weapons which were being used. For example, there were explosive fire bombs, I remember, dropped at one time, and the butterfly bomb. We made films explaining how these functioned and what they looked like, which went out in one of the series of one-reelers put into the cinemas one a week, I think, all through the war.

Then there was a series of films directly for the Ministry of Information on the strategy of the war. These had to be done very fast for showing in the cinemas as part of the weekly series, and there was an attempt to show the public what was going on in the Middle East, which was a complicated area, and this was done largely with animated diagrams. There were two or three of them only, but quite interesting because they were an attempt to show the British government's or British forces' view of the strategies which were involved on both sides, given a new development in the war like the Japanese war beginning.

For the navy we did all these antisubmarine films. They were rather a different character because they were for showing to personnel who had been cleared for security, and they were really instructional and training films to explain to naval personnel how these antisubmarine weapons worked and how particularly antisubmarine weapons, various forms of depth charges or projectors for throwing depth charges, worked in relation to Asdic, which was detecting the whereabouts of the submarine. These were very exciting to do and were made in the research establishments that were working on these things. They were done at Shell, and Rod Baxter, who still is working with me here, had a lot to do with these.

The radar films came a bit later on. I think we did the radar films for the Admiralty, rather surprisingly, to start with. They were films on the early radar principles and, again, training films to help people use radar equipment.

There was another series made for the Petroleum Warfare Department. The Petroleum Warfare Department was an extraordinary department set up during the war to look into all the possible ways in which oil or oil products could be used to help fight the war. The kind of thing we made films about were great barrages which were going to be, as it were, ignited along beaches, which might be exposed to enemy invasion. What they did was to bury projectors in the sand and connect these with oil pipes to central reservoirs of petroleum, and if a landing force appeared and the enemy came ashore, this would be ignited and you'd get great walls of flame along the thing. Whether this, or any of it, is still secret, I don't know. Then there were great canisters of inflammable liquid — probably gasolene, I suppose — concealed in hedgerows, so that if a tank came along, somebody from a distant point would press a button and this would be ignited in the throne of the tank. Oh, quite fearsome weapons, they were! Whether any of these were ever used I don't know. They were almost all defensive, but they were part of a complex system for protection against invasion, and we did a great many films showing weapons under test, some of which worked and some of which didn't, and showing installations and how the installations could be controlled and put into operation. That was another series.

We did one or two films at Shell for the Ministry of Labour on new skills in the workshop, trying to improve the efficiency of people who'd gone into the factories — women, perhaps, particularly — to teach them simple bench skills. This was an idea we had ourselves at Shell, but it didn't really catch on.

That would be about the size of it, I think. We did some films for public showing about the efficiency of arms workers. Grahame Tharp directed and I produced a film on the Stirling bomber which was really much more a theatrical-type documentary to show the skills that went into the making of this bomber, how efficient it was and new and exciting. It was a kind of morale-boosting film.

Quite a number of these Home Defence training films and services training films went into the cinemas as sort of prestige documentaries, but mainly they were for specific educational-training purposes.

The only other thing worth mentioning is a series of films we did at Shell on the psychology of recruitment. We did a film which Basil, I think, originally produced, called *Personal Selection: Recruits,* which was about the principles which ought to be followed in choosing recruits for the army, to assess their qualities and psychological characteristics and other things so that they got into the right niches. The second, more complex, difficult one, which I produced and Geoffrey Bell directed, called *Personal Selection: Officers,* contained some very interesting psychiatric interviews with young men, mostly privates, who'd been chosen for promotion. . . .

But the achievement was really not in the making of any individual film. Some of them were selected and got a certain amount of acclaim, went into the cinemas, perhaps, and got written up favourably, but that didn't really matter nearly as much as the fact that the Ministry of Agriculture had been able to improve the efficiency of British farming with however many films, and the Ministry of Home Security had been able to support public morale with some contributions, which they made for nontheatrical and theatrical showing, to an understanding of what the threat was and how people could defend themselves individually or collectively against bombing and so forth. Although Grierson could scarcely have foreseen it in these terms, I'm sure that this is what ultimately came from his belief that it's the film policy that counts, rather than the content or style of any individual film.

Apart from producing films in Britain during the war, Basil Wright enacted his increasingly familiar role as Grierson's ambassador.

Wright: While I was at Film Centre, I was seconded twice, with the agreement of the Ministry of Information, to go to Canada: the first time in 1942 for a very brief trip (four or five weeks) and the second time, the next year, for seven months. The first time I went over, it was because Grierson wanted to indoctrinate me to become the London editor and presenter of the World in Action and Canada Carries On series, which were being much misunderstood in Whitehall. So I came back carrying the gospel with me and with the official position of London editor, so that I could go to the Ministry of Information and argue with them about how they wanted to treat the Grierson films from the National Film Board.

The second time was when Grierson, by now wartime information officer as well as film commissioner, said to Beddington and the MOI, "You know that the misunderstanding, psychological misunderstanding, between the British government and the Canadian government is really appalling. Can't you get somebody over who knows about propaganda and mass communications? I want him to examine the climate of opinion in Canada and then reinterpret it back to England." I travelled all over Canada, except for some ghastly interruption because I got acute appendicitis and had to go into hospital. I lost a great hunk of journeying, including a visit to Hollywood, where I was supposed to lecture to all the screenwriters on wartime films. I didn't make any films, although I suppose when I was in Ottawa I gave advice to a lot of snotty-nosed youngsters like Sid Newman. . . . Nice boy. He often comes down here, but, you know, they were all funny little creatures then, learning their job.

Paul Rotha was at Film Centre at the beginning of the war. In 1939-1940 he directed The Fourth Estate, *an ambitious documentary about* The Times *newspaper, which took what was probably by prewar standards a refreshingly detached attitude towards its Establishment subject, although today it seems fairly conventional. It was not shown at the time, however, ostensibly because it was unsuitable in a wartime context.*

The following year he formed Paul Rotha Productions.

World of Plenty (1943).

Rotha: When in 1941 I set up my own unit with several others, including Donald Alexander, we declared a policy that we would make films at the commission of the British Ministry of Information, but we would not make films about the combat fronts. We would make films about what was happening in Britain under the influence of a world war. This was accepted, and all the films we made in the subsequent years were about such things as day nurseries and public health and schools and education and so on. Never once did we make a film about any of the [armed] services.

We worked on the proverbial shoestring. The GPO film unit became, as you know, the Crown film unit, and they were in many ways "the luxury unit." They had cameras. They were moved down to Pinewood Studios. They had unlimited film stock and so on. The independent units, such as my own and such as Realist, had none of these privileges. We had no special equipment. You couldn't buy cameras because they were all wanted for the war, for the army units. Film stock was rationed. Our technicians were under deferment, and those under thirty, of course, were called up. I can say that with my own unit we were working literally with the halt and the maimed and the blind. Yet at the same time we were called on to make about a hundred films a years, which is pretty heavy pressure.

When the idea cropped up in 1942 to make a film about the problems of world food, its production, its distribution, and its eating, Eric Knight, my dear friend who was in this country at that time, collaborated with me, and we wrote a script for a film which later became *The World of Plenty* and had very worldwide distribution.

Now when it came up that I should make this film, I had, I think, eight films in production for which I was responsible. But I still had to make this major film. So we devised a form of experiment, that this film should be slightly — only very slightly — derived from the American Living Newspaper technique, whereby we would have a sound track of arguing voices and cut this to edited material. This was an experiment which fortunately came off, I think. But it was pure experimentation because of shortage of time in this case and shortage of materials, as well.

Instead of the visuals being taken from fresh material, they were in the large taken from libraries. So Eric Knight and I wrote a fairly detailed right-hand page to the manuscript, with exactly what the voice was going to say. This altered all the time, of course, but that's the nearest I think I ever had to a script in documentary.

Pretty well all the shots of food production and of distribution and supply, and all the shots of consumption were stock material. The only new material in the film were the camera interviews with outstanding personalities, of which obviously the most important was the late Sir John Boyd-Orr.

Wright: Paul Rotha did this distinctive thing of developing his own particular style in *World of Plenty*, *The World is Rich*, and *Land of Promise*, a very, very difficult and dangerous way of film making because it didn't permit any form of escape for the audience. This is why there was such an attempt to stop some of those films, particularly *World of Plenty,* on the part of various authorities. It was too near the knuckle, because if you ask the audience to answer that sort of question, the answer is going to be very embarrassing to authority. That's why these films, of course, are so important.

Oh, he had a tremendous boldness about him at that time. And he got people. He got Boyd-Orr absolutely, you see. He was giving Boyd-Orr what Boyd-Orr wanted, the platform of a world machine of propaganda for this very simple deal — food or starvation — which we've still got with us.

Basil Wright is not exaggerating the spirit that emerges from World of Plenty. *This is a marvellous film, which I still think Rotha's best. His achievement is the more impressive in that he relied so heavily on library material.*

Rotha: This material is very difficult to find, and I'm not telling anybody how I find it because this is a sort of black market. But I happen to have my fingers on material all over the world in various libraries, and I know where such material does exist. It's very difficult to get, and, once you get it, it's even more difficult to use because the countries concerned don't like you to use it. For example, in the successor film to *World of Plenty, The World Is Rich,* there are famine scenes in Bengal which, I mean, are quite devastating. The Indian government raised absolute hell to prevent me using these. They couldn't, and I used them. Where I got them from I'm not telling, even to this day, but I did get them, I used them, and nothing happened.

The same thing happened on my *Life of Adolf Hitler* film, of course. . . . But what amazed me about the Hitler film — a great deal of material I wanted to use came from films which the Nazi party had made themselves for their own use, not in cinemas but in clubs and nontheatrically, and obviously had never been shown outside Germany — but these were the property not of the West German government, as I thought they were. They were the property of the executors of the Nazi party, and I learnt for the first time that there was such a body as the executors of the Nazi party, and we had to pay copyright to these people. Being a man of very strong principles, I took the material. I had it duped. I used the prints, and then I refused to pay. Nothing ever happened, I might tell you.

Harry Watt's return to the Crown film unit was brief. In 1942 he left documentary to join Ealing Studios as a feature director.

Watt: We had considerable confidence by this time that we were better film makers than the features people, and of course the trade had suddenly woken up to it, after ten or twelve years of contempt. When their best efforts with all these phoney studio war things were being panned and at the same time our pictures (I'm talking particularly about *Target* and *London Can Take It* and these others) were getting marvellous write-ups and marvellous distribution, they suddenly realised that something was wrong. They began to say, "Jesus, we'd better get hold of some of these boys." And this, of course, pandered to our conceit. . . . But I would never have gone to Ealing if we hadn't made the great mistake of taking on Ian Dalrymple as producer.

With Cavalcanti I used to resign about once a week, and Cavalcanti just laughed and said, "Shut up, you stupid idiot. Get on with the work." And I went back to work. I did this once too often with Dalrymple, and Dalrymple happily accepted my resignation. I rather regretted it, but Ealing were pressing me to join them, and I thought, "All right, bugger you, I'll go and join Ealing and join Cav." But, I mean, the moment I did it, I rather regretted it.

Wright: Apart from the fact that some of the documentary people like Harry Watt and Sandy Mackendrick (he and Roger McDougall ran a sort of documentary group, particularly a script-writing group) went into features bringing the influence with them, feature people began to see the point about the documentary approach, for instance a feature boy like Anthony Asquith. Indeed, during the war you got strange doublings-up when Jack Lee made the submarine film *Close Quarters** at Pinewood Studios and Asquith made a submarine film called *We Dive at Dawn* almost at the same time and more on location than in the studios. You did get this curious blurring of distinctions between documentary and feature during the war.

Dalrymple: A rather annoying thing happened to us about the submarine film. For a long time the navy wouldn't play with us at all. . . . With the permits we managed to set up the Royal Air Force film unit, and the army already had two or three cameramen of their own, but they did play ball with us a lot in giving us facilities and that kind of thing. The navy we could never get anything out of at all until finally there came this submarine picture idea, but before we were allowed to make ours they gave a contract to Balcon at Ealing to make *We Dive at Dawn* which was a theatrical-type film, as opposed to a documentary-type film, but, of course, in the nature of things was pretty nearly dramatic-documentary. It was supposed to be what you might call a feature entertainment film, and we were not allowed to do ours until they'd done theirs. So Ealing Films, you see, would more or less have scooped the interest in that particular one. But ours, I think, was used also for training and that kind of thing. It was quite a good film.

Wright: When Noel Coward was scripting *In Which We Serve*, he had two sessions with me. I got him a hired theatre and I showed him a selection of British wartime documentaries, and he saw them all carefully and took notes

*Jack Lee's *Close Quarters* (1943) was a feature-length documentary produced by the Crown film unit.

and used this as part of his buildup. In fact, if you look at Ealing, Mick Balcon is no fool. He did the same thing, you know. A film like *San Demetrio, London* came from documentary.

It was a time when the feature film, not merely here but in America, too, had to take note of the importance of actuality. The war made people face up to these things, and it was a question of whether you ignored it or whether you made something of it which was human, heroic if you like, but at least made people feel their participation in the great events through the small events which were happening. I mean, the realism of the films made under the services is one thing, but if you take a film like Launder and Gilliat's *Millions Like Us*, that was made by two people who'd really dived headfirst into the documentary conception and come up with this very simple — I haven't seen it for years — but at the time it was a very moving, very beautiful, very true film.

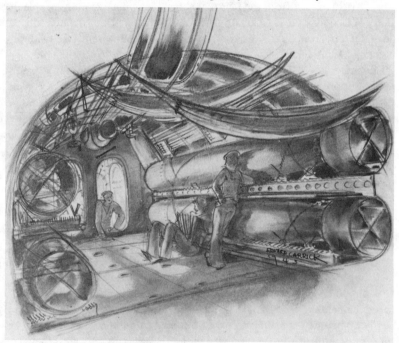

Edward Carrick's original set design for the submarine in
Close Quarters (1943).

Rotha: Jack Beddington, that admirable man, when he was the director of the films division at the Ministry of Information, had the idea of bringing together what he called the ideas committee. This consisted of a number of writers and directors from feature films and a number of directors and others from documentary, who met round a table over beer and rather lousy sandwiches, once every fortnight. He started this about 1942, and it went on throughout the war. We would talk backwards and forwards across the table for about a couple of hours, and then we'd go down to the theatre and see some films, and this was a very healthy and excellent thing. It broke down the barrier which had existed between feature and documentary. I'll give you an example of that. My unit had made a film called *Night Shift* about women working in a factory in South Wales (by the way, I saw it again the other day, and it stands up very well). This was shown one night after the ideas committee meeting, and Frank Launder and Sydney Gilliat saw it, and it gave them the idea to make a feature film called *Millions Like Us,* which was highly successful and completely based on the documentary *Night Shift.*

Humphrey Jennings, during the war.

Another example was Carol Reed's *The Way Ahead,* which was, I think I say in one of my books, entirely based on a film called *The Common Lot,* a two-reeler which Carol saw and which gave him the idea of making *The Way Ahead.* But a lot came out of this ideas committee. Balcon was a member of it and all the leading boys, Charlie Frend and the rest of them. And the man who should have the credit for it is Jack Beddington.

Humphrey Jennings was with the Crown film unit right through the war.

Dalrymple: When the blitz started, about the second night the house next door to where he was living was obliterated, and Humphrey very naturally had a bit of a shock. So I said, "Why don't you come down for the weekend?" I happened to be living in a place called Chorleywood, just a chance that I was there then. I hadn't sort of intended to be there during the war. He came down, came into the house; the door banged behind him, and he nearly passed out promptly. So my wife said to me, "Why doesn't Humphrey live here for a bit, because it's not very pleasant up there in London." So Humphrey did, for two and a half years. Of course, he was out on jobs most of the time, and he merely came back to us as a sort of home base, because his wife and children were in America (they'd been evacuated).

He had a wonderful sense of humour, a wit, and the one thing he loved doing was debunking pomposity. If he didn't aim to do so, it just came automatically with him in so amusing a fashion that life, despite the bombs and so forth, was an absolute joy with him around.

During this period Humphrey Jennings, with Stewart McAllister as his editor, evolved his style. With Heart of Britain *(1941),* Words for Battle *(1941),* Listen to Britain *(1942), he brought a new inspiration to British documentary. Most of the elements were there already – the idea of creatively interpreting actuality, the techniques, the sounds, even some of the shots (for Jennings is alleged to have been quite shameless about using other people's material without so much as asking their leave) – but only Jennings thought how to pull it all together in a way that made poetry of it. How did it happen, and what were the stages of discovery? What was going on in his mind as he made the remarkable transition from propaganda to art?**

Dalrymple: We didn't talk about that at all. We talked about the war and about how stupid this, that, and the other was. And, anyway, he wanted a bit of relaxation because he was working all hours. The whole time we were associated, he was never idle for a moment.

Wright: When he was talking aesthetics, he was talking about all the ideas for his book *Pandaemonium* and about William Blake and the industrial revolution and that sort of thing, but to me he didn't talk very much in what you might call theoretical terms about film. He would talk in theoretical terms more about drama or painting. I always found him very reticent about actual film making, his own film making.

---

*The best exposition of Jennings's development and the interrelation of his many varied ideas and interests is contained in Robert Vas's documentary film about Jennings made for BBC Television's Omnibus programme and first shown in 1970.

Cavalcanti: Oh, but he was still so young. He would have written about it, I am certain, and the contribution would have been epic.

Legg: I'm not sure that he knew what he was at himself. I don't know if he knew where he was going. He had certain very pronounced views about life and history, and Kathleen Raine, at least, believes that he eventually came to the conclusion that the whole of the industrial revolution and the last two hundred years in this country had been a disaster which would never be surmounted, but I don't know. Do you remember that thesis that Isaiah Berlin once expounded that there was a certain kind of artist, writer, painter, who hopped from subject to subject, of which he instanced Shakespeare as one. There was another kind of creature who spent his whole life pursuing one end, one purpose, one channel, of which I think he instanced Tolstoi. It was a very interesting idea. I think Humphrey was one of the former. He hopped, and if you look for some sort of great continuity of thinking, of evolution, of aesthetic approach, I'm not sure that it was there.

Watt: I got on very well with him, although he was an intellectual. But I never really worked with him except on *London Can Take It.* He worked very much on his own. He would disappear and reappear at the office – a skinny, chinless fawn. He was the only person who could come back and rave about what he'd got, and be right about it.

Dalrymple: I was always in trouble with the London end because there was never any script. That wasn't the way Humphrey worked. He'd have a bit of a note on an old envelope or something, a few words to remind him of various things. So part of my job was really to protect these people from being harassed from the London end who, quite rightly, wanted to see a little end product.

From the time of *London Can Take It,* followed by Harry's *Target for Tonight,* they were reassured that things were going to happen. And Humphrey was very much liked by the civil servants in the ministry – I mean, the little department which was the contact with us, the ordinary professional civil servants, apart from Beddington and Bernstein, who were in charge of the whole thing. There was one particular man called S. J. Fletcher, who was our real contact in the ministry, and he was always fighting for us. He'd been with the GPO film unit, and he was quite marvellous. One or two were not so good, were rather stupid, and somehow or other they were switched to something else!

Jackson: Humphrey would interpret a situation in disconnected visuals, and he wouldn't quite know why he was shooting them, probably, until he got them together. Then he created a pattern out of them. It was as though he were going out to collect all sorts of pieces, cut already, for a jigsaw puzzle, and wasn't quite certain what the picture of that jigsaw puzzle was going to be until he had it in the cutting room, and here he was enormously helped by McAllister.

Dalrymple: Humphrey and McAllister had a strange effect upon one another. Humphrey was frightfully well organised in shooting. He'd have the most marvellous luck, too, because sort of symbolic things happened the whole time; and because he'd been a painter and in fact was still dabbling with paint when he had a moment, he had a wonderful gift for choosing the exact place to put the camera. So he'd go out and shoot madly and all the stuff would come in to McAllister, and McAllister would brood over it on the Movieola. When Humphrey had finished shooting, he would join McAllister in the cutting room and nothing would happen for weeks, apparently. You wondered when the hell anything was going to emerge, and of course London end got a bit restive. Then all of a sudden, overnight, somehow everything went together — doink. And there was what I thought a mini-masterpiece in each case.

Jackson: It was terribly like a painter in a way; it wasn't a storyteller's mind. I don't think the dramatic approach to a subject, in film, really interested him very much. It was an extension of the canvas for him. Patterns, abstractions appealed to him enormously, and those are what people remember most, you know: *Listen to Britain,* the cornfield waving and the sound of the Spitfire going over, more evocative of 1940, 1941, than reams of dialogue. Humphrey got it in three shots. That's a special talent that can create for all time an evocation of that kind.

At the time it was made, however, Listen to Britain, *like* Spare Time *before it, did not escape adverse criticism from inside the documentary movement. Reviewing it as film critic of* The Spectator, *Edgar Anstey described it as "an expensive Crown Film Unit production . . . which will not encourage anyone to do anything at all." His review went on: "It sets out to assemble a varied collection of characteristic British sounds ranging from a piano recital at a National Gallery lunchtime concert to the clatter of a falling railway signal, and to illustrate the skilfully constructed jigsaw with an appropriate (and beautifully photographed) set of visual images. This is an aesthetic enough conception in all conscience, but by the time Humphrey Jennings has done with it it has become the rarest piece of fiddling since the days of Nero. It will be a disaster if this film is sent overseas. One shudders to imagine the effect upon our Allies should they learn that an official British filmmaking unit can find time these days to contemplate the current sights and sounds of Britain as if the country were some curious kind of museum exhibit, or a figment of the romantic imagination of Mass Observation."*

Anstey: I was often unfair, I think, in my criticism of Humphrey's work in those days because I felt that some of his films were a bit sort of dilettante. In the purposes which they did then so well serve, they proved not to be, particularly overseas. But I had no doubt at the time that he was the most artistically gifted — I think, really — of us all. He and Basil Wright, you could say, were competing there, but I think Humphrey had the edge.

Listen to Britain (1941)

I always thought that certain films of his — in particular, *Fires Were Started* — were masterpieces. *Listen to Britain* I had some doubt about, because I thought it was too indirect and oblique. On the other hand, it turned out — and my wife was able to tell me this afterwards because she was in North America at the time — that it had much more influence than *Fires Were Started* or *London Can Take It*, which he didn't make. *Listen to Britain* had enormous influence overseas. There were a lot of people besides me who were a bit sceptical about it here because one felt there was a certain amount of fiddling while

Rome burned. But then he dealt with Rome burning, you could say, in *Fires Were Started.* Oh, he was a great, great film maker. He and I used to argue and disagreed about a number of things, and I think he always felt that I was a little unkind about *Listen to Britain,* but I did praise other films of his with enormous enthusiasm which I generally felt. He was a great, great film maker.

Fires Were Started (1943).

Ian Dalrymple produced Fires Were Started *(1943).*

Dalrymple: Harry once said to me very shrewdly and wisely, "We must try to get Humphrey to do an action picture, because everything is so static with Humphrey. All his setups are static. The people are static."

So there came a time when things had quietened down. The Germans had taken all their aeroplanes to go and hit the Russians, and after May 1941 we were more or less at peace so that one could take many more risks in the blackout and that kind of thing, and it was suggested that a film should be made about the national Fire Service.

Unfortunately, we had a lot of fights at the other end because they wanted it shorter and they thought it too deliberate here and this kind of thing, and Humphrey did not like his work being mucked about. So I was really between two fires the whole time. However, in the end we got it in a way that Humphrey could accept, albeit with misgivings, and the ministry could accept.

Bernstein, particularly, was concerned because he had to persuade the theatres to take it.

To me, to this day, it is one of the films of the war, one of the others being of course *Western Approaches* which Pat Jackson sat in the sea for about six months making.

Western Approaches *(1944), like* Target for Tonight, Close Quarters, World of Plenty, *J. B. Holmes's* Coastal Command *(1942), Jennings's* Fires Were Started *and later* Diary for Timothy, *was a feature-length documentary, a kind of film not made in any quantity until the war.* Except for the compilation films made by the service units, such as* Desert Victory *(directed by Roy Boulting, 1943),* Tunisian Victory *directed by Frank Capra, 1944),* The True Glory *(directed by Carol Reed and Garson Kanin, 1945), most of the wartime feature documentaries came from the Crown film unit.*

Before Western Approaches *Pat Jackson had directed the documentaries* Health in War *(1940) and* Ferry Pilots *(1942).* Western Approaches *still stands as one of the finest feature documentaries of the war.*

Desert Victory (1943)

*There had been documentaries of considerable length before. *BBC: The Voice of Britain* ran 56 minutes, *Contact* 42 minutes, and *Song of Ceylon* 40 minutes.

Jackson: "Western Approaches," I hadn't realised, was a great sea approach to England. I didn't know what it was until I discovered in the Atlantic. I thought it was a sort of technical expression. It didn't relate to anything at all.

The first thing, of course, I went to sea in convoys. I went up the east coast convoy a couple of times, went to Gibralter. And what was really terrifying was that it was so deadly dull — deadly, deadly dull: just the horizon full of ships, and they'd never seem to move. They went at four knots, five knots, which was a slow convoy, and occasionally a destroyer would rush down the line. But it was static. It was so dreary. You get used to a convoy after the first ten seconds. Right, come on, boy! Nothing more! So how on earth to bring the subject to life? Really, I was in a terrible state about it. For two months I hadn't an idea in my head, and I went back to the studio to see Dalrymple. I was going to say, "Look Dal, I'm terribly sorry. I can't see this at all. I'm afraid I've failed you."

I got halfway to the studio, and suddenly it hit me. What would happen if a submarine used a lifeboat as a decoy and a straggler from the convoy picked up the message from the lifeboat? You've got the three elements which represent a convoy in the battle of the Atlantic interacting on each other. I went straight back. I'd solved the real problem of how to tell the story of Western Approaches.

Then came the technical problems. As it was rightly supposed to be a document about an aspect of the Battle of the Atlantic, I said we must try and have the real people who fought it, and that meant no actors. Dalrymple agreed. So I went up to Liverpool and sat in a pub near the Shipping Federation and got to know the publican. I had an agreement with him that, if I gave him a wink, there was a face behind the bar that I'd like to meet and talk to. I was there for three weeks and I found a possible forty men, officers and ordinary seamen. These forty I brought down to Pinewood. I put them in a half-section of lifeboat in the lot, in a field behind Pinewood, and I gave them stones to act as though they were the rations for the day, to see how they were going to react to this extraordinary setting. Three or four of them immediately left. They said, "Sorry, Gov! I can't face this. I'd rather go back to sea and risk the torpedoes. I'm feeling sick." I said, "Well, that's all right. Fine." We got some of the men from the forty, but I still hadn't the eighteen or nineteen that we needed for the lifeboat. Back I went to my pub, drank more gallons of beer, and eventually got the lifeboat crew.

It was getting on towards the beginning of September, late in the year. We got all the help we could from the Blue Funnel Line, which supplied the lifeboats with great platforms fore and aft so that we could get the camera on. But we were three weeks down at Holyhead before we'd shot a shot. The technical problems were so difficult. The platforms at the end of the lifeboat put the boat out of trim. When we put weights in, to bring the boat into trim, the boat became so sluggish that it was slopping water over. The water was creating shorts in the cables and everything else. But eventually somehow we licked it.

Pat Jackson (right) making *Western Approaches* (1944).

The men were marvellous because they were relaxed, I think for the reason that *we* were in *their* element. We were the ones who were being seasick and looking stupid. So they were able, as it were, to play the hosts. The dialogue was very carefully written in the script. It had to be because certain situations had to be put over, and the only way they could be put over was by prepared dialogue. Some of them learnt it word for word. They felt more secure learning it. Others, rather more adaptable, particularly this fellow Banner, just looked at it and said, "Well, I see what you want. I get the feeling. I can put it in my own words, can't I?" I said, "Of course," and he put it in infinitely better words, because they were his words from the depths of his experience of thirty years at sea. Then the others listened and caught on, got the style from this chap Banner, saw how he was getting the sense of the salt, and they all did it that way.

But it was a very long job because we were going out several miles from the Irish Channel, to get out of sight of land. We took very little food; food was only sandwiches. I think we were the best part of four to five months doing those lifeboat sequences, which I suppose comprised about a third of the film. It would have cost astronomical sums if there had been actors, of course, but the men were not getting much more than their normal rates of pay if they'd been serving in the ordinary merchant ships, and of course the unit was being paid very little in these days. This is the method of film making which I would still like to employ, but it's very hard nowadays for economic reasons. It's coming back a bit, I think. The new boys are beginning to use that technique again.

Making *Western Approaches* (1944).

Clifton Parker wrote the score for Western Approaches.

Jackson: He saw the film one afternoon at Pinewood, and half an hour later he came into my office, where there was a piano, and sat down and played the melody. Astonishing, quite extraordinary!

Dalrymple: One element which was most important to us was music. As we were dealing with the people who did the actions, and not professionals, and as we wanted to keep the commentary down as much as we could and as we couldn't play dramatic scenes with dialogue, music was obviously all-important. And we had the services of Muir Mathieson, who at the time was the leading film conductor, actually sort of producing music supplied by the composers, knocking it into shape, and exactly fitting it. He was an absolute genius at this. So through him and through an arrangement we made whereby the composers would accept the token fee of £50 or something (because the money we got to make films was negligible) but kept the rights of the music, we were able to use Vaughan Williams and Bax, a number of the younger lot too. We were able to get some marvellous music, and of course we used classical music to a certain extent, obviously.

After Western Approaches *Ian Dalrymple left the Crown film unit.*

Dalrymple: I hung on in the latter stages of *Western Approaches* because we were having a little trouble in the cutting room and we had to change the editor because he wasn't really understanding what Pat Jackson was up to. In the end Pat really edited the film with his sister, who acted as an assistant.

In his letter of resignation (dated 10 May 1943) to Jack Beddington, Dalrymple recorded that during his period with the Crown film unit, it had produced eleven features or featurettes and eighteen shorts. Three additional features and a short were in an advanced stage of production, and script preparation had begun on a further two features, a featurette and a short.

He gave the following reasons for tendering his resignation: "In the first place, the large reduction in earnings I had to accept for official work has now, after three years, made it difficult for me to meet my private commitments.

"Secondly, it seems possible that a new impetus might be beneficial from the point of view both of the Unit and of the Films Division.

"Thirdly, the present constitution and functions of the Board of Management or Control seem to me to be unsatisfactory. In the first place, it does not manage; secondly, it is not permitted to control; thirdly, the representation of the Administrative Departments is limited to points of information and is not on a level of responsibility: and fourthly, although we have on the Board an eminent representative of the Trade, we are not using him either as an adviser, on the one hand, or an advocate, on the other.

Fifthly, the commercial exploitation of our films is exposed to the mercy of the whims and wangles of private distribution, with the result that the same old artificial conditions are created to prevent the producer even recovering his cost. The attitude of the Distributor or Exhibitor is either that a film is too difficult to be popular: or so popular that he should get it for nothing. Where a 'difficult' film proves popular, as it almost invariably does, it is prevented by the usual devices from receiving its proper revenue. In these conditions, if they remain uncombatted, it is no longer possible to invent a programme of production which will at once serve the needs of war publicity and not be a burden on the Treasury."

Dalrymple: There was a new director general, Lord Radcliffe, and when he took over he had everybody in and gave us a great talk on what we were supposed to be doing. Well, I thought this was a bit much, considering we'd been doing it for three years. I didn't want to be then told, three years later, what I should be doing, and one of the things I thought we'd been doing was to sustain the morale of the population until such time as action took over. So I said, "Don't you think in a way that we've been taking the place of the action which is coming and sustaining the morale?" And Radcliffe said, "Oh no, that's not what you've been doing at all." So I thought, well bother that!

Another thing was that at that time the Beveridge Report had come out, and there was the fact that we should be thinking about what we could do in the difficult period after the war. I made one or two suggestions, but nobody would listen to them at all at the time. They said we must get on with the war. In fact, you see, we'd done our job then, really, because after that it was merely a matter of the newsreels recording what was in fact happening of a positive nature. . . .

We felt if we were going to be any good at all we ought to be studying the problems of peace, of social reconstruction, the health service, what was going to happen to the mines, the new atomic power that was coming in, and all that kind of thing. We ought to be studying it seriously. But no.

Another thing was that we'd accumulated a great deal of material which from a historical point of view would in the future be very illuminating. . . . I suggested to the ministry that if they allocated me about £3,000 a year for this project only, we could compile from our material, filling in a little bit where necessary, a ciné-history of the war from the inside, from inside England. I don't mean the fighting part, at all. But after a time Jack had me in, and he said, "I'm sorry, Dal. *They* don't like history." So a great deal was lost and scrapped. You see, the raw material, according to the purposes, of course, was cut and handed out there and then to the newsreels. There was no favouritism, and each one was chopping about as they wanted. It was everybody's, from the Ministry's point of view, whereas they should have kept a blueprint of the whole of the stuff before dishing it out.

In 1944 Paul Rotha Productions made Children of the City.

Rotha: One of the films which we were asked to make in 1944 (towards the end of the war but the war was still on, and this is important to remember) was commissioned by the Scottish Office. It was one of a group, and this particular film was to deal with juvenile delinquency in Scotland. This film, which was very successful and had big distribution in America particularly, was directed by a woman called Budge Cooper, and it attempted to go really seriously into the reasons for delinquency in children. But, apart from the film's success, the important thing is that such a film could have been made whilst the whole of this country was at war. I can't think of the Americans doing this, and certainly the Germans wouldn't have done. I can't imagine the French doing it, or any other country doing it. But in time of war it was possible still for British documentary to make films about social problems of this kind. I saw the film again not very long ago, and I think the analysis of the causes of child delinquency which are expressed in this film made in 1944 are as relevant today as they were when the film was made. In fact, as you know, when we make a documentary film on this kind of subject, a lot of research is spent originally in analysing the problem and drawing up almost a social analysis report on it. And when Miss Cooper and I drew up this report on child delinquency in Scotland at that time, the Department of Health in Scotland asked if they could keep a copy because it was the best report they had ever had in this way.

After Children of the City, *Paul Rotha Productions was replaced by two new film units, Rotha's Films of Fact, which made* Land of Promise *for the Gas Council, and Donald Alexander's* DATA.

Paul Rotha directing Marjorie Rhodes in a scene for *Land of Promise* at Nettlefold Studios, 1944.

Rotha: When I made my film about housing and the whole problem of housing, *Land of Promise,* in 1945, there were a number of sequences which I could very well have done in the actual houses, but it would have meant taking lighting, of course, obviously, synchronous cameras and London-bus-type location recording equipment. Therefore in those days it was much more economical and efficient to build the kind of set I wanted in a studio and shoot it in the studio. It was a question of economy, more than anything. Had it been today, well, obviously I'd have taken a tape recorder and a walkabout camera.

But I remember for *Land of Promise,* we saved up and kept enough money somehow to have a sound truck down in a public house just off Fleet Street, on a Sunday when it was closed. We shot the whole ending sequence there with John Mills and Herbert Lomas and Miles Malleson, because in *Land of Promise* I used well-known actors because I wanted to put a point across. I do not believe — and I may well be in a minority in this — that documentary just has to go to the actual to be documentary. I think it is the social purpose that matters. I said this, I hope very clearly in my early book way back in 1936, in which I claim that, for example, Pabst's very great film *Kameradschaft,* the mining film, was in its way a social-documentary film, and I always maintained this very strongly.

Taylor: Some documentaries are made in studios, but, you know, it's not really where they're made. I mean, during the war, we made a series on ana-

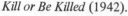

Kill or Be Killed (1942).

esthetics* (because at the time the teaching of anaesthetics was abysmal), a long series of farming instructional films, a long series on gardening (growing food in gardens). Alex [Shaw] and I, between us, produced a very good series called Your Children and You — *Your Children's Eyes, . . . Teeth, . . . Ears, . . . Sleep.*† It was all that kind of film we were making. We are also making propaganda films. We had people like Len Lye,†† who worked with us all through the war. And Frank Sainsbury made quite a number of propaganda films, but they were usually slanted from the documentary point of view — what we considered the documentary point of view.

At the Crown film unit, Ian Dalrymple was succeeded by J. B. Holmes and later Basil Wright, who was producer in charge from January 1945 to January 1946.

Children on Trial (1946).

*The Technique of Anaesthesia series was sponsored by Imperial Chemical Industries from 1944.

† Your Children and You series for the Ministry of Health began in 1945 and continued for several years after the end of the war.

†† Len Lye's *Kill or Be Killed* (1942) for Realist, is a strange, compelling film in black and white, which gives a simple lesson in unarmed combat the stark quality of a primeval struggle for survival.

Wright: You have to remember there was a tremendous reversal during the war in which the documentary boys got Pinewood Studios, which were then the biggest and best equipped in the country, and it went very much to their heads, you know, the hell with location. I remember when we were shooting *Children on Trial,** the ridiculous sight of a reconstruction, on the biggest stage in sight, of a very small slum room in Liverpool. I went into the studio, and I strongly recommended that it must have four walls and they mustn't take the fourth wall away or they'd be cheating. They could have shot it, as they would be doing today, in an actual slum room. They didn't because they had a studio — well, partly that, partly of course that conditions in wartime were difficult. Let's be fair about that.

Meanwhile, Pat Jackson had signed a contract with Korda.

Jackson: When we finished *Western Approaches,* the Ministry of Information really didn't know what to make of it at all, and so they asked Korda, who was then honorary adviser to the ministry, to have a look at it.

One morning my sister and I were in Theatre 2 at Pinewood, and in came Korda wearing a funny trilby hat and mackintosh, very charming, and he said, "I've come to see a film called *Western Approaches.* I'll sit here, Take no notice of me. Start when you like." So the lights were dimmed and we started, and there was my sister biting her fingernails at the same rate as I was biting mine. After an hour and twenty minutes the lights came up, and he was very flattering indeed, liked it. He was then with Metro Goldwyn Mayer, Inc., and he put me immediately under contract.

I said, "I'm awfully sorry, Alex, but I can't take this contract up because the war is still on officially, and this is the only bit of war work I've done. I don't feel that I can leave this until the war's over." He said, "That's all right, dear boy. You come when you want to come, but it's a pity because I have a very nice subject for you, which you would likely do very well, called *Bricks upon Dust. . . ."* I read *Bricks Upon Dust,* and it was a beautiful subject and I would have loved to have done it. But alas for me, Basil Wright had asked me to do a film on the Beveridge Report, and of all unfilmable things in the world, the Beveridge Report was surely the one. I was six months struggling with the Beveridge Report and then I forgot all about the Beveridge Report and wrote a script, but it was never made although I completed the script. The ministry liked it but was frightened of it because it was an exceedingly radical document indeed. But it was all a dramatically conceived piece, no commentary in it whatever.

So there were six months of my life wasted, by which time Korda had been sacked by Metro, who didn't renew his option, and so my one and only ally in Metro had gone, and I was signed, sealed, and delivered to Metro and

*Children on Trial (1946) was directed by Jack Lee for Crown.

they wouldn't release me. I left the Crown film unit thinking I must try and do something, and the fact that I was then under contract to Metro meant that no English company wanted to use me because they would merely be building up, they thought, my reputation for the benefit of Metro. So I, quite naturally, was dropped from every British studio, and Metro in England were doing no films at all. So there I was, signed in a little pigeonhole, incapable of working.

Humphrey Jennings as he appeared in *Lilli Marlene* (1944).

During the last months of the war Humphrey Jennings shot A Diary for Timothy. *Unlike* Fires Were Started, *which had been a commissioned subject, this was Jennings's own idea.*

Wright: He came up with that idea and sold it to Jack Holmes, my predecessor, because it was already started when I got there. Well, he really sold it to Jack Beddington, because Jack Beddington had very considerable confidence in Humphrey as an artist.

I was the producer in a fog of bewilderment. I didn't know what Humphrey was doing. I used to go and see the rushes every morning, and I'd say, "Yes, what are you going to do with that, Humphrey?" He said, "Oh well, you know, we're making the film backwards, aren't we?" which was true because he was shooting every day for *Timothy* and he'd say, "When we've finished shooting we'll find out what it's all about, won't we?" We did. For his individual achievements, Jennings to me comes tremendously high, particularly with *Fires Were Started*, though I'm very fond of *Diary for Timothy*.

Jackson: Humphrey was a very incredible character — I mean, a delightful man but always out on his own particular limb. In many ways he was a very cold man, you know, with great charm. But it was a cold, analytical, brilliant mind. I never think of Humphrey as being very sort of concerned with getting humanity on the screen. It happened with *Fires Were Started* because the subject was so strong that the characters he chose just came out. But this was not his primary interest, I think. His primary interest was more abstract.

He was a very changed man, funnily enough, when he came back from Burma. This was 1950, I think, shortly before he went to Greece. We just happened to meet up in Piccadilly one day and we had lunch together. He said, "I sat on an ox cart going through the jungle from one village to another, and it took us two days. An extraordinary thing! It gave me a different sense of time and a different attitude to all my problems and everything else that I thought was important." He said, "The people were wonderful. My goodness me, they were fascinating. I never realised how important people are."

A Diary for Timothy (1945).

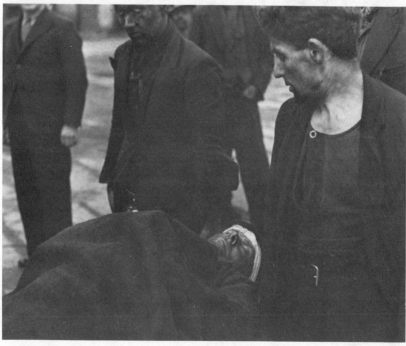

Elton: If you regard films as a mystique, well he has some of the qualities of this, and the Film Institute find in him elements perhaps which are
closer to their, in my opinion, rather phoney ideals than my attitude to realism.
But he is a superb film maker, so don't let's get away with that, particularly
Fires Were Started, which for a moment combined his great sense of Britain
with what was going on. I think *Diary for Timothy* has much to be said for it,
but it began to peter out then. His identity with England (England I say,
specifically, rather than Britain; he was a very English Englishman) for a
moment came to a head in *Fires Were Started,* which is a very great picture.
But it was perhaps a culmination of elements which had come from many different sources, and this perhaps shouldn't be allowed to be forgotten.

Rotha: I think Jennings's work can be overrated. I think it has since its
day. But at the same time I rate Humphrey very high, particularly *Fires Were
Started.* . . . Some of the others I'm not quite so happy about. It's difficult
ground for me. He's a little bit more poetic than I am, as you probably know. . . .
He deserves a very important place in the story of British documentary, of
course. I would couple with that the editing which the late Stewart McAllister
did on Jennings's films. This is very important. Right from *Spare Time* onwards, McAllister contributed a very great deal. Of this there is no question at
all. In the use of sound, especially, McAllister was a very, very remarkable
collaborator.

Legg: I think that Humphrey probably represented the final development
of the poetic line, as we saw it in this country. That's not to say that it couldn't
have been taken farther, but I think it wasn't taken farther and that he carried it
as far as it was taken here. Now, that's only one aspect of it. There's the whole
of Arthur's scientific thing, which is another. There's the whole instructional
thing, which is the third. Humphrey was only concerned, really, with one aspect
of things. But I think that, in so far as he represented that particular approach,
he was the culmination of it, probably.

*During the war British documentary reached the peak of its achievement,
and aesthetically at least, this now seems largely due to the work of Humphrey
Jennings. Talent apart – and he had more talent than most of the others – Jennings was a different kind of person, dedicated to his own individual development, rather than the development of documentary as a whole. Alone among
the documentary directors who remained in documentary until the end of
the war, Jennings did not take on the responsibility of producing, with its in-
cumbent obstacles to personal creativity. His whole approach, in fact, ran
counter to Grierson's idea of group collaboration in the interest of public service (and also, of course, in the interest of gaining prestige and influence both
for documentary itself and for those who upheld it). It is therefore hardly*

surprising that Jennings came in for more criticism from the school that produced him than from almost anyone else.

On the level of propaganda, influence, helping Britain to win the war, the documentary achievement is practically impossible to assess. Ministry of Information films were shown both in the theatres and elsewhere and, according to The Factual Film, *at one point the weekly five-minute films distributed free were reaching a cinema audience in excess of 20,000,000. How did the cinema audiences regard these films? Were they affected by them in any way, or did they just take them as fillers-in before the main feature?*

Most of the feature documentaries and other major documentaries (like the shorter films of Humphrey Jennings) were not distributed free but were given a theatrical release through normal commercial channels. Some of them, according to The Factual Film, *were "box-office successes; for example,* Target for Tonight, Coastal Command, World of Plenty, Merchant Seamen, Fires Were Started, Today and Tomorrow,* Desert Victory. " But* The Factual Film, *published two years after the war, provides neither a complete list of such films distributed up to the end of the war, nor any figures indicating the revenue from them. The fact is that very few figures seem ever to have been available, and any figures that might be quoted (like those given to Ian Dalrymple by Brendon Bracken in 1945) are unconvincingly low and, in my opinion, simply reinforce the feeling that emerges from Dalrymple's letter of resignation, that documentary never really got the chance to compete with the commercial industry on anything like equal terms. This is the battle that Grierson decided not to fight when he hit on the idea that there were more seats outside the theatres than in them, and it is a battle that has never been fought on behalf of British documentary.*

About the documentaries shown commercially during the war, the most we can therefore say is that the titles mentioned above and some others like Western Approaches *and* The True Glory *(another highly distinguished production, made by the service units under the direction of Carol Reed and Garson Kanin) were very successful indeed.*

The nontheatrical scene expanded enormously during the war. The Factual Film's estimate of the total audience reached by the MOI's nontheatrical distribution in its most active war year (1 September 1943 – 31 August 1944) was 18,500,000, but this is less, one cannot help observing, than the potential cinema audience in Britain in any single week at that time. Was the other audience immeasurably more attentive, interested, influenced? Only the members of that audience itself can say.

Today and Tomorrow (1945) was produced by Ralph Bond and directed by Robin Carruthers for World Wide Pictures and the MOI. It had a commentary by Arthur Calder-Marshall and music by William Alwyn.

7

The Post-War Decline

*The war in Europe ended in May 1945, and in July 1945 a Labour govern-
ment was elected in Britain. In October 1945 John Grierson came to Britain
on the government's invitation to advise on the future of official visual-in-
formation services.*

Rotha: One or two of us, primarily Grierson and myself, were very operative behind the scenes politically with the Socialist government, and when the
1945 election results came in with a huge majority for the Labour government,
we optimistically thought that the new government would have a really imaginative, progressive attitude towards information services — not only film, but
all information services. We were very bitterly disappointed.

The thing came out, unhappily as happens in politics, through a complete disagreement between Ernest Bevin and Stafford Cripps. Cripps had always believed in documentary, in British documentary, that is. In fact, Cripps
once said to me, "I think that the showing of British documentary during the
thirties and during the war years has been a contributory factor to this
enormous 1945 result in the election." Cripps commissioned Grierson and myself to write a memorandum for a complete policy of the Labour party towards the film industry, the industry as a whole plus information services.*
Cripps accepted this, but it never became policy because Bevin, only Bevin,
in a stronger aggressive position as he was at the time in the Foreign Office,
was able to defeat it. Well, I won't dwell on this in detail, but it was from then
onwards that I think (now, this is a highly personal point of view and certainly
not agreed to by a lot of other people) British documentary went into its
decline from, and this is my interest, a social point of view. There are exceptions, but not very many. I think, from then onwards (I'm talking of 1946,
1947) the majority of the films — and many have been made — were made by
directors and technicians whose main interest has been the technical interest
in making the films and not the purpose of the films themselves.

*This report, *The Government and the Film Industry,* was published in *Rotha on
the Film* (London: Faber and Faber, 1958).

After the war the Ministry of Information was transfigured to become the Central Office of Information [COI] — very simple words, but they mean a great deal, because instead of the Ministry of Information having the freedom of its grant from the Treasury, the Treasury again resumed complete financial control over what was spent and how it was spent. The result, briefly, was this. The Central Office of Information had no policy whatsoever, in terms of making films. I won't talk about all the other things, publications and so on, but in terms of films they had no policy whatsoever. If, for example, the Ministry of Health came along and said, "We want a film on such and such a subject," the central office merely said, "Yes, what sort of film do you want?" The Ministry of Health then said, "We have a committee set up to say what kind of film we want." Well, I don't have to elaborate on what happened, do I? You know perfectly well the kind of films which were made in those desperate years. It was a big battle. It was fought very hard, and in the long run it came down to a battle between ministers.

Wright: Grierson came over from Canada in the latter part of 1945, and I said to him that I was being driven mad at the Crown film unit, that I couldn't stand it, that I didn't like being the landlord of a huge studio like Pinewood and coping with all these temperamental people, and that I'd had enough trouble and misery being a producer all through the war. I was, in fact, a film director.

Grierson said, "Yes, I entirely appreciate that," and he then went off to the Ministry of Information and by some means known only to him, he arranged that if I left Crown film unit I should become personal adviser to the director general of the Ministry of Information, in relation to the reconstitution of the ministry for peacetime, in other words, the fact that it was then turning into the COI. . . .

To me it was one of his most dramatic and superb conjuring tricks. I went to him saying, "I can't stand this any longer," and he waved a magic wand and produced a new situation for me. Obviously, he must have started with Jack Beddington because they had a tremendous love-hate relationship, rather like Grierson and Flaherty, you know. They were always quarrelling, but he must have gone very high up to get anything of this sort done. But you have to remember that his position in Canada was a very influential one and was noted as such in Whitehall. I mean, at the end of the war he wasn't just National Film Board. He was in control of all Canadian information services. He was just below ministerial level, so he had at that time prestige and influence. All the crises hadn't happened — the witch-hunt, spy trials, and so on. They were to come.

In January [1946] I left Crown and I went to the Ministry of Information, which was in that London University building in Bloomsbury, and in fact moved into Jack Beddington's office, Jack Beddington having left the ministry and gone back to his other work in public relations. I was on a small committee.

... There were just four of us, I think, and our job was to make the recommendations as to what should happen to the Ministry of Information in peacetime. We strongly recommended in the direction of something of the nature of the National Film Board of Canada, and we particularly recommended that the ministry must remain an active and not a passive body. We'd agreed on this, and we'd more or less rehearsed it in front of the DG, who was the chap who's now Lord Radcliffe, and in fact the Treasury had been intervening quietly in the background because they'd been longing to take their revenge on what had been done to them during the war in terms of information. And this report which we had very carefully written and backed up with all our opinions was completely switched round into the COI, which was then, and still is, a passive, spineless body upon which other government departments trample and out of which very little good has come, with all due respect.

In his foreword to the third edition of Documentary Film *(1951), Paul Rotha quoted the following from a manifesto sent in December 1946 by the British documentary group as a whole to Herbert Morrison, then responsible for the COI in the House of Commons: "Since the Central Office of Information took over certain functions of the Ministry of Information in April of this year, experience indicates that, as far as film production is concerned, the new machinery is not working with the smoothness and speed which is required by an efficient information service. The documentary film-makers have been as anxious to contribute to the successful operation of the new Government information services in peace-time as they were during the war. The record of Government film production since April 1st, however, does not measure up to past achievements nor to the demands of the moment. No major film, comparable with those produced during the war, has been completed. Delays and obstructions have been increasingly characteristic of the commissions which the documentary units have received. This decline can be attributed to a number of causes, which in our opinion require urgent investigation."*

In the same foreword Rotha wrote: "We should remember, of course, that times were changed. No longer did the Labour people want films to expose bad housing conditions: Land of Promise *was uncomfortable to the Labour Ministry of Health! They wanted films to instruct local authorities how to build pre-fabs. The emphasis had passed from attack to construction; it was too early to praise. What could and should have happened under Government guidance was for the larger documentary themes to have taken Britain's place in the world community of nations. A start was made (if I may say so) with the F.A.O.* The World Is Rich,* but it was never pursued and that film itself, with its high hopes and fundamental arguments, became a source of embarrassment to its official sponsors."*

---

*The World Is Rich (1946-1947) was Rotha's successor to *World of Plenty*. It was produced by Films of Fact for the COI.

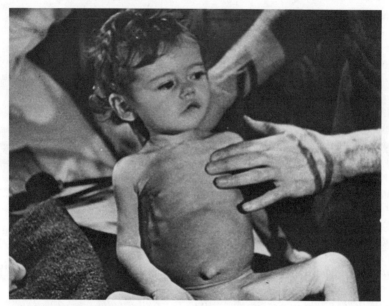

The World is Rich (1947).

During 1946, Grierson was in New York trying to set up International Film Associates with Stuart Legg.

Legg: This vast panorama of material which was available to us officially during the war obviously dried up. But what we were going to try to do was to perpetuate World in Action, or something like it, into the peace, with the problems of peace and so on, around United Artists because they had distributed World In Action and given it 6,000 theatres in the States and Latin America. It had enormous distribution. . . . We were going to try and do this from New York and feed it into the United Artists machine, but for various reasons it didn't work.

One of the reasons this project didn't work was that Grierson became the victim of an anti-Communist witch-hunt. Basil Wright was in New York to negotiate to be the British representative of World in Action just before the witch-hunt started.

Wright: There were a lot of people in Ottawa who deeply resented Grierson's success and Grierson's forceful method of doing things and so on. And like so many other people he got caught up in this ridiculous anti-Red, anti-Communist scare which swept through America and Canada after the war. All that happened was that one of his secretaries was found to have had some sort of relationship with this Russian spy in Ottawa. Whereupon, everybody leapt on it, with all the anti-Grierson things, the trouble being that Grierson was already planning his New York headquarters for World in Action with Stuart and United Artists.

The Americans, who are far more anti-Red than the Canadians, picked this up in a big way, and the attack was absolutely as vicious on Grierson as it was on the Hollywood Ten, although circumstances were different because he was not in fact being formally accused by any government of having done anything. But you know what the libel laws are there. . . . He was exposed to a tremendous amount of violent attack and it was, for all I know of it, extremely serious and definitely – quite apart from other problems of finance and tactics and legalistic things – it was a very serious blow to the World in Action programme, the project for it.

Legg: We tried to get this thing off the ground in New York, but it didn't succeed and it obviously wasn't going to in terms of peacetime limitations. Grierson, I think, realised this, and he was asked to go to UNESCO and he went there.*

Meanwhile, at the Crown film unit things were getting worse.

Taylor: I stayed on at Realist until the end of 1946, and then I went to Crown as producer for two years, which was a very difficult time, really, because Crown had fallen to pieces, you know. There was a big boom in the commercial industry, and practically all their best people had left. Well, they all had. There was no one left. When I went there, I think they had eight directors on the establishment, the civil service establishment, and four scriptwriters. And only one director had ever made a film, and none of the scriptwriters had ever written a script. They were completely new people. None of them had really done any film work at all, and we took over Beaconsfield Studio in that very cold winter. It had been an aircraft factory, and it was an absolute ruin and Wimpey's or someone was in trying to rebuild it. It took two years to rebuild this tiny studio. Absolute bloody shambles it was!

Crown had also gone very much off on the entertainment line during the war. Most of them had their eyes on becoming commercial directors and had dropped mostly the ideas that documentary was about. I mean Pat Jackson, Harry Watt, Jack Lee, and Jennings, they all went to the studios in the end, you know, which was a terrible loss, really, because they were all very skilled people.

And then Grierson had started the expansion of documentary into Canada, Australia, and New Zealand, which also took a lot of people from here. . . . A lot of women had been trained, but nearly all of them got married and stopped

*Grierson went to UNESCO on the invitation of its first director general, Julian Huxley. In 1947-1948 he was director of mass communications and public information for UNESCO in Paris.

work. . . . I'm not criticising or complaining about the people going off, but I'm saying that it was a tremendous loss because each of them could have been a growing point for documentary.

Jackson: We wrote a letter to Rank, a lot of us, saying, "Please don't let this tradition of film making die because we really have put documentary on the map, the international map." It was before I took up my contract at Metro. Jack Lee and I were then, I suppose, the senior members of the old Crown. We could see what was going to happen with the civil service. We knew that our days with the Crown film unit were numbered before absolute strangulation took over, and we knew that Rank was coming into British films in a big way, after his religious films. He had just taken over Pinewood and was going to come in when the Crown unit left, and there was no programme of films announced.

The letter was received, I think I heard afterwards, but not really considered very seriously. The answer to what we were asking for was [the film "magazine"] This Modern Age, which Rank thought was a fair enough contribution to an analysis of the everyday scene. But, of course, it was not the style that we wanted at all. I mean, March of Time was doing it far better. It was really a rather poor reproduction of that.

Anstey: I got funds from Odhams Press to produce two or three items in the Rank magazine, This Modern Age. This, so long as it lasted (it only lasted about a year), was quite a worthwhile thing. Some of This Modern Age magazines I think were up to March of Time standard, but others weren't.

I had a chance to make the second mining issue because I'd done one on the March of Time, and this one was called *Coal Crisis.* * It was about the nationalization of the coal industry. It went into the cinemas and did very well. What remains particularly in my mind is the discussion I had with Arthur Rank, himself, after it was finished. Some other members of the production committee which ran This Modern Age were clearly a little bit nervous about it, because it made a clear case for the nationalization of the coal industry, which was at that time imminent, really. It had been sponsored not by them but by Odhams. Therefore, they had to be cautious about attempting to stop it or change it. On the other hand, the magazine was under their auspices and was going out as a Rank screen publication, in the sense that it was a monthly film magazine. So, when the time came for the finished film to be examined by the committee, which was a normal procedure, nobody showed up, to my surprise, except Arthur Rank himself, who was chairman of the committee. I showed him the film, and he cross-examined me about it and finally said, "Well, if you assure me, as you have, that everything said in this film about

Coal Crisis was made in 1947. Anstey produced it; John Monck directed.

the present condition and the economics of the coal industry is as you depict it, then we must put it out. A lot of my coal-owner friends," said Arthur Rank, "will probably never speak to me again or not for a very long time, but if it's true we must show it." And indeed he did. . . .

I think most people who met Arthur Rank had a considerable affection for him and admired him, but in his situation as something of a right-wing political figure and a very rich man operating in private industry, I thought that his attitude did him a lot of credit. . . . He was a very remarkable man, I think, with enormous integrity and great conscience.

In 1947 Documentary News Letter *became* Documentary Film News.

Wright: *Documentary Film News* went on but, like documentary, gradually running down slightly, the sense of urgency being turned off, the water going from hot to lukewarm to cold.

In 1948 Grierson was invited back to Britain as film controller at the Central Office of Information. He asked Stuart Legg, who had meanwhile been in New York making documentaries, particularly for the United Nations and their new agencies, to return, too, as associate producer at Crown.

Legg: Crown was going through a lot of internal troubles. I think possibly that the balance was getting a bit upset in the direction of the film makers. There were things like the Crown charter, eruptions from the ballerina end. . . .

Taylor: Then I fell out with Grierson over the future of Crown . . . I'd reorganised Crown. I thought it was a bad thing having it under one producer, the kind of prima donna, as it had always been up till then. I reorganised it on what I thought documentary lines were, which was one producer to produce feature-length films: Donald Taylor was producing the feature-type stuff, but it was documentary feature-type stuff. (I mean, Phil Leacock made a film called *Out of True,* which was about mental health — it was that type of thing.) Stuart Legg was producing kind of journalistic stuff. (He made a very good series, one-reelers and two-reelers.) I can't remember, I think there were five producers. There was an educational producer. And then Grierson and I didn't see eye to eye on the control of Crown. He wanted the control directly to him, and he wanted a civil servant in charge of the administration of Crown, and a supervising producer there. This was the system they'd had before, and it hadn't worked.

I didn't devise the new Crown. . . . Alex Shaw was a producer there for a year before I was there (Alex Shaw was one of the original documentary people, and he'd worked for Strand Film Company and was a very, very good film maker), and Alex drew up a thing that he called the Crown charter, which

made the producer at Crown film unit the equal of the director of films division.
To me it was the perfect way of doing it, but Grierson, of course, had a lot
more experience of working with the civil service, and he was most likely right.
I don't know.

Legg: I think a number of people thought, "Ah, Grierson's coming back.
This is going to be the resurrection of everything." It wasn't. I don't know
what the reason was.

Grierson, I think, reached the peak of his creative career in Canada. You see,
he found Canada extraordinarily sympathetic to his personal makeup. There he
was, a Scot who had come to England. In some ways England had given him
what he wanted in the EMB and GPO, but he was always anti-Establishment,
and in Canada there was the whole Mackenzie King outlook on life, which was
very much to regard England as something on the other side of the Atlantic,
the Statute of Westminster and all that, each in every respect independent. I
think that Grierson found this was what he was looking for; an anti-Establishment man found in Canada a sense of independence and a will to independence
that was sympathetic to him, and everything worked like magic in those circumstances.

Now, when he came back, somehow it didn't spark any longer. I think
part of it was not Grierson but the fact that the bureaucracy was growing.
The bureaucracy was becoming immense in this country.

*Edgar Anstey had been working on a project for the oil industry in Vene-
zuela, followed by an investigation for the Colonial Office for a film to be
made about the West Indies.*

Anstey: I was very excited by my trip round the Caribbean for the
Colonial Office, and it didn't take me too long to decide what the film I
was going to recommend needed to be about, because here — and it may still
be a true statement — was a part of the world which seemed truly integrated.
I mean, racial prejudice just didn't seem to exist there. You had endemic
Indian groups, Negroes, white people from all over the world, living together
and sharing responsibility for the community, Negro lawyers of great emi-
nence, Indians very distinguished people in the professions.

So I came back to recommend that the Crown film unit . . . should make
a film about social organisation in the Caribbean and particularly about trade-
union organisation, which was at a very advanced stage, and where you got
members of different races working together in trade unions and having great
influence on governments, providing members of government, a very close
relationship between government (this was before independence, of course)
and trade-union leaders. I came back and wrote all this down, and Grierson
mustn't be blamed too much if there's any question of blame, because he was
a bit remote then from the whole thing, perhaps, in the COI, but my pro-

posals could scarcely have fallen on stonier ground. Nobody paid any attention, and what they finally came up with was the one thing which I was absolutely determined should never be made, and that was a film called, I think, *Caribbean,* which was virtually about the Trinidad festival, full of sort of comic coloured people, dressed up and dancing, and absolutely no reference to social organisation or the fact that there were a lot of mature citizens there or that they were integrated. But what I resented most bitterly about it was that you were left in just as much ignorance as I'd had before I went there of the fact that the society there, in Trinidad perhaps particularly, also in Jamaica, is being run by Indians and Negroes. There was no hint. Everybody was out on the street, leaping about. It had a wonderful sound track and it was beautifully edited and it didn't mean a damn thing.

Legg: I left Crown finally in 1950 because, again, we were making a monthly series for the theatres in which I had to be certain of my completion dates for release, and I simply found I couldn't make them. The bureaucracy of departments was such that he, she, it had to see the film. Committees had to see them, and I couldn't guarantee release dates to the distributors. I think Grierson felt rather the same. And so the return, the resurrection didn't work. I left Crown in 1950, and the year later it was abolished to save the stering area!*

Meanwhile, time was running out for Humphrey Jennings, who did not live to see the end of the Crown film unit. But the few postwar films he made lacked the inspiration of his wartime work. A Diary for Timothy *was followed by* A Defeated People *(1945) and* The Cumberland Story *(1947) for Crown.*

Watt: People were tired and just wanted to forget the war. That's why I still can't understand why in God's name they started to make — and spent a fortune on making — a film about a mining disaster at the end of the war, when we'd had dying and killing for six years. It seems to me a madness. I've no idea why they did it, but I imagine that was one of the big coffin nails, *The Cumberland Story.*

After The Cumberland Story *Jennings left Crown to join Ian Dalrymple's company, Wessex Films.*

Taylor: I was running Crown when Jennings left. He was much more a kind of art film maker, a film maker for film making's sake, although he was more than that, I think. He was a very good film maker, but he went off with Dalrymple to make features. . . .

*The Crown Film Unit was abolished in January 1952.

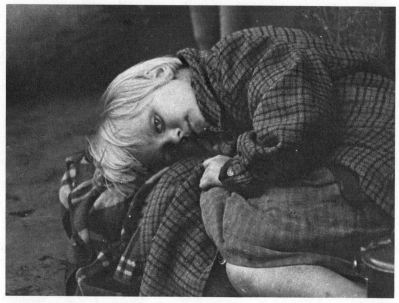

A Defeated People (1946).

Dalrymple: I was always hoping, though I didn't know whether it was going to be a great success, that Alex [Korda] could find something for him, because Alex admired his pictures very much but at the same time they weren't really his cup of tea. I mean, naturally he was much more interested in feature films and in artists, whereas we only used the actual personnel.

Jennings never made a feature film. If he had, it would, in Ian Dalrymple's opinion, have been "a very different kind of feature."

Dalrymple: I think one of his ambitions was to make a film of *Hamlet*, but it wouldn't have been done in the way that Larry [Olivier] would have done it, with the emphasis on what was more the stage technique. It would have been an imaginative film, and I should think would have been totally lost on the audience.

So, after the war he came to my company and was working on one or two things that we had to do. One was to be a great picture of what you might call the decline and fall of the British Empire. But at the time the commercial industry was going through one of its continual dips, and the money simply wasn't there. So, really, what it ended up in — what was sort of salved from it — was Humphrey's Festival of Britain film.

For Wessex Films, Jennings made Dim Little Island *(1949) and* Family Portrait *(1950) for the Festival of Britain. In September 1950 he was killed when he fell from a rock on the Greek island of Poros. He was 43 years old.*

The Cumberland Story (1947).

   Dalrymple: After the Festival of Britain film, there came this assignment
from the public-relations side of the European Economic Commission and the
Marshall Aid organisation, who wanted six films made on what had been done
under various titles like "transport," "housing," "food," "power," and the last
one of all wasn't quite so sort of literal and specific, called "health." And
they put it to the ministry that they wanted about fifty percent profit. So
Humphrey brought it along to me and said, "Would you do it? At least it's
something to do."
   I'd got a lot to do at the time, but Humphrey hadn't, so I took it on and
for very little profit margin, because it was a £100,000 contract in the end. I
think when we came out we'd lost about £2000. We had to accept a rather
literal and straight commentary from the man who commissioned it on behalf
of the EEC, and do our best in the shooting to make it not quite a magic-
lantern picture, and Humphrey thought if he chose the health one it would give
him a chance because Greece came into it and so forth. It was quite an organisation because there were six separate units, and the organisation of the units
wasn't exactly done per subject but per [geographical] area, so that everything
in which Scandinavia was involved, or France, went to that unit; there was
one going to Greece (of course, Humphrey's); there was one in Central Europe
doing Switzerland, and, needless to say, we ran into the most appalling weather

everywhere except probably in the Mediterranean. . . . Then there was this awful blow of Humphrey falling off the cliff. He hadn't even started shooting. He was still doing his reconnaissance.

By the time the Crown film unit was abolished, at the beginning of 1952, there is fairly general agreement that British documentary had gone into a decline, or even perhaps died. Grierson called it "the dereliction" and said it happened "from the end of the war."

Grierson: The good thing went with television to the BBC. Oh, that's where the tradition went. I think Edgar Anstey at Transport kept something going in a permissive way, gentle and good, not with very great driving force because he didn't have much money. But the BBC, I think, on the whole took over the best of the documentary tradition, not just in terms of news, news in depth, social things like *Cathy Come Home* and many other social things besides that (it's always been good on the social front, both nationally and locally) but also in the sort of spirit that invaded *Z Cars*. If you look at the real names behind *Z Cars* you'll find a cross-fertilization from the early documentary movement. *Z Cars,* of course, is a very good example of the sense of fidelity to local atmosphere and the local thing . . . for what it's worth. . . I mean it's still *Z Cars*. . . .*

English documentary had a very vivid life in film form during the thirties and during the war. It's had a very good life on television . . . but, really, I don't think there's been any contribution by Britain to documentary in the last ten years, of any new sort. It hasn't given any great leadership in the matter of the use of film by the backward countries. I don't see us sending out people to teach the people in these various countries, as we ought to be doing. I mean, I read yesterday that half the people in ACTT are unemployed. Damn it all, the country should hire them all to go and teach people elsewhere. . . . The whole thing's wrong. If this country had any spirit at all, it wouldn't stand for technicians being unemployed. It would send them out to teach. If there's nothing to do here, there's plenty to do elsewhere.

Legg: I think the documentary film as we knew it then is virtually dead. It's so nearly dead it doesn't make much odds one way or the other. It isn't

*There have been over 500 episodes of the highly popular police series *Z Cars* (crime patrol cars with the call-sign "Z for Zulu") which began on BBC TV on 2 January 1962 and continues, with diminished vigour, in 1974. Although fictional, its north-country location and emphasis on everyday authenticity (particularly the ordinary lives of policemen) has given the series a strong documentary flavour. The cross-fertilization from early documentary, to which Grierson refers, is indirect. The series has exercised the talents of many writers both new and established, and directors who have worked on it include John McGrath (who directed the first episode and a number of others), Herbert Wise, James MacTaggart, Don Taylor.

entirely. I think that certain things are still going on that are valuable, but it's so much more enormous now, and the balance is so thoroughly upset. I wouldn't say it's dead. It's gone elsewhere. It's gone into the BBC and that sort of thing. It's played its part.

The war was the turning point. You see, up till that time it had been a relatively small effort oriented to one or two or three people. There was Grierson's thing. There was Rotha's thing. There were one or two others, perhaps less important. Relatively small, very cohesive around different orbits, and essentially a minority movement, rather dedicated, it was not without a political purpose, obviously, and political reference. It was a progressive movement essentially. It was harnessed to things like the need for more housing, the need for cleaner air, the need for better nutrition, and so on. These were matters of great public moment in the thirties, obviously.

The early part of the war, I think, was marked in the information-propaganda field in this country by a competition not unlike that between Walter Creighton's film and Grierson's film of ten years before. The fantasy thing, I think, was tried, the feature form was tried as a means of propaganda, and documentary was tried — all with a view to finding the key to address the British nation in time of war as far as films were concerned. By and large, documentary won that battle hands down, and the whole of the film effort of the Ministry of Information became very largely geared to documentary production in various forms and under various aegises. Well, it made some remarkable films, obviously — *London Can Take It, Target for Tonight,* and so on.

Come the end of the war, it had grown enormously. There were many more people in it because in time of war, money is no object. The civil service goes mad, and the Treasury pours out money, for once in its life. Then at the end of the war it became even larger, with people being demobilized who wanted a new way of earning a living, who didn't want to go into the normal, dreary channels of life, who sought something rather odd and peculiar. So it found itself with many more recruits, people coming out of the services and people who'd been in the service units. Secondly, not very long after the war many of the objectives which it had fought for before and advocated became matters of legislation. They were at least on the statute book. They were at least in the minds of the Labour party. So it was no longer a minority movement. A minority movement had become a majority movement, and there is nothing like a process of that kind for taking the wind out of sails.

It had to find something completely new to work for and to fight for. At the same time, I think its success during the war tended to make it a favoured instrument of industry. Many more films were ordered, put into production, and produced. The COI, I think, overproduced. Industry began to overproduce. The result of all this sort of thing was to dilute. It was bound to be that. Objectives got lost. I think that many of the people who came into it after the war didn't understand how it really worked, the balance between sponsor and film maker, for instance, and I think it did become largely a matter of saying, "Film sir, nice film sir, yes here's your film. Would you like ten close-ups or twelve?" A lot of it became rather servile. The government over-produced, too, and it became a sort of vast, pulpy mass instead of a small, co-hesive spearhead, or a number of spearheads.

I think there was a considerable effort, and a very successful one, in developing at least two new forms of sponsorship within my particular pur-view. One was the development, which Arthur Elton had started, of the technical scientific film, the narrowing of the gulf between science and society. This was not social documentary of the previous era at all but something which was peculiar to Arthur, and he developed it on an enormous scale, rather as Grierson had developed the sociopolitical approach before the war. The other was the outward movement into the emergent world and the very large effort which was made there in locally-formed and locally-staffed film units, particu-larly associated with the oil industry.

Taylor: There were a tremendous number of sponsors and everyone plunged in to cream the market off. There were short film companies (I mean, no one blames them — they were there to make short films and to make some money) with no more purpose behind them than that. A lot of the best people went. We didn't really succeed in training up more people. For some reason or another, we didn't get succeeding generations of people to go on. There were a few. I don't know, maybe the idea itself was out of date and had fulfilled its purpose.

But the same thing has happened in Canada now. They're making all sorts of things that really have nothing to do with what the Canadian National Film Board's about — well, to me, anyway.

One of the things about film is you get a kind of cycle. A thing grows and matures and then dies, like Ealing Studios, which had a very short life, about seven years. They started off with terrible films. They made wonderful films, then they made terrible films, or bad films again — and this usually works, you know. I mean, Grierson, on his previous experience, managed to batter the film board into a thing that kept its shape much longer than any-thing else, really. But I think that people like Edgar and Basil and Elton and myself have not succeeded in bringing on more people. In the event, it didn't matter because they came on in another way, through television.

Watt: I feel perhaps that if I'd stayed in documentary, and Cav had stayed (maybe this is very conceited) the gradual disintegration of it might not have happened perhaps so fast. . . .

What would have happened to documentary if I'd stayed on, I don't quite know, but one very important thing did happen, and that was that suddenly from the service units, which had been gradually forming after they saw the success of the Crown film unit, came brilliant and wonderful films like *Desert Victory* and *Burma Victory*. The moment they appeared, the real thing, the front line shot by real army men who were being killed while doing it, the reconstructed documentary as such, was dead, to my mind. (This didn't prevent large numbers of feature films, war films, being made and being very successful, but the public accepted them as a story with a hero, some well-known actor leading his troops to Dieppe and rescuing the girl. . . . The public loved this stuff.)

This, again, when these came out, influenced me very much in changing. I was going to make a reconstructed war documentary in Australia. That's what I was sent out to do.* It was an association between the Australian government and the MOI, and it was through the MOI that I was sent. But it was quite obvious to me that the reconstructed war film was finished, and therefore I tried to find a war story that wasn't a war story, and I was lucky enough to find *The Overlanders,* which was a good prestige film for Australia. It was wartime, but it wasn't fighting. If I'd stayed on in documentary, I suppose I wouldn't have realised this at first and would have wanted to go on making something like *Western Approaches* if I could have made it as well. I would have wanted to do that, and most likely have fallen flat on my face.

Wright: I think there are five or six factors all combining to a rundown of documentary.

First of all, exhaustion set in because you've got to remember that we had a manpower crisis during the war. A very large number of documentary people were called up, anyhow. The intensity of work during the war was absolutely tremendous. Mental exhaustion, if not physical, certainly was there.

Secondly, the situation for the making of documentary films deteriorated rapidly after the war for a number of reasons, of which the principal was the election of a Labour government, because we discovered by bitter experience that all the good sponsors were bloody capitalists, and even in the mid-thirties or late thirties the nightmare was to have to make a film for the co-ops or something of that sort, because they were so hidebound. They were so stupid, and you could never get any sense out of them at all. They didn't understand anything about the motion picture. I remember, after the great election after the war, saying to a lot of colleagues at a meeting, "Now our troubles are starting," and they were. Then that was compounded afterwards, of course, because Churchill was hoodwinked into abolishing the Crown film unit, and this all came from the other side of the picture, which was the Treasury taking its revenge on the Ministry of Information because, during the war, Churchill gave Brendon Bracken at the ministry more or less carte blanche. He said information is important, and so the Treasury had to pour out money, which they deeply resented, for the Crown film unit and for the MOI. So there were a lot of things stacked against us in that direction.

Another point, the third point, was that like all movements in the arts,

---

*Watt went to Australia in 1945 to make *The Overlanders* (1946) for Ealing.

you start by being wild men, then you become established, and then you become old-fashioned. Just as the French impressionists were first of all regarded as raving lunatics, then they were very popular, and then they became old-fashioned (although their effect is seen to this day on railway posters and hoardings and that sort of thing), I think by 1946, 1947, we were over the peak.

And then simultaneously there was coming up television. And it's very interesting to note that television is done by people who were not brought up in film documentary. This is to me quite understandable because tempo is so entirely different. The few times I've had anything to do with television, it's horrified me because I've always said if I make a film it takes as long as it does for a woman to have a baby. And on television, you know, you have to take a pill.

Edgar Anstey, although claiming to be personally unaware of a crisis in documentary after the end of the war, had not very much that was positive to say about this period. In 1949 he set up the British Transport film unit, which he headed until his retirement in 1974.

Anstey: I suppose that the volume of film that was being made inevitably dropped off, but many of the films that we'd been doing in the last couple of years of the war were directed towards the establishment of the kind of peacetime situation which we all thought might be possible. So I think, with many sponsors, as with gas, for example, there was a direct transition into the peace. I did a film (Max Anderson directed it) called *Words and Actions,* which was about the nature of democracy. This was sponsored by the gas industry before the war was over. It was almost entirely about the peace, really.

There was less film making, and, of course, units like Crown were affected, naturally, because it wasn't possible to persuade people that the non-theatrical film-showing arrangements, the Central Film Library, Crown, should go on straight into the peace, as they should have, because in fact there was even more work for them to do. But postwar economics being what they were, axes fell . . . and, of course, the MOI became the COI. Then the COI was cut back and so on.

But if a lot of people were in personal difficulties (this should not happen, of course, in a perfect world), it's not so surprising because the number of people involved in film making had become very large towards the end of the war. A lot of people still in the services were making films, you see, There were all the service film units, and those people were bound to get demobilized quite soon, and there wasn't the same call for films from them. So I would have thought that there was a crisis, in the sense that some people found that what they'd been doing was no longer required, rightly or wrongly. But I wouldn't have thought that the crisis was any more serious than one has experienced in the last two or three years. I wouldn't have thought that unemployment was as high then as it is now amongst film technicians.

I think most people were quite excited about the chance to build when the war was over, and I think people were very balanced emotionally, intellectually — emotionally much more balanced then because one of the things about the war was that it's very good for emotional balance if issues are as simple as they were then. So I think people were in good heart. Morale was strong, and everybody knew what he wanted to do. There was a certain amount of frustration about doing it. There were one or two very minor things — for example, I got very interested in these films on personnel selection and I had hoped — and a number of psychiatrist and psychologist friends of mine believed — that industry would start to look at people as individual persons and deal with industrial personnel problems with as much care, solicitude, as was being accorded to the services towards the end of the war. But this didn't happen, sadly. I mean, film would only have been a small aspect of that, but films, as I discovered, could play an enormous part in this examination of personality in relation to job. But that was one of the things that went by the board. Nobody yet quite knows why. And I suppose there was a little bit less being done about technological research in film because, with the war over, there wasn't the same drive towards technological research.

A lot of people are always bewailing the fact that today is not yesterday. I mean, the golden age of documentary, the thirties — people talk as if masterpieces were being made every five minutes then. In actual fact, the volume of production in the thirties was much more considerable than anybody allows for. I think that in retrospect the important films are remembered and the less important films are forgotten, and so there's a tendency to believe that in the thirties twelve magnificent documentaries were made. Actually, these are the twelve documentaries that survive in our memory, and there were probably a hundred and twenty others that are completely — and probably rightly — forgotten. The same is true during the war. The same, I'm sure, is true today. But when you're very close to it, you don't see the thing in a proper perspective. I think there are probably as many outstanding documentaries made today — more, I would think — than there ever have been before, if you take into account the television output.

Arthur Elton, associated with Shell right through the years from 1936, also experienced no crisis.

Elton: Eighty-seven film libraries, every film in thirty languages — it's the biggest single core of films made from a single-minded point of view that there is in the world, I think, the National Film Board of Canada excepted. Empire Marketing Board gone, GPO gone, Ministry of Information gone, Crown gone — Shell stuck to it. That's their importance: a theory, a consistency, an attitude that has never varied.

Anstey: There's absolutely no doubt that the view of the Shell Oil group which is held in the world is conditioned in some measure by the distinction and objectivity, and humanity, too, of the films that the Shell film unit has made over these years. And we hope that the view of British Rail here and the other nationalized transport industries, is being conditioned internally and externally to some extent by the work that's being done by film. This is what Grierson was really all about: providing any organisation, any corporate body, with a communications arm, with a voice.

After he left the Crown film unit, Stuart Legg became a free-lance.

Legg: People brought me films to mend which had gone wrong, and I got out my plumber's bag of tools and tried to help on that sort of side. People brought me a lot of writing to do, scripts and, more particularly, commentaries. Then, one day, Arthur Elton who had been head of production in the Ministry of Information during the war and had then gone back to Film Centre, particularly looking after the whole Shell film programme which by that time was becoming large, asked me if I would come in with him on certain of the Shell films which he didn't think were particularly his cup of tea. . . .

Shell, in company with many other oil interests, were moving into new fields, in the sense of oil itself becoming a base for chemicals and therefore beginning to impinge on social affairs, economic affairs, agriculture, health, all over the world. This was becoming a very important part of their work, and Arthur asked me to come in to look after and develop this whole socio-economic side. I did this gradually, bit by bit, and then became very much involved in it. And this led to the Shell films like *The Rival World,* which Bert Haanstra directed; and *Unseen Enemies* on health and disease; *Food or Famine,* which was about the pressure of population on resources. They were films of very great scope, and Shell were wonderful in supporting that width of view.

By that time I was back in Film Centre and became a director of it. When Arthur was offered the post of controller of information of AEI (the electrical combine), I took over Film Centre as chairman. The whole oil industry thing became enormous . . . in the Middle East, in Latin America, in Singapore, and elsewhere, and this whole business of instruction, of information of one sort or another, particularly in the emergent countries, became a thing I was very interested in.

There came a point, however, when I think a number of things came together. These things always depended on personalities. You can say that there is a formula for sponsorship which depends on a balance — you can put it in those abstract administrative, organisational terms . . . but it's personalities that count in the end, because there are so many intangibles, so many needs of understanding of subtleties on one side and the other. Where you had a sponsor who was an artist in this business of using creative people, all these intangibles and subtleties somehow looked after themselves. There was tremendous understanding between each side.

Now I felt that, one way or another, this was becoming more and more difficult, not in oil, where it was always good, but in other fields which I looked after as well. It was becoming overloaded in the direction of industrial bureaucracy, managerial this and that, efficiency which was very often the reverse of efficiency, and a general hardening of the arteries, infinite uncertainties about whether a film was to go into production or not and under what circumstances, and I felt that the game was not worth the candle.

To cut a long story short, Arthur said that he would like to come back. I said that I would like at least to step sideways, that I'd always wanted to look again at my interest in history and geography. So he took Film Centre over, and I virtually moved out. I now have really very little to do with films. I do writing instead.

Is a new basis for sponsorship needed?

Grierson: No, documentary is concerned in the last resort with the creation of loyalties. Therefore, every concern of a national or international or even local order, every concern involved in management, in instruction, is involved with whatever establishes loyalties and creates the world power of people. So the loyalty of sponsorship is always there, an inevitable relationship of documentary. . . .

Now, there is a new basis for sponsorship today, but it will always be of the same logical nature. The sponsorship is not by accident. It is always and has always got to be logical. It must be in the interest of the sponsor to be concerned with documentary film; otherwise, there's no use asking him. Now the trouble with the people today is that they don't know how to sell the relationship, because they are not as tutored as we were in the political and economic relationships of things.

The documentary film in Britain has failed for lack of an intelligentsia. It hasn't got an intelligentsia today that can really go and tell the people in sugar or the people in some other commodity why logically they are concerned in a particular educational or inspirational purpose.

This, however, might be a guide to a new phase of sponsorship. I've said that there has been this concern — not only in Canada but certainly in Canada we have it, with the distance between the local community and the central governing body, the distances, the gaps presently appearing in the democratic process, so much so that people are crying out for what they call participatory democracy, and they're crying out for some way of solving the problem represented in the streets by the protest movement of one kind or another. Note, they are encouraged to do so by the presence of the mass media and the fact that they can get plenty of publicity if they make enough noise. So that there's a situation aggravated by the mass media, the fact that people are rather inarticulately seeking to express themselves in this modern democracy.

Now how can we fill this need? Well, we can obviously do it by developing local television: the expression "We've got to have, not local *pre*sentation" (that's to say, presentation of the local case by some faraway landlord like the BBC) "but local *repre*sentation" (that is, presentation of the local story by local people, which is a very different thing). Presentation is not representation, and that's where the BBC is making the biggest mistake of its life. . . . No matter how much noise you make on the BBC, you're after all being edited by outsiders, just as, for example, I'm doing this tape and I know that this is not me at all because you're going to edit it. I'm going to be edited by an outsider, and I will not be represented. I'll merely be presented.

However, the lead to sponsorship in this situation is that the development of the local television thing will immediately raise the question of who is going to give an account of the stewardship in the local community. Now, in every local community — let's take a small town, for example — there'll be a Chamber of Commerce, there'll be a Rotary Club, there'll be schools, there'll be Parent Teachers Associations, there'll be a university, possibly. Well, think of all the people that are there with their organised representational councils or gatherings. They will all want to have a piece of the local expression, won't they? They'll all want to have a say in the making of the films, or at least a film to make. If they don't get on television, they'll make a film. . . . Now who's going to pay for all these things? Well, I should think that one of the almost inevitable sources of finance will be the people who run the local industries. They are the new sponsors. . . .

What's been wrong with sponsorship from the beginning is that the film makers have not been imaginative enough about where the sponsors could be served by the cinema. They've been quite content, the poor bastards — and poor bastards they very often are — to make just a catalogue of events and products, flattering the sponsor. Well, they've sold their birthright in doing that.

What other directions might British documentary have taken?

Grierson: I've already mentioned the poetic gap. There's always room for poetry, and it seems to me the saddest thing in the world that England, that has after all in its greatest aesthetic tradition the tradition of poetry, had not produced an equivalent line in visual poetry, in the film. I don't know, it may be that England is not visually equipped for it, but anyway we did begin in the thirties and I very much regret we haven't gone on in England.

Legg: If the point of crisis was the end of the war, one of the things that needed attention was the form of presentation. . . . You see, the poetic form . . . had been developed up to a certain point. . . . Then you got this rather urgent sort of social reporting side which had been taken up, and various other by-products. Now I think one of the things that needed looking at was a completely new approach to presentation, film method, about that time, and I think there was a clue — and this is very much a personal opinion.

Out of the war came one or two remarkable features, documentary features: *Target for Tonight, Fires Were Started, Western Approaches, Cumberland Story,* and one or two others. They were semi-story films; there had been one or two before the war, like *North Sea.* Now, I have a sort of idea that that was one of the ways to go, that perhaps there was overproduction of all these rather mundane, ordinary sort of films which might perhaps have been concentrated into rather more unusual, extraordinary features, story features. I don't say you'd call them features in the normal sense, but four-reelers, five-reelers, maybe six, which renewed the whole approach. I think that's one possibility which might have happened, and, no doubt, there are others. But it went stale, you see. The form was the same, and it needed a whole new vitalizing process of presentation which just didn't happen. . . .

I didn't contribute to anything, as far as presentation was concerned, very much not. Again, I think possibly because I basically wasn't really interested in film. The innovators are a particular kind of people who have to have a certain ambience and a certain climate and all that, and perhaps it wasn't present either on the sponsorship side or on the producers' side. I think, certainly, that one is to blame. It's one's fault to some extent.

Jackson: It was very noticeable that the Italian cinema suddenly reached its greatest peak by continuing exactly where we left off. If you look at *Paisa* and Fellini's work, there's an exact extension of what the Crown film unit had done. And from that moment on, our story-documentary technique finished, and the Italians then took it on, and there's an element in cinema which is completely dead in this country.

Why did more of the documentary movement not go into features?

Wright: We were far too interested in making a new sort of film which wasn't a feature. You see, documentary films exist now. They didn't exist in those days. The idea of constructing a film on the pattern of *Night Mail,* for instance, or on the pattern of *Song of Ceylon,* had never occurred to anybody. We found by painful experiment how to do it because of a little film called *Coal Face,* without which some of the sound track of *Song of Ceylon* and practically the whole of *Night Mail* would never have existed. There's a little test-tube film: the first time Auden and Britten worked together; different uses of the sound track in relation to the picture. So there really wasn't time to think about going into feature films. If you went into feature films, you were doing something else. You weren't doing documentary.

You have to remember that the British film industry was in a most frightful mess at the time. I mean, apart from Anthony Asquith, what was there? Well, Mary Field and Percy Smith doing *Secrets of Nature,* and they were under the same umbrella as Asquith. They were under Bruce Woolfe, you see. Mick Balcon, apart from bringing on Hitchcock, hadn't really got cracking in a big way. In fact, he didn't until he got the sound studios, both Gainsborough and Gaumont British at Lime Grove. . . .

There were young men who were working in the feature industry already, who jumped in Grierson's direction very quickly. Arthur Elton was working for Gainsborough, and as soon as he became conscious of the EMB unit, he was round on the doorstep very soon.

Basil Wright never moved out of documentary. From 1946 he was producer at International Realist, the London-based company formed to make films for Grierson's projected New York setup. Only one film, Bernard Miles

Waters of Time (1951).

Paul Rotha making *World Without End* (1953).

on Gun Dogs *(1948), was produced specifically for this setup, but International Realist went on. It was in the same building and loosely linked with the Realist film unit, and did "selected sponsorship jobs" including* Waters of Time, *directed by Wright for the Port of London Authority as a contribution to the Festival of Britain in 1951, and* World Without End, *codirected by Wright and Rotha for UNESCO in 1953. Shortly after that, Wright was advised by his accountants that International Realist was making so much profit that "the most convenient thing to do would be go into liquidation before we went into the upper company tax bracket." So International Realist went into voluntary liquidation. "It suited me," says Wright, "because I didn't particularly want to run a company. I was getting tired of running companies." Wright has since directed or produced the occasional documentary.*

Wright: There have been certain feature films I would have liked to have made, but they were what you might call fairly specialised. In fact, none of them ever came off.

No, I've never had any particular desire in that way. I think I used to find in the old days, in the thirties, that you could spot people in the unit who were there in order to move into features. There were others who were there, in a way, to stay. Humphrey Jennings was his own self to himself. He merely wanted to be able to make his sort of thing, and the Crown film unit setup was just right for him. He didn't want to make feature films in that sense, I don't think. His films were his particular films. Because he died so young, you never know what he might have done later, but I never saw any signs in Humphrey of wanting, in a conventional sense, to make feature films.

Arthur Elton remained in documentary, at Shell and Film Centre, until his death in January 1973.

Elton: I have always been enormously interested in feature films. I've never made one. I've handled a certain number, partly because I worked in the studios as an assistant and partly because in the war I was in charge of some of the films at the Ministry of Information other than the Crown films, and that put me in touch with feature people; features were under our guidance in different ways.

I've always had a passionate interest in them, but I've never made one, and I'm inclined to think that a big, complicated documentary film is much more difficult to make than any known feature film. That's a private view. perhaps not shared by feature directors.

John Taylor remained in documentary, mostly free-lancing. He has his own production company, and has been making films for various sponsors over the past fifteen years, mainly on subjects connected with conservation and the environment.

Taylor: Maybe I'm not adventurous enough or something, but I was committed to documentary at a very early age, and I've not thought of ever going to the studios or anything like that. I didn't see documentary's future in that way.

You know, they condition rats to go through the door when the bell rings, and if you're conditioned young enough, you go on.

Edgar Anstey remained in documentary, at British Transport.

Anstey: I was never really interested in going into features. I talked with Mick Balcon. Mick Balcon had the notion at one time that this is what I should have done. He was always very interested in documentary.

I rather resent the notion you get around that documentary is a stepping-stone to features, because, for me at any rate, and I think for all the early people, we regarded features as being just a kind of play-making — you know, a rather inferior sort of thing. They were just entertainment, whereas what we thought we were doing was making much more exciting — certainly much more important — things, bringing them alive for people, sort of communicating all kinds of truths which were much more difficult to communicate but much more important for the health of society. That is what we thought and, I suppose, still think in some ways.

Grierson: Using film in a purposive way was exciting. . . . It was exciting new aesthetic territory. People were not only finding the art of the cinema, but they were finding themselves as artists. Not only that, but the subject matter itself was very exciting, and so in some cases was the new range of technological discovery, new range of scientific discovery, and the implications of scientific discovery. They were dealing, in some cases, with the future of new countries or the future of underdeveloped countries. There were all kinds of intrinsic interests in the pursuit of documentary. . . .

I suppose some of us could have gone into the big time if we'd wanted, if you call that the big time. But I never thought of that as the big time. I would have thought of that as the small time, going into show business. To me, the big time was public service, and I think something of that spirit was shared by many people there, that they really believed in public service. It's been difficult for you people to appreciate today, because nobody can think of the COI as being associated with the excitement of the film in the public service. I can't think of anything quite shabbier than the film activity of the COI. It's almost at the far end of the scale, as far as we're concerned.

Cavalcanti was equally at home in features and documentary. His first experience of documentary had been with the French avant-garde and not with Grierson's movement. After leaving documentary, he made a name for himself in features at Ealing Studios.

Cavalcanti: I think documentary is a good school for feature directors; in fact, I don't think people should start touching feature films without passing through documentary. But then, as I told you, my conception of documentary is of something very well thought out — that's to say, the reportage is very different from the actual documentary film, and it's a pity that TV has diffused a bit the idea of documentary and somehow hasn't contributed much to it. With the brilliant reportage they present, they haven't made the documentary advance at all.

Really, you must know there was a certain snobbery about documentary. People were very proud. In fact, I think they despised me a bit because I have the same pleasure in doing features I did in documentary. But most of the boys who couldn't get into features sort of made themselves important, I think, by saying they despised features, which was a lie, you know.

Pat Jackson worked mainly in features from the end of the war.

Jackson: I suppose there was a certain prejudice from the commercial world. Why should they employ a documentary director unless he could prove that he could, in their terms, handle their medium, which was to get at the heart of the story and tell it in terms of dialogue, conflict, actors, and artists. And they said, "Oh, these boys are all right. They've handled farm labourers and this, that, and the other. They can take some pretty pictures, but I'm not going to put 'em on the floor. They may cost me a fortune." So there was a prejudice on their side, and there was a certain prejudice on the documentary boys' side because they thought, "This is contaminating, and we must stick to our documentary principles. We mustn't get corrupted by commerce." So there was a sort of shying and looking at each other askance, but the Crown film unit was lucky. Let's not forget that. We got the plums. Therefore, we got the breaks, whether we took advantage of them or not. We got the breaks commercially, where a lot of the other boys didn't because they didn't have the money. We were able to show that we could, possibly, manage to handle story in dramatic terms, whereas other units which didn't have the financial backing or the subjects as showy as the ones the Crown film unit got, weren't able to show it. They probably had twice the ability that we had, but the moguls were going to say, "Well, what have you done? A five-reel documentary on coal mining. Well, that's very nice, but thank you very much. I'm not going to give you Deborah Kerr. No, thank you, you might waste a fortune."

I think that was probably the reason. I know that there have been some documentary film makers that wouldn't have touched features with a barge pole anyway, because they thought it was wrong. Jolly high-minded of them. Splendid, but a pity if they had something to contribute.

Paul Rotha remained essentially a documentary director, but after 1950 he made three feature films which might be described as story documentaries: No Resting Place *(1953),* Cat and Mouse *(1957), and* The Silent Raid *(1962).*

Rotha: In the thirties, and certainly during the war period, I don't think the documentary people wanted in any way to go into features. They recognised there was something completely different, a different world, not only in terms of technique but in terms of subjects.

I probably kept touch with the feature film industry in the thirties more than any other documentary person. I had many friends in it. I mixed, and I talked with them. At one time I had long talks with Alexander Korda with a view to setting up a unit within his company, London Films. It came to nothing. Most projects with Korda came to nothing, anyway, because at the end there was never any money there, although he'd talk wonderfully to you with his Canalettos on the wall and so on. But I was always interested in trying to take the whole documentary idea and method much wider than the short film, which it was confined to, to a large extent up to that time in England. I think you've got to remember that Korda had one great ambition in his life, and that was to achieve "prestige" (in quotes), and this prestige could be achieved by collecting names. Hence, in my book, *The Film Till Now,* I talk about the rose garden at Denham (this is just before the war). The rose garden is simply symbolism for the names like Marlene Dietrich and Robert Donat and all the rest of the people he collected round him. Many of them did nothing; they never even made a film — and if they did, they were very bad films — but nevertheless Korda had to have his great prestige. And, amongst other things, Korda saw that in British documentary there was a prestige thing to try and attain. Hence, I think, my talks with him, but then it all came down to nothing because there was never any money.

Grierson: I wouldn't work with Korda because his mind wasn't related to mine in any way except in terms of painting. He was very, very good on painting. But oh, no, no. Korda was terribly interested in money. I mean, he was fabulously good at money, so good at money that some of the best stories in Hollywood were the stories of Alex and money. . . . Oh, he was pretty sharp, and as a businessman rather gorgeously imaginative in some of his financial deals. No, he wasn't for me, but as a person to know he was a person I was very happy to talk with, very happy indeed.

Jackson: I suppose it's true to say that the leaders of documentary simply weren't geared to become commercial producers. I mean, handling that kind of finance is in itself a different sort of problem. Going into the city to get a quarter of a million pounds is not something that I suppose would have interested Grierson very much. Nor would it have interested him very much if he, in getting his quarter of a million, found that strings were attached and that the film that he wanted to do was going to be watered down to an extent, or that ingredients were going to be put into it because it was now a commercial enterprise, which took away the very reason why he wanted to make it in the first place.

In other words, there is an inevitable element of corruption in terms of a film's content if it becomes a commercial enterprise for the big circuits for which you're going to make a profit. And the strength of documentary was that, of course, it didn't really matter a damn whether it made a profit or not. It was sponsored money, which was set aside by a government department because it was considered a public service. Documentary was a different experience altogether, a different world . . . There was a freedom which was quite matchless. You were given a subject, and you were left to get on with it. Your producer was there to help you if he could, and if he couldn't, well, that was just too bad. You went on, and you were free, unfettered completely. And if it was a botch, it was your mistake and nobody else's.

But this is not so in the other world. (I'm talking about my experience; I dare say things are different now.) You're not free about your cast necessarily, and you're not free about the ingredients of the story, or how honest you can be with the story. There was a lovely story that [Joseph] Janni and I wanted to do, about delinquency in Liverpool, and this would have been one of the first coherent statements about this problem in screen terms. It was a novel by a schoolteacher, *No Language but a Cry.* It was going to be a follow-up to *White Corridors,* 1952, 1953, something like that. We'd been hunting, Jo and I, for a story and found the story, and I thought it was marvellous and I'd done a script. I could see every shot. I knew exactly how we were going to shoot it. So did he. But the green light was not allowed to flash unless we gave it a happy ending, and if you had a happy ending to this particular story, as I told them, you might as well not make it. It would have taken the impact away completely. But no. So that was never made.

Jo went to do *Romeo and Juliet,* and I still struggled on to get *No Language but a Cry* made. Mick Balcon had a bit of a guilty conscience because he was still on the board of Rank and had slightly advised against making it because he couldn't see it being a commercial success, so Mick applied to Group 3. This was after Grierson had left Group 3; Greenwood was running it, and he was prepared to make this film. Then suddenly, by ill luck, he decided to send the script to the censor. This was before Trevelyan. Wilkinson's day, and it was the censor who stopped the film being made because he said, "In my opinion, films of this kind about such problems as we are facing in Liverpool merely exacerbate the problem and do nothing to alleviate it. I will not guarantee a certificate if you make it."

That was the final straw. A great shame, because it could have been a very powerful film, carrying on the tradition we've been talking about. Right in line with Jack Lee's *Children on Trial,* this would have been a further development of it, because we would have taken the cast from the gangs of boys I'd got to know up in Liverpool.

So there it is. It's an industry first, and a very cumbersome one, and if there's any art in it, it's very much away down the field.

Harry Watt has also spent the greater part of his career in features.

Watt: I suppose I'm looked upon as having had a reasonably successful career in features. I made some films that are not completely forgotten, but I would say quite frankly that I regret that I left documentary.

As creative work it was so much more exciting, and there was so much of the communal effort about it, the camaraderie, the lack, basically, of jealousies. Of course, we had our jealousies and our rows. We had enormous rows, but they were tremendously friendly rows. They were never kept up, and no one's dignity was ever hurt by them. . . .

In features, *Overlanders* was a happy film, but not the other ones with these enormous units — sixty, seventy people all fighting for themselves (naturally) and fighting to get on and backbiting, and you discovering you had spies everywhere. Everything you did and said was being reported back to head office, and they were watching you like hawks. You were generally just in this rat race.

Documentary was not a rat race, and I got out of this life in which I was happy and never earned more than ten pounds a week. And although certain times, perhaps, I was happy, I never was really happy in features, and that was one of the reasons I retired early and tried to get back into documentary. I was happy making *Maria,** and I made it cheaper than the young boys would have made it because I'd been so brought up.

One of the reasons why my films made money at Ealing, too, was that I'd made remarkably inexpensive films. I couldn't get out of my system ever the documentary tradition of saving money, and of course I used a lot of nonactors. But, I mean, I made *Nine Men* with practically all nonactors for certainly under £30,000, and it went out as a first feature. I made *Where No Vultures Fly,* the Royal Command picture, for £140,000. It made a fabulous fortune. *Eureka Stockade* was an expensive picture because we had terrible trouble, weather trouble, and it was a big cast, and big crowds, and it wasn't a success. I suppose it made money. But my films did make enormous amounts of money for Ealing, largely because they were cheap, and this was the documentary training.

There was a good deal of the documentary tradition in Pat Jackson's White Corridors, *with its mixture of nonactors and actors, including Godfrey Tearle, Googie Withers, James Donald, and one of the seamen from* Western Approaches.

Jackson: That was the first time that a film at Pinewood was shot in six weeks, with Christmas in between. (I sound as though I'm going glorious. I'm not. It just happened to be one of those subjects which we planned very, very carefully.) The average had been nine to ten weeks. And this caused a bit of trouble because the unions didn't like this very much. If films were going to be made in six weeks where they had normally been taking ten, this, so they thought, could be a threat to employment, instead of realising that this was a way of increasing production. Fortunately, it was a success, and it made a lot of money for Janni, and established Janni. A very happy picture.

But Western Approaches *has remained Jackson's favourite among his own films, rightly.*

Jackson: *Western Approaches* was a different experience altogether, and that will always be my favourite. Of the commercial world, certainly my

---

*People Like Maria (1958), a documentary for the World Health Organisation, directed by Harry Watt.

favourite is *Birthday Present*. I think it was reasonably honest, a fair statement of a problem that could have hit any of us. . . .

The Birthday Present *had its London West End opening during the Asian flu epidemic of 1957, and got only a short run.*

Jackson: None of the independent exhibitors in England booked it because they gauge their bookings from the success of a show in the West End, and at that time the difference between profit and loss was whether the independent exhibitors took the film. So the film didn't make money. Consequently, it was considered a failure, although most of the notices were very good.

Dalrymple: In those days you really had to make films that appealed to the family to be successful, and therefore there was nothing like the same realism or the same pathological angles which seem to be so popular today. And I don't think that on the whole the people in documentary were madly interested in making what you might call pop films. They all had their own rather forceful ideas, if not politically, anyway socially, sociologically, and that's what they were all interested in. They all wanted to improve the world and that kind of thing, and not just entertain it. In those days — it was before TV had really established itself and certainly before commercial TV came in — people still went to the theatres as families and for the lighter form of entertainment.

Wright: Documentary led to a lot of change in features: it's not the same as the talent going in. You only have to look at the feature films during the war to see the influence of documentary. And I think there's no doubt, even before the war, of the impact of the documentary people, who were doing what people nowadays take for granted. . . .

The causes are being proclaimed now more and more through the area of the feature film. You might say that the younger generation in feature films today are doing what the younger generation used to do in documentary in the old days. I don't have to harp on the example of *Easy Rider*. It was made for nothing and made a tremendous profit, whereas *Zabriskie Point*, which was Hollywood's answer to *Easy Rider*, was made for a damn fortune and no good.

From 1951 to 1954 Grierson was joint executive producer of Group 3, a production company set up by the National Film Finance Corporation as a training ground for young feature directors. His best productions were The Brave Don't Cry *(1952) and* Man of Africa *(1953), but by the Grierson standards in experiment and innovation Group 3 was something of a benighted operation.*

The Brave Don't Cry (1952).

Grierson: Well, Group 3 was, of course, a great success in some ways. The idea was invented by Harold Wilson, and it was an employment agency, rather. There were a great many people out of work, as today, and it was felt this was a very big waste of young people. So Group 3 was set up to give young film directors an opportunity, and of course there went with it the idea of young writers, young actors, young actresses, and so forth. Well, let me say that it was a total success in the sense that it made a lot of money before it was finished. This was, of course, in spite of the fact that we were given the wrong end of the stick in distribution from the very beginning because we were government money and it was felt we were the thin end of some fearful nationalizing wedge, and so we were given a very, very bad break by Rank Cinemas. But in spite of that it actually made money, and made money for the government.

One contribution to that was, of course, the fact that we had the film of Mount Everest, which was a great success because the climbing of Mount Everest happened to be successful and it happened to coincide with the coronation. We were on to a box-office winner with that one.

But the interesting thing about Group 3 is that, while it was started to give young film directors a chance, they made the problem very difficult for

me by giving me a studio at the same time. Now, a studio means that you've
got to keep your plumbers going, your electricians going, and so on, and so
you are haunted by this awful feeling that you've got not just the employment
problem of young film directors and young film actors, but you've got the
employment problem, much more seriously, of electricians, plumbers,
plasterers, and carpenters.

There we had, in fact, an economy which called for the making of
films for £40,000 to £50,000. I think once or twice it went beyond. After
my time it went to £60,000, but the thing was, £40,000 was the basic
figure. So you had to be on and off in six weeks. Now, once you go on
and off in six weeks, that means that you can't start playing around as experi-
mentally as you might suppose. You can't be experimental about your writers.
I remember playing with Whiting at the time, and well, Whiting cost me a
lot of money and I never quite brought him in, and he was a very great writer
indeed, John Whiting. But when you think of the other writers that I
missed, I missed them because I hadn't time for them. I needed people who
could write stories that would give me a surefire timing and give me a good
bricklaying, from the point of view of storytelling. In other words, I was in
the manufactory of pictures, in spite of all the ideals.

Nonetheless, we did have great good fortune. The stories were at least
decent stories, but we missed Pinter. The BBC could afford later on to experiment, take a long time, and so they brought in people like Pinter. I missed
Pinter although I knew about Pinter. I missed various people because I had to
play surefire.

What we did do — there must be some gift in the system — was that we
got Joan Collins by accident, and we got Kenneth More by accident, and we
got Peter Sellers. There were all kinds of people began there. You'd be utterly
astonished if you look at the list of the people who started with Group 3;
we provided the names for the next ten, fifteen years.

So it was oddly enough, in the thing that nobody expected that we were
most successful — that is, in the finding of new faces for the cinema. I would
say that, on the whole, it was successful from a Board of Trade point of view.
It gave employment. It did develop talent. It kept a great number of people
employed that wouldn't have been employed, but note, it kept a great number
of electricians, plasterers, and plumbers employed that wouldn't have been
otherwise employed. And it gave me no sleep at all for years because I was no
longer concerned about film making but keeping plasterers alive. . . .

It was an experiment that had its own limitations set upon it from the
beginning, but it was one that nobody need feel ashamed of. And it made
money. This always pleases me, the fact that I've never done a commercial
film that didn't make money.

8

Reflections on Past and Future

How important was the British Documentary Movement?

Dalrymple: It was the glory of the British cinema. . . . It was unique in the world at the time, and sort of led the world in that kind of work.

Rotha: I don't think the films themselves are the least bit important. What is important is the sort of spirit which lay behind them.

Grierson: If I were going to talk about the thing that gives me the biggest kick, looking back on documentary, it was the absolute discipline of the documentary people in the thirties. Nobody stepped out of line, because they knew that divided we would perish but together we could stand. And we were disciplined, of course, for a purpose. We were *engagé,* and the first thing about being *engagé,* is discipline.

Cavalcanti: We were very far from the Korda complex. . . . It was very different from the mentality of today. For instance, nobody ever thought of inscribing me for a pension or anything like that. All the work I did for the GPO, as well as for Ealing in England, I was never inscribed. So I get to a very dangerous old age, and I have not a pension.

Watt: The idealism and the belief that we had, whether rightly or wrongly, that we were creating a new art form, and battling against the Establishment and the opposition of the trade — every facet of the trade — was tremendously stimulating. And there was an enormous feeling of camaraderie, of people working together towards an object. . . .
You never compromised in documentary. You did your best, but you never compromised. You compromised, perhaps, a little bit politically. I mean, you did not come completely out with your political beliefs, but I can emphasise again that the implicit thing in those films of the early thirties, particu-

larly where we were showing the workers of Britain as the most important citizens in the country, was a tremendous political contribution which the modern people don't appreciate.

Grierson: Remember, there were no working class on the screen when I started out. I was the first guy to put the working class on the screen, believe it or not.

Cavalcanti: People are still impressed by their experiment, but I think that one of the things documentary did — and I think it was a very valuable one — is that in England since Shakespeare the working classes were considered as comic relief in the theatre and in films, and little by little documentary imposed the workers as dignified human beings. I think that perhaps is the most important result of the documentary movement.

Grierson: The day I declared — and I did declare — that there was more seating capacity outside the theatres than there was inside the theatres, then suddenly the whole vista was changed in one sentence.

Wright: I think that the great discovery of documentary was that you could set up, not merely production but a distribution and exhibition system which had nothing whatever to do with the machinery of the entertainment film industry, and this was Grierson's discovery. . . . This was the great contribution of documentary.

For me, personally, the peaks of certain films as aesthetic seem to be most terribly, terribly important. But it is the fifteen three-reel films on the technique of anaesthesia, the twenty-four films on simple gardening, the films for schools, and this and that that added up to a tremendous parade of films made not merely with technical skill but with tremendous forethought in terms of scripting to make them box-office in their own sense to the people to whom they were shown — this to me is the achievement of documentary.

Jackson: I should say that we like to think the documentary movement had an enormous effect, and I suspect the honest truth is it had absolutely no effect whatever, certainly not on the commercial cinema.

I think it had an enormous effect on the methods of teaching and an enormous effect, probably, out in the colonies and the dominions, in far-flung parts of Empire in the old days. I should say that as a means of getting information to very primitive societies, it had an influence. But in terms of cinema today, commercial cinema, it had none at all, I would have thought.

W. H. Auden: I am sceptical about the importance of the British documentary movement, in the sense of its subsequent influence. I mean, I don't find people detecting the influence of GPO films in other directors' work.

Jackson: I should say that documentary cinema has possibly had an influence on television, that our method has affected the way in which documentary television programmes are put together, been a bit of an influence and probably a bit of a help, a bit of a guide. I wouldn't put it beyond that.

Legg: The thirties was a very creative period. . . . In painting it was a very exciting period: Picasso was at one of his peaks; Braque was painting wonderfully. . . . T. S. Eliot, Ezra Pound, Auden, all the English poets of the thirties were beginning something very new. The whole of the surrealist movement was happening. . . . Now, I think the documentary film in a way was one such movement, and those kinds of movement have an influence which lasts and which may be transformed into other things and taken up in other contexts and circumstances. They themselves die.

It has been taken up by television, I think, very largely. I suppose there were certain techniques which documentary sort of invented (particularly in films like *Housing Problems*) which became perfectly normal, regular television methods. No doubt, they've been carried very much further in television, but they sort of germinated themselves in this particular style of film making, which, in turn, was related to particular needs of getting certain things onto the screen. . . .

The Shell thing continues strongly. The Transport thing continues quite strongly. But the ordinary sort of documentary that's produced now for some industrial sponsor, no. I can't sit through them. They're dreary. Transformed into something else, yes. You've got the National Film Board of Canada. You've got the Commonwealth film unit in Australia. You've got the Malayan film unit. You've got the whole development in India. It's gone elsewhere, certainly, and sometimes in very lively ways. There are now film units in certain of the emergent countries, I think, in Africa and so on, to which documentary from here has contributed.

But, as Groucho Marx once said, turning to the camera at a moment of desperation, "You can't expect all the jokes to be good and to go on all the time." After all, the National Film Board of Canada began work in 1939. You can't expect all the jokes to be good for thirty years. Same with the Shell film unit. Same with Transport. Same with them all. These things rise up; they develop; they are exciting in their birth and their emergence. . . . They rise to a peak, and then they decline. This is what's happened to documentary. It's passed on certain things which are valuable and lasting.

Grierson: How would I evaluate the progress? Well, I'd first of all talk about the great extension of its fields, the wider and wider exploration of the documentary film all over the world. You see, we started in England, but the great thing was that we started with an international front. We started the Imperial Institute, thinking at first of exchanging films between the dominions and the colonies and the mother country, as we called it then. And

out of that experiment of the Imperial Institute we got ourselves a view
which involved the building up of film production all over the Empire. . . .

We began with scratch films, films that came from all kinds of sources and
were no good whatever, and as soon as we saw them, as soon as we made a
catalogue of them, we knew very well that we could do better. So we began to
think of organising ourselves, the documentary movement here in England, which
we did, and that was a wonderful development because it concerned the fidelity,
loyalty of a great number of people.

And then, of course, we became like missionaries. We built up in the colonies. We built up in the dominions, and then there came, of course, the National
Film Board of Canada. There came the Film Board in Australia and New Zealand
and so forth. There was this from the very beginning of documentary, this
sense of building up all over the world. . . . The great thing about documentary
is not what we did in England but the fact that we happened to light a bonfire.
And the bonfire blazed in England, but people got the idea and started lighting
a similar bonfire elsewhere, the trick being that, of course, documentary is of
use to governments, is of use to serious people for all manner of education, for
all manner of exposition, for all manner of illumination, for all manner of inspiration. And so it lights up different people in different ways in different countries.

The greatest thing of all to me, and where I would really finish up
by laying emphasis, has been the use of the film for simple purposes. That
is, not only in teaching, but in the teaching of health, not just the teaching of health and medicine but the teaching of health and medicine at the
most primitive and primary levels, the use of the film to educate the starveling
peoples, the up-and-coming peoples.

I'd say the greatest achievement of documentary today is what it has done
and is doing in the less privileged countries, not least, of course, in countries
like India. . . . That is the great field. . . . We are no longer concerned just with
the cineastes and the arty-tarty people, the sort of people in that *Sight and
Sound* ménage. We're concerned with putting the camera and projection into
the hands of the doctor-teachers at the most primitive levels, the midwives, the
agricultural organisers, the agricultural teachers. We're concerned with decen-
tralizing the means of production, taking the myth out of it, taking the mystique out of it, and making the documentary film a living tool for people at the
grass roots.

*Grierson had just returned from India, where he was preparing a survey
on communication for the Canadian government, to be made available to
other countries concerned with aid programmes.*

Grierson: There's no question at all that the biggest thing that will
happen is when something really serious is done in a country like India. India
has got 550,000,000 people. Well, all the mass media together, that's to say
radio and movie, only arrive at an audience of 100,000,000 people. That is,

450,000,000 people are outside the range of the so-called mass media. Well, there is a whole world for the documentary film to take over, in the hands of educationalists of all kinds, in the hands of village leaders of all kinds, 450,000,000 people in India, alone. . . . I think I must be the first person to lay my finger on that point, that all these mass media together only arrived at 100,000,000 people and 450,000,000 people were living on word-of-mouth. . . . And, of course, once you get into the word-of-mouth business, you're in very different territory. You're in with all the teachers then . . . and if the teaching force begins to arm itself with the serious use of film as a power of expression for democratic purposes, then you've got yourself a very, very big development indeed, which makes all our developments of the thirties in England look like two cents. Oh, I think there are far bigger things happening than anything we dreamt of.

In a social revolution like the social revolution of India, you've got teachers all over the place, teaching sanitation, teaching health, teaching progressive agriculture of one kind or another, teaching community development in various ways. Now, wherever you get a teacher, you get somebody using his mouth. In other words, there's a conveyance by the mouth or by illustration and what they're doing is working up from the illustration of the blackboard to the use of the Epidaiscope to the use of the magic lantern (which is basic to India anyway, about 2,500 years old, to my knowledge, in India) to the use of the comic strip (which, of course, again is 2,500 years old in India) using five or six different illustrations to tell a little story. You get children doing it quite automatically in India.

But you go from there, of course, to the filmstrip and from there to the local film, to the film making process on the 8 millimetre or 16 millimetre level. When you talk about illiterate, you haven't got any reflection of the vitality of that particular process. In fact, the more I see of the word-of-mouth process in India, the less I'm concerned about literacy per se. There are so many vital ways of communication that you can skip the business of reading and writing. The travelling theatre is to me a marvellous thing in India, where it's got echoes of German expressionism sometimes, ancient Greek theatre, Elizabethan theatre — in fact, I went to one show in Calcutta, and it looked to me like the old Lyceum. It was a melodrama of the most Victorian order, but every now and again it ran off into Greek recitative, Greek chorus, and into all kinds of effect that certainly didn't belong to the Lyceum. The word-of-mouth world can be a very vital world, but the moment you add the film or the filmstrip you've added a very vital instrument indeed.

Elton: Films were first of all the poor man's entertainment. They began by taking the place of the music hall and so on, and the upper classes, who stuck to the theatre and things which were for exclusivity, looked down on films for a very long time. Then films were taken up by everybody, but today they are often regarded as something exclusive and only to be understood by people of a special kind, witness *Sight and Sound,* which perpetually tries to separate the film as something which can only be understood by the privileged, whereas I believe in the film as a companion with the other arts.

I believe it has an immensely long history, that, in fact, it deals with a succession of images and that movement is merely a local, recent addition to something that goes right back to the Stations of the Cross and to the cavemen. The moment people took two pictures and put one beside the other, you began on film. This is very close to another theory of mechanology by a French philosopher called Jacques Lafitte, in which machines can be easily considered as having laws of their own and developing on evolutionary lines. I have a paper on this subject.

In his paper "Notes on the Film Considered in the Light of Mechanology," Arthur Elton said: "So far as I know, Lafitte did not study the film as a machine and, as such, an important member of a large mechanological series, embracing a host of related machines, and evolved from simple origins, long away in time. Yet, at one point, he hails ethnographers, art historians and archaeologists as

Arthur Elton, photographed by W. Suschitzky.

being the first mechanologists, urging that their methods should be applied henceforth to the study of all machines. So, by extension, it is not impossible to add to Lafitte's short list, students of the film, but not, I must add, film critics. For film critics are almost always dedicated to the film, considered as a unique and lonely phenomenon, divorced from all other media of art or communication, a kind of mirror of fantasy, a sort of anthropomorphic dream.

"By parting the film from its early origins, and from other members of the series to which it belongs, critics have not only narrowed the film. They have made it infertile. They have blunted the film as a means of universal communication. They have detracted from its incomparable powers of analysis of contemporary and historical events.

"The result of such social and aesthetic drives to isolation has been that the film is almost universally regarded as belonging to a special class of its own, categorised by 'movement.' Yet, in the series to which the film belongs, 'movement' in the sense of stimulated physical movement is quite a late and specialised development, and perhaps of less importance than a deeper and more far-reaching principle that I call 'successivity.'

"The concept of successivity can best be understood when one remembers that a film is nothing more than a succession of still pictures or 'frames,' usually photographs, sometimes drawings — quanta of movement as one might call them. As a film is projected, each frame modifies the impression created by the previous frame, and conditions the viewer's reception of the succeeding one. When the content of any particular frame is close in space and time to that of the frames on either side, the effect of sequential projection produces an illusory sense of physical movement, superimposed by the mind on a succession of still pictures, Even if the succeeding frames differ from each other substantially in content, space and time, on projection sequentially, each image will continue to modify the effect of the preceding one. Though the illusion of physical movement will not be provoked, another kind of movement within the mind will be established, as image piles on image.

"Even in a conventional movie, the effect of cumulative intellectual movement is constantly present, and is usually dominant. . . .

"Film is the present manifestation of a mechanological series with a direct line of ancestry through photograph and lantern slide, through zoetrope, praxinoscope and thaumotrope, through peepshow, panorama and Eudophusikon, through the camera obscura and camera lucida, through the sequential paintings and frescoes of the seventeenth century and the Middle Ages, past the Stations of the Cross to the drawings of the cavemen. Branches of the same mechanological series embrace the theatre, the opera and the dance. The construction of a ballet and the construction of a film often have much in common. In certain types of film-making, there is a very strong affinity between arranging visual images to establish a particular set of facts or ideas, and editing words and lines of words to express particular ideas with accuracy. Even

*the printed page can be argued to be another branch of the series to which
the film belongs. . . .*

*"With the fructification of the mechanological series that contains the
film, with new techniques appearing almost daily, from cassettes to holo-
graphy, these communication machines are among the most powerful influ-
ences in our social environment. The problem that faces us all is this. Can
these instruments be wrested from the hands of those dedicated exclusively
to commerce and, for financial ends, to the artificial manipulation of emotion?
Or can the new science of mechanology place these immensely powerful
machines of communication in safer and more responsible hands?"*

*Documentary ideas could sometimes be far from simple, but, apparently
as a matter of policy, experimentation with the films themselves ceased long
before it reached this kind of intellectual level.*

What role should documentary play now in Britain?

Grierson: Oh well, what role it's got to play here wouldn't interest me
very much because I think there's such a thing as priorities and what's happening in England's not half so important as what's happening in China. I mean,
really, really! This is a fat country, a fat and lucky country. It can afford even
to stop working every now and again. It can afford all kinds of unemployment
because it's so comfortable. It's got such a cushion of comfort. But no, the
priorities for me are elsewhere, and they're wherever the poor people have got
to build up their resources, and wherever they've got to build up their defences
against the encroachment of other countries.

What future for British documentary?

Wright: On the assumption it still exists? I think it's changed so much. I
think the whole area of *cinéma-vérité* has been far more powerful in people's
approach than you can think, and it's very much tied up with the instant stuff
you get on television.

Come to think of it, who is making documentaries now? You know, real
documentaries. I'm asking myself. Organisations like the National Coal Board
and, of course, Edgar Anstey's British Transport have a distinguished record,
but this is not the future. This is the standard thing. Documentary is a thing now
which is used; it's now automatic. When we began, it was very unusual for a
film projector to be anywhere near a school. Now in the schools, it's automatic
that they show films and they have language laboratories and they have tape
recorders. So, if you really want me to answer, I don't think documentary's
got any future. It's got a past and a present. If it has a future, it will be some
new developments started by a new genius — I mean, of the type of Grierson,
who will take the existing factual informational film area and give it a good
shake and start something else off, as I believe Rouch and the Maysles bro-
thers and Leacock in fact did with *cinéma-vérité.*

From left, Henri Storck, Jean Lods, Basil Wright
and Joris Ivens at Council Meeting of International
Association of Documentarists, Paris, 1969. Photo
by Virginia Leirens, Brussels.

Rotha: Obviously, I'd like to think there's a very great deal of hope. It
depends, and this is an old cliché, but it depends on the young people and
what they want to do. I can't help feeling that some of the younger generation
are terribly in love with the technique of making films, rather than the subjects and purpose of these films. I'm all for good technique — heaven knows
I am — but I only believe it's important if it's put to a specific purpose. What
I think is maybe lacking in documentary (at any rate, in this country — I
can't talk for other countries) is this specific purpose. After all, with our union,
excellent though it is, most of our technicians in documentary are getting excellent wages and I hope they're all safely, happily married and have families
growing up and all the rest of it. But I think they've rather lost that drive and
that energy and that initiative which perhaps we had in the thirties. Maybe
this is a little bit lacking today.

    The other day I was asked to see two films about the Barbican site in
the City. I saw these two films. You know, the colour's all right and the camera's tilted sideways and all this silly nonsense, but these films did nothing.
They said nothing. They were completely unimportant. After the showing
was over, I turned round to the man who produced, not directed but produced,
these films, and I said, "How much do the flats in the Barbican cost?" He
said, "I don't know." I said, "Why the hell did you make the films, then? I

can tell you what they cost because I happened to live near the Barbican and I applied for a flat there ten years ago and couldn't afford it. So they've jolly good technicolor, nice cutting and all the rest of it, but what the hell do your films talk about? What do they say?"

This is what's gone out of film making. You see, there's Anstey sitting there at British Transport. I saw a whole battery of his films the other day. They're very well made; technically they're excellent films. I couldn't fault them. But at the end of them you just say, "What do they mean? What do they say? What importance are they in the year of the Common Market?" I saw a whole lot of Elton's films at Shell. They again are extraordinarily well made technically, but what do they build up to? What do they say about what's happening in the world today?

The National Coal Board films, again very well made, are more important because they are not made for public audiences. They are made for within the members of the coal mining fraternity, and they're films about safety and so on. These are doing something which is important. This is obvious, and these I'd except from my general criticism.

But what else is there? Where else are they coming from? Units are making TV commercials. . . . I can't think of any important films being made in the last ten years which will compare with the kind of films we were trying to make thirty years ago.

Taylor: The thing that seems to me to have gone wrong with the documentary idea is that people have gone off after art forms just for the art form's sake. They have deviated from the main line, which is communications and being of service to people. I mean, that's really what Grierson saw films as, a service to people.

Anstey: In the thirties we didn't regard anything we did as aesthetic experiment. Communication was the overriding thing. We thought we were finding new methods of communication. As the medium develops and becomes more sophisticated, the new methods of communication open to us are bound to become fewer, really. . . . I mean, almost all possible methods have been explored now, I suspect, and one can break new ground but by very small differences, as compared with the enormous differences that were open to us in the day of *Housing Problems*, when all you had to do was to take synchronous-recording equipment into a slum house and you'd done something new.

Cathy Come Home represents a new documentary departure — if you like, a move into feature — but it was a legitimate new step. If you're assessing the documentary achievement over the last five years, you could probably find a great many films which match up in their attempt at pioneering with the early work, I think, bearing in mind that you can't make the same jumps forward. I mean, we had this wonderful chance: a relatively small group of people with the whole field open to us.

Legg: Shell is still doing good work. One or two other industrial sponsors are. The Transport tradition is still lively. But, on the whole, I think the interesting work that is being done now in the realist context is perhaps not coming from organised documentary but from unorganised, from people venturing on their own, combining their resources now and then and being able to produce such films as they can. . . . Some very interesting experimental work has come out from that, as well as a lot of nonsense. But the original thing has risen to its peak, declined, and is no longer seen as it was. The younger people now who perhaps would have gone into documentary in its former, inspired days, have gone elsewhere. . . .

I think it possible that there are certain circumstances under which one might see a renewal. Documentary is very much influenced by outside events. It is an instrument of information, of propaganda, and to that extent it's dependent on needs of communication. It usually is in greatest demand in times of difficulty, in times when there are real problems to be explained, to be informed about. Now it's possible, I think, that the governmental role of it might return to some kind of inspired work if things began seriously to go wrong. If, for instance, there were other depressions, if there were crises. You can say that it reached one of its great moments of triumph in the war. Heaven forfend that we should see that again, but it does thrive on unrest, on difficulties, where governments feel they've got to communicate.

In the industrial field, it has become increasingly difficult to make good film work because of the growth of industrial bureaucracy. All this search for efficiency, for managerial reorganisation, for these schools of management, is beginning to give industry a new kind of image and a nasty kind of image. Industry is becoming po-faced. Now, this may bring about a reaction. It seems to me perfectly possible that industry may turn round one day and find that its image is very bad, and that there will be a rethinking of the whole attitude to the public. If that were to happen, then things like films would become important again in their wider contexts.

Elton: Documentary moved to television, very properly. The best documentary, or much of it, is now television. Television, however, has given it a kind of journalistic element because it's easier to do. The more you can have of a person talking on the television tube, the cheaper. The film maker has to solve problems of presentation. You have to get the ideas over in pictures, but much BBC stuff is illustrated talks. They're the greatest journalists in the world, but they have to some extent lost, or have never acquired, the means of pictorial presentation. They're not interested in the pictures, as such. There's a depressing lack of pictorial logic about them. . . . Even the Kenneth Clark series,* which is immensely important because it brought these great pictures into everybody's sitting room, was more of a presentation of a lec-

Civilization, BBC TV, 1969.

ture than it was necessarily a study of the pictures. This is not a criticism either of Kenneth Clark or of the BBC, but there are other ways of handling that kind of theme, which I think is almost beyond them. There is a dimension which I think they've never been able, or never wished, perhaps, to explore. It's very probably lack of time and possibly lack of money, too much to do and too many hours to fill. I think they do a brilliant job, but one must say that there is a certain absence from the television screen of things which one would very much like to see there, and which the cassette, of course, may bring back.

Cavalcanti: Until television settles down, until the cassettes come, you won't get things put in their right place. I don't think so, and I am frightened to die before it's put right.

The importance of film institutes, cinémathèques, the importance of the film clubs, of the specialised cinemas — all that is showing the way into the cassette state, when people with a TV set can have films, like they have gramophone records of the symphonies. I think that is going to put everything right.

Why did the documentary movement not go into television when BBC TV was beginning in the thirties and forties?

Dalrymple: Because the BBC wouldn't have us. They didn't want any of these disgusting, vulgar, commercial people on the one hand, and they didn't want another set of highbrows and intellectuals, who said plenty to them, thank you, on the other. They didn't want to take advantage of this experience of making films, and in due course they built up their own marvellous documentary units. I mean, some of the BBC documentaries I have watched absolutely fascinated me. I think they're marvellous. They had a little bit more money, of course.

But it was the other way round really. People all wished to graduate from TV to films, because the actual salaries were higher in films, and in a way a film lasted longer: it takes a long time for a film to percolate all round the world, whereas on the BBC you've had it that one evening, with maybe a repeat.

Wright: Of course, I'm much older than some of the other people, but it is interesting that very few of the documentary people transferred themselves to television, and when Paul [Rotha] went to BBC to do their documentary thing, it didn't work. Now, mind you, there are other reasons for it not working, but one of the reasons — because he called me in and I did a whole programme with him and I was only pulled through by some people who were there who were television-minded. (Norman Swallow pulled us all through on that, but he was thinking television. He wasn't thinking movie. I was thinking movie all the time.) Of course, he did have a very difficult time with Cecil

McGivern. It ended up in a blow-up, of course. But, without going into personalities, I think there was this difficulty for documentary people in adjust-
ing to the television idea.

Rotha was head of the BBC documentary department in 1954-1955.

Rotha: I didn't ask for the job. I was invited by the BBC to be head of
what was to be a new department. . . . I was given six or seven writers and
producers, as they call them in television (directors, in film terms). They were
a very good bunch, indeed — creative ideas, good technical accomplishment,
and very, very hard workers. They had to be. We put out, I think, something
like ten hours of screen time in a week, and I was very proud of the programmes,
mostly on social matters one way or another, which we put out. Our department was number 2 on audience-research ratings every week. News came first.
Documentary came second. Then came sport, then live entertainment, and,
way down the list, drama and so forth. Week after week I was very happy to
see that we had very high ratings indeed. Of course, there was no commercial
television, no competitive television in those days.

But, as time went on, over the two years I was there I found it became
more and more difficult from a policy point of view. Now, this has got nothing
to do with the boys and girls who worked in the department — they were excellent — but with the people higher up in the hierarchy of the BBC. I can give
you a very good example right away. We were at that time putting out a programme called "Special Enquiry," which was a monthly, forty-five minutes,
and dealt with an important problem each time. We decided one month to do a
programme on British railways, and in the strict BBC attitude we took both
sides — what was wrong with the railways and what was right with the railways.
I had approval from my boss at that time to make the subject, and we started
work. We hadn't been on the filming for more than two or three days, at I
think Liverpool Street Station, when I had word from the controller of programmes, Cecil McGivern, who's now dead, to say I was to stop all work. I
said, "What do I do, then? I can't make an alternative in this short time, and
besides there isn't the money." He said, "All right, we'll put in an old film
instead." Anyway, I had to stop work, and I asked him when I saw him next,
"What's the reason? I must have a reason. Why was the programme stopped
after it was in the brief?" "Well," he said, "the two generals were on the telephone together." By the two generals he meant the head of British railways and
the director general of the BBC. . . .

This went on on a number of subjects. It went on over subjects we had
about Cyprus and about the slums of Glasgow, and eventually it became very
unpleasant for me to have to keep cancelling what I thought were extremely important programmes, and, quite frankly, I got out.

From 1957 to 1968 Grierson produced and presented the series This Wonderful World for Scottish Television.

Grierson: I've always worked for governments, except when I went on television. I did that for the commercial people. That was only because I knew old Roy Thomson from away back in Canada. I'd retired by this time. I'd retired for, oh, ten days, I think, when he called me up and said, "Listen, I've got to find a highbrow programme. You're it."

So I set out to do a highbrow programme, according to Roy Thomson, which turned out to be a lowbrow programme. At least it turned out to be a popular programme.

These programmes introduced the work of new film makers from all over the world. They were not in themselves an original contribution either to film making or television, but it is depressing to discover that already they no longer exist. All but one has apparently been junked by the company that sponsored them.

Grierson: I always think of documentary as having certain fundamental chapters. The first chapter is, of course, the travelogue, that is, the discovery that the camera can go about — it's peripatetic. The second chapter is the discovery by Flaherty that you can make a film of people on the spot — that is, you can get an insight of a dramatic sort, a dramatic pattern, on the spot with living people. But, of course, he did this in respect of faraway peoples, and he was romantic in that sense. The third chapter is our chapter, which is the discovery of the working people — that is, the drama on the doorstep, the drama of the ordinary.

But there is a fourth chapter that's very interesting, and that would be the chapter in which people began to talk not about making films *about* people but films *with* people. That was the beginning of *cinéma-vérité,* when people started going down and getting close to people, not as Flaherty did. Flaherty didn't really know what was going on among the Aran Islanders; he was too distant from them. But when the people went down and made *Housing Problems* in Stepney, they knew the people, and you could recognize right away that this was a new relationship entirely between the film makers and the films, that they were making films with the people and that they were, well, very close to the people indeed. That's, of course, the real beginning of *cinéma-vérité,* and any effort by anybody else to say that *cinéma-vérité* has any other origin than in *Housing Problems* and the English documentary school, is just nonsense.*

Of course, the French are always finding phrases and discovering terms

*The origin of *cinéma-vérité,* like that of documentary itself, is of course often attributed to Dziga Vertov.

for things, but generally about ten years late, like, for example, *musique concrète*. When that started appearing and I was one day in Cannes invited, I think by Jean Cocteau, to hear this amazing new world of *musique concrète,* I laughed if I did not sneer because it's something we'd all been playing with a long time before, maybe twelve years, something like ten years before. We'd Britten and all sorts of people involved.

However, the next chapter, this making films with people — you've still got the problem that you're making films with people and then going away again. Well, I see the next chapter being making films really locally, and there I'm following Zavattini. Zavattini once made a funny speech in which he thought it would be wonderful if all the villages in Italy were armed with cameras so that they could make films by themselves and write film letters to each other, and it was all supposed to be a great joke. I was the person who didn't laugh, because I think that *is* the next stage — not the villagers making film letters and sending them to each other, but the local film people making films to state their case politically or otherwise, to express themselves whether it's in journalistic or in other terms.

So there you are. These are the chapters.

The interesting thing, of course, is the confusion over *cinéma-vérité.* We've all known about the possibilities of the cinema, of the camera, for intimacy, and we've all been aware for a long time how you can intrude on intimacy. You can turn the camera into a Peeping Tom if you want to, but who wants to? I mean, what kind of mind wants to? It didn't take *cinéma-vérité* to discover dirty pictures. In the selfsame way we've all known that if you asked an embarrassing question, you could always get an embarrassed reaction to the embarrassing question. We've always known that. But if you start making that a sort of tool of your trade, as the Film Board of Canada was doing some four or five years ago, it's becoming an ugly process and it should be stopped because you are really invading privacy, and in fact you may go beyond the law. So that *cinéma-vérité* is interesting, but it's mostly on its positive side, of course, that it's interesting, in so far as these intimate revelations do tell you something positive about things. But it's so open to exploitation by the provincially-minded or by the second-rate — and the trouble with the second-rate getting hold of a means of production like film is that they, having second-rate minds and second-rate approaches, will fall victim to all these temptations to get a sensation at any price, because they don't know how to get a sensation otherwise. Because they're not poets, because they're not dramatists, then of course they can always make dirty pictures.

Will professional film makers be involved in the next chapter of documentary?

Grierson: If a doctor is making a film about medicine, about an operation, about family planning . . . it will be professional, bound to be professional so long as he keeps the camera steady. It's a doctor making it. I don't want any so-called professional film maker coming between that man and making an exposition, a piece of teaching. He's a doctor. He's a teacher. Therefore he's a professional, period.

Epilogue

John Grierson died on 19 February 1972. The interview he gave for this book
was probably his last. He rarely gave interviews and only agreed to this one
because his close friend and former colleague Stuart Legg particularly asked him.
After I left him he sent a message, via Stuart Legg, to the effect that I should do
a very different kind of book from the one I appeared to be planning. Instead
of approaching the subject in such a personal way (he had especially disliked
a question I asked about his own greatest achievement), I should explore the
whole economic and political background out of which documentary had
sprung.

The idea is absolutely characteristic of him and because I did not follow
it up (because far from it I related his interview to the other interviews in
ways that interested me) his prophesy that he would be merely presented (not
represented) has proved correct. Everybody quoted in this book is presented
rather than represented in the sense that I, and not they, chose what to leave
out and what to put in where. On the other hand, the book is constructed in
the true documentary spirit according to Grierson's own original definition
of documentary as "the creative treatment of actuality" — and I can say that
over the years since I embarked on it my constant concern has been to try to
make the balance fair.

Grierson's final verdict, his dismissal of the professional film maker as
someone who merely gets between a teacher and the thing he is trying to
teach, is in line with his suggestion that I should prepare a book which was
not about film making at all. He had turned full cycle since the beginning,
and documentary as Basil Wright understood it when he said it "meant a
chance for Len Lye, a chance for Norman McLaren, a chance for Richard
Massingham" no longer interested him very much. The fact is that documen-

tary in this sense has died (the Len Lye's and Richard Massingham's of today, if they get a chance at all, get it on television due to nothing but their own talent or persistence) and Grierson was shrewd enough not to spend the latter part of his life trying to resuscitate a corpse.

The clearest evidence that this is the true state of affairs was provided by Lindsay Anderson and Karel Reisz's Free Cinema endeavour in the late 1950s. Then, as probably now, a number of interesting British documentaries were being made but rarely or never shown. This was the main reason for mounting the Free Cinema programmes at the National Film Theatre. Not all the work included in them was British: there were, for instance, early films by Truffaut and Chabrol; but the programmes of films made in and about Britain included early work by Anderson, Reisz, Tony Richardson, Claude Goretta, Alain Tanner, Robert Vas — a great deal of it photographed by the same promising cameraman, Walter Lassally. It could have been a second generation movement, except that there was nothing to sustain a movement, no method of financing one, no future outlet for any films it made. So this time everybody almost immediately went off separately to find his own solution in features, the theatre, television — and of course the screenings at the National Film Theatre probably helped a little.

According to Anderson, Free Cinema was "always rather strongly resented by film makers in this country and particularly by the old guard of documentary, none of whom ever did anything to help us. There were one or two friends like Basil Wright — but Basil wasn't really then producing films — and I would say that the documentary establishment were definitely hostile. They were hostile to our principles because we weren't a follow-on of the Grierson school. We were less sociological and propagandist than Grierson, and there wasn't much love lost between us."*

Certainly the Free Cinema group were not following on from Grierson's later teachings, but there is a case for seeing them as the true heirs of his original movement as it existed until about 1937 and, apart from a certain kind of dedicated and experimental approach to film making, apart from techniques which had never been used in Britain before but had recurred of course during the intervening years, there was nothing to inherit from that. Nothing (except television which has always lacked a Grierson at the head of it) has since been able to offer the opportunities that the GPO Film Unit offered in the mid-1930s. Grierson was quite simply in no position to help a later generation of British documentary film makers solve the problems that he had turned his back on twenty years before.

It must also be put on record somewhere in this book that, talented as some of Grierson's original protégés undoubtedly were, it seems they were just not talented enough or sure enough to develop the thing they had begun.

*Quoted from *Lindsay Anderson* by Elizabeth Sussex (New York: Praeger, and London: Studio Vista, 1969).

Instead (apart from those who went into features at a time when the industry was geared almost exclusively to family entertainment and therefore gave them little scope) they followed Grierson's line which was, in very general terms, to work for the extension of the territories occupied by documentary rather than the development in depth of documentary itself. Probably nothing that might be described as a movement in the arts has produced less major art than the British documentary movement. But this is not the last word on the subject.

When Free Cinema ended, the final manifesto read: "Free Cinema is dead, Long live Free Cinema." The same could have been said, even more aptly, of British documentary in the late 1930s when sociological aims took over from aesthetic ones. Like the Knights of the Round Table, the members of the movement in fact disbanded and went out into the world in search of the holy grail — and so the idea of a kind of purity was able to persist unsullied by the feuds and jealousies that were otherwise just about to erupt. Moreover, by not entering what Harry Watt called the rat race, by not attempting to compete in an environment where compromises were virtually inevitable, the Grierson school succeeded in preserving the documentary idea virtually intact and untainted to this day.

This, and all the material problems that go along with it, is the main inheritance. As Grierson said "the word documentary belongs to everybody now . . ."

Index